D0567421

DATE DUE

MAR 6 1992

DISCARDED
SDSU LIBRARY

DISCARDED
SDSU LIBRARY

UPI 201-9509   PRINTED IN USA

Good Work at the Video Display Terminal

DISCARDED
SDSU LIBRARY

LIBRARY
COLLEGE LIBRARY

Good Work at the Video Display Terminal

....

A Feminist Ethical Analysis of Changes in Clerical Work

....

BARBARA HILKERT ANDOLSEN

....

The University of Tennessee Press
Knoxville

DISCARDED
SDSU LIBRARY

HILTON M. BRIGGS LIBRARY
South Dakota State University
Brookings, SD 57007-1098

HF5548.2
.A73125
1989

#19554341

Copyright © 1989 by the University of Tennessee Press / Knoxville
All rights reserved. Manufactured in the United States of America
First Edition.
The paper in this book meets the minimum requirements
of the American National Standard for Permanence of Paper
for Printed Library Materials.
∞
The binding materials have been chosen
for strength and durability.

Library of Congress Cataloging in Publication Data
    Andolsen, Barbara Hilkert.
    Good work at the video display terminal : a feminist ethical
analysis of changes in clerical work / Barbara Hilkert Andolsen.—
1st ed.
        p.   cm.
    Bibliography: p.
    Includes index.
    ISBN 0-87049-618-2 (cloth: alk. paper)
    1. Office practice—Automation—Moral and ethical aspects.
2. Clerks—Effect of automation on.   3. Video display terminals–
–Health aspects.   4. Sex role in the work environment.   I. Title
HF5548.2.A73125   1989
331.25—dc20   89-4884   CIP

To William Hilkert and Alan Andolsen,
who have shown me that moral judgment
is a business skill, and to
Daniel and Ruth Andolsen,
who will carry on the struggle for justice.

Contents

•••••••••••••••••

•••••••••••••••

••••••••••••••

Acknowledgments

··················

··················

··················

I am grateful to Harvard Divinity School's Women's Studies in Religion Program for the opportunity to pursue this project while a research associate during 1984–85. I am thankful to the Ford Foundation, which supplied funding for the research associates' positions. My fellow research associates Phyllis Blum Cole, Sylvia Marcos, Ada Rapoport-Albert, and Emily Erwin Culpepper provided thoughtful comments, encouragement, and support in abundance. The program's director Constance Buchanan created an environment in which we could do good work.

I particularly appreciate early research support for work investigating office automation from the National Records Management Council, under Chairman Robert A. Shiff.

Scholars who have studied office automation generously shared their knowledge with me. I am particularly thankful for conversations with Roslyn Feldberg, Judith Gregory, Bradford Leach, Harley Shaiken, Jeanne Stellman, Mary Murphree, and Cynthia Costello.

I benefited from collegial support from Harvard Divinity School faculty members, especially Ralph Potter, Sharon Welch, Margaret Miles, Arthur Dyck, Robert Franklin, Gordon Kaufman, and Preston Williams, and from Weston School of Theology faculty members David Hollenbach and Edward Vacek. Lisa Sowle Cahill and Lorine Getz helped me make important contacts in the Boston area. Constance Parvey shared her lovely Boston home with me.

I thank my colleagues in the Department of Religion at Rutgers University, especially Henry Bowden, James Turner Johnson, and James Jones. Mahlon Smith was helpful in arranging for my research leave. I also appreciate the encouragement provided by my women's studies colleagues, particularly Mary Gibson and Judith Gerson.

I received valuable assistance from librarians at the Rutgers University libraries, the Harvard University libraries, especially the Harvard Business School library, Gardner Sage Library at the New Brunswick Theological Seminary, the library at Weston School of Theology, Union Theological Seminary Library and the New York Public Library—the Astor, Lenox and Tilden Foundations.

My warmest thanks go to my husband Alan. I developed an interest in the human impacts of office automation through discussing his work as a management consultant in administrative and office systems. Alan has been a sounding board for all the ideas in this book. He has been a tough editorial critic and a patient technical advisor about data base management and word processing difficulties. In addition, he has done his share and, at times, more than his share of the mundane work necessary to keep a family going, while I researched and wrote this book. Most importantly, his commitment to justice for all persons in business life has shown me that the struggle for justice in the workplace cannot be accurately described as a clear-cut battle between the sexes.

I also want to thank Jose Enrique and Maria Louisa Martinez for the help with child care which made this work possible.

Finally, I thank Grace Ahmed and Cecelia Nodine, the secretaries in the Department of Religion at Rutgers University. Day after day, they show the competence and the human relations skills which this book acknowledges as very valuable resources for our joint productive endeavors.

Introduction

·················

·················

·················

$\mathbf{T}$his book presents an ethical analysis and evaluation of changes in clerical work which are occurring in conjunction with the implementation of office automation systems. The choices which human beings make in the course of designing, implementing, and operating such systems will have important consequences for human well-being. Human choices about these technologies will help determine whether a large group of women have opportunities to participate actively in the economic realm and whether the terms of their participation will be equitable. In this book, I explore elements for a normative theory of "good" work—one appropriate to the experience of clerical workers. In other words, I struggle with the question, why is good work important for human flourishing, including the human flourishing of data entry clerks and secretaries?

Office automation is the process whereby technological tools are incorporated into office operations in order to increase office workers' efficiency and effectiveness. The use of typewriters, telephones, and calculating machines in office settings is a form of office automation. However, this book examines office automation systems which make use of computer and associated telecommunications technologies. Telecommunications is a term which refers to a group of technologies which permit the transmission and reception of analog and digital data over distance. (The human voice is an example of analog data.) Among the earliest telecommunications devices were the telegraph and the telephone. Telecommunications technologies are increasingly important in office automation because they provide the networks which link together various computer devices.

In most larger organizations, *office automation is an evolutionary process* in which earlier computer applications—initially restricted to certain routine, high volume, information processing operations—have spread to other areas of the organization and have also been superseded by newer, more sophisticated systems. Thus, many clerical workers whose work is being automated do not face a single transformation of work patterns, but rather a process of continual change.

Office Automation and Women's Well-being

The choices made in the course of implementing automated office systems have important consequences for the well-being of women. While office automation systems are beginning to affect the work of virtually all white-collar workers, early office automation systems have been targeted toward enhancing the productivity of clerical workers. In the United States, clerical work is a critical category of women's work. Eighty percent of all clerical workers are women, and almost one out of every three women working for wages is classified as a clerical worker. Moreover, in drawing attention to the impacts of office automation on the well-being of clerical workers, I am raising issues which should be of interest to anyone concerned about the well-being of the American worker, for "the typical American worker is no longer a man in a hard hat. She is a woman at the typewriter—or, rather, at a [video display terminal] keyboard."[1]

Those who have a special concern for the well-being of women who are socially disadvantaged for reasons of race or ethnic identity should also be concerned about the impact of office automation on clerical work, because it is a major source of employment for young minority women.[2] Clerical work is the largest category of employment for Hispanic, Native American, and Asian/Pacific women. For African American women, clerical work is second only to service work as a source of employment. The last two decades have seen an important shift in the composition of the clerical work force. Younger minority women, especially younger African American women, have been moving into clerical occupations in large numbers. By 1981, young minority women were as likely to hold a clerical job as were young white women. In fact, young white women were beginning to move out of clerical occupations into skilled blue-collar, technical, professional, and managerial jobs. It may be that young African American and other minority women are gaining increased access to clerical employment at the very time when office automation threatens to have a negative impact on many of their jobs.

Office Automation and the Global Economy

Office automation is proceeding during a time of fundamental economic change. Since World War II, there has been an accelerating trend toward global economic interdependence. The use of computer/telecommunications technologies is an essential element in the growing global economy. Without computers, it would be impossible to gather, process, store, and retrieve the huge amount of information necessary for multinational business operations. Modern telecommunications links make it possible to transmit economic information across the globe almost instantaneously. Thus computer/telecommunications technology is one factor which makes possible the internationalization of production and finance.

At first, computerized information systems facilitated management oversight of *manufacturing* sites in other nations. Electronics manufacturing was among those industries which were "in the forefront of this migration to developing areas."[3] Third-world women, working in export-processing zones in the developing nations, assemble the computer equipment used to automate the jobs of first-world clerical workers.[4] Now, however, companies are beginning to use computer/telecommunications technologies to shift routine *clerical* operations to other regions or nations.

During the last two decades, competitive pressures in the global economy have intensified greatly. There is tremendous pressure on many businesses to keep their costs low through capital investment, which increases the productivity of both their factory and office staffs. It is often to the benefit of managers and stockholders to transfer less skilled labor operations (now beginning to include routine clerical labor operations) to areas with low wage rates, low unionization, and/ or government policies which are favorable to business. Workers everywhere are confronted with a highly mobile capital investment system which makes the achievement of justice an ever more complex challenge.

The Diversity of Clerical Experience

Throughout this book, I discuss clerical workers. However, that occupational category is a very broad one. The experiences of clerical workers are very diverse. Clerical workers include secretaries, typists, word processing operators, reservation agents, file clerks, bookkeepers, office machine operators, telephone operators, social services clerks, bank tellers, and data entry operators. They work in firms of very different sizes. A clerical worker may be the only general office worker in a small business or one of a large number of clerks performing highly specialized tasks for a multinational corporation. Clerical workers work in all industries. Those who work in information intensive sectors of the economy—such as banking or finance, insurance, and government—are often confronted with more elaborate office automation systems than clerical workers working in other sectors. While it is useful to consider the impact of new technologies on this largest occupational grouping of women workers, it also important to remember the multiplicity of women's experiences within that broad category.

This volume concentrates on clerical occupations as women's occupations. In the United States, 80 percent of all clerical workers are women. Moreover, some specific clerical occupations are even more heavily sex segregated. Women are 99 percent of secretaries, 97 percent of receptionists, 92 percent of bank tellers, and 91 percent of data entry operators.[5]

There are male clerical workers. However, many of these men are clustered in a handful of clerical positions, such as postal clerk, shipping clerk, and ticket agent. There is little information about those men who work in traditionally female clerical job categories. It is not clear whether this smaller number of male workers is threatened by similar negative impacts of office automation. To the extent that they are, we should be concerned about their well-being also.

Introduction

This work focuses primarily on the impact of office automation on clerical workers in the United States. However, international economic pressures are driving the automation of clerical work in many of the other advanced industrial nations of the world. Some of the less developed nations are also beginning to automate some clerical work. In fact, nations such as Barbados, Korea, and mainland China are even performing a small but growing amount of clerical services for export to corporate customers in the more developed nations.

This book examines the social problem of providing good work for clerical workers in the information era. However, the issues raised here are not necessarily limited to clerical workers in general or female clerical workers in particular. An increasing number of management, professional, and technical workers are using computer/telecommunications technologies as tools for their work in offices, too. Issues such as technological unemployment, computer monitoring, or VDT safety concerns affect not just clerical workers, but many other workers as well. Computer systems design policies which enhance management control over the work process, create greater social isolation on the job, or increase stress in the workplace affect factory workers as well office workers and male workers as well as female workers.

Still, I contend that the particular configuration of issues confronting women who are clerical workers deserves sustained ethical analysis. This book seeks to examine and to evaluate the intersection of gender with the organizational status and power of clerical workers. Unfortunately, serious scholarly attention to the specifics of such women's work lives is still relatively rare. There is still a tendency to incorporate women within some "generic" whole in a fashion which ignores or obscures some specific dynamics operating in the workplace experiences of women. Indeed, too quickly subsuming women into the generic "men" or even "workers" contributes to the social invisibility of questions about justice for clerical workers.

An Uncertain Future

Office automation is still in a relatively early stage. The more serious human dislocations accompanying this technological transformation are only now beginning to be apparent. Indeed, while there have been several government, business, academic or union-sponsored studies of the impact of office automation, the changes underway are not well understood. At present, we have a rather tentative grasp of the social implications of office automation.

Moreover, office automation is a continual process. Therefore, the social impacts of that process change as the technology itself changes, as certain office automation applications become more widely dispersed throughout the economy, and as new applications are developed. There is a real risk in attempting to describe the future impacts of such a rapidly changing phenomenon such as office automation.

Whether office automation will exacerbate future unemployment levels depends upon a complex interaction of variables in the future. The employment effects will not just be the result of labor-saving potential inherent in the technology, but also of such factors as the rate of growth of the labor force, the rate of female participation in the labor force, the amount of capital available for investment in office automation systems, and the degree of international competitive pressure on labor costs. Therefore, the impact of office automation on future employment levels for clerical workers is conjectural and highly controversial. To assert that office automation may result in the elimination of a significant number of clerical jobs over the next two or three decades is intentionally to fix attention upon the more pessimistic among a wide range of employment predictions—all of which are highly uncertain. In this book, I deliberately present a "worst case scenario" concerning labor displacement resulting from office automation. If that scenario should be realized, the suffering of clerical workers and potential clerical workers will be massive.

Implicit in this worst case scenario is the assumption that the labor displacement potential inherent in office automation technologies is high and the assumption that, under protracted conditions of instability and sluggishness in the global economy, pressure will be intense to reap the benefits of office automation in the form of lower labor costs, rather than enhanced services. It may be that the high potential for labor savings offered by office automation technologies will not be realized, in part, because many office automation systems will be poorly designed, incompetently administered, and ineptly used. However, it is a mistake to rely primarily on organizational incompetence to protect the jobs of clerical workers. As an ethicist, I insist that we should take seriously the possibility that a large number of clerical jobs could be eliminated by the year 2000, for the human impact of such massive job displacement could be devastating. It is important to consider what social choices need to be made *now* in order to prevent the further economic marginalization of a large group of women.

It is not just predictions about the future impact of office automation on clerical work which are uncertain. It is difficult to gather reliable descriptions about even the *current* consequences of office automation for clerical work. Of the relatively few social science studies investigating clerical work and automation, several involved interviews and observation in companies where the management was "enlightened" enough to welcome researchers. Such studies cannot give us information about the working conditions for clerical workers employed by less benevolent companies. One major study about stress and clerical work relies on data collected from surveys published in four major women's magazines. The respondents are not, therefore, a "representative sample." In spite of the shortcomings in the information presently available about the impact of office automation on clerical work, it is urgent to encourage broader discussion about the social consequences of this technological transformation of women's work. Public attention to this phenomenon is crucial, because office automation may have a major impact on the well-being of a very large number of women.This book discusses three potential problems raised by office automation: the displacement of a large number of workers, especially socially disadvantaged workers; the redesign of the remaining jobs in a fashion which interferes with worker autonomy and sociality; and increased occupational health risks.

Potential Problems

Office automation may pose a serious threat to women's employment opportunities. Computer/telecommunications systems may permit employers to sever the link between a rising volume of information to be processed and growth in clerical employment opportunities. Since the beginning of this decade, employment for clerical workers has grown less rapidly than employment in other occupational groupings. After the turn of the next century, there could even be an absolute decline in the number of clerical jobs available in comparison with 1980.

Patterns of serious job loss may be hidden because of the high rate of attrition in many clerical positions. Companies may choose to avoid clerical layoffs by abolishing positions while they are "vacant." Such hidden job loss should be a matter of social concern, for jobs which are abolished after one employee leaves are not available for other persons who are new to the labor force, who are reentering the work force after a break in paid employment, or who change jobs. Opportunities for work are also affected when permanent, full-time positions are redefined as part-time or temporary jobs. While some clerical workers welcome the flexibility offered by part-time or temporary jobs, such jobs also have serious drawbacks, which must not be ignored.

Office automation not only restricts the number of full-time, permanent clerical positions available for qualified workers, it also contributes to the elimination of lower-level technical, professional, and managerial jobs which have served as crucial gateways to higher level positions for some clerical employees. Office automation is one factor contributing to a situation in which obstacles to upward mobility are all but insurmountable for far too many clerical workers.

Some clerical jobs will be eliminated as a result of office automation. Many of the remaining jobs will be changed in complex ways. The results of office automation are ambiguous for the well-being of many clerical workers. Some aspects of clerical work have improved; other aspects have deteriorated.

In early, large-scale office automation operations, work was frequently fragmented. Clerks were required to handle meaningless bits of coded information according to rigidly defined procedures. In some cases, office automation systems allowed management to exert greater control through heavy-handed machine pacing and intensive computer monitoring. In too many cases, such facilities continue to exist. In other cases, however, automated clerical jobs are now being designed to provide more variety and responsibility. Some of these new jobs include routine tasks formerly performed by professionals and managers. Compared to the professional jobs, the enhanced clerical jobs are subject to tighter managerial control, but compared to previously available clerical jobs, they offer more variety, increased autonomy, and higher pay.

However, jobs which require heavy use of computer terminals may isolate workers from others. With interactive computer systems, almost all requisite information is available through the computer, so workers rarely need to consult one another. Such social isolation may diminish the quality of work life for clerical workers; it may also weaken workers ability to band together to transform the conditions of their work.

Additionally, prolonged use of video display terminals (VDTs) to perform clerical tasks appears to be connected with a variety of physical discomforts and health risks. Bodily discomfort, including eye and musculoskeletal problems, are associated with work in poor office environments. Such health problems seem to be exacerbated by poor job design. Occupational stress is, perhaps, the most critical job-related threat to the health of clerical workers. A lack of autonomy on the job is a crucial factor associated with hazardous occupational stress. Office automation systems can be devised which include features such as machine pacing and computer monitoring, which increase both rigid managerial control and employee stress levels. Office automation equipment can also be used to decrease burdensome, routine tasks and to give workers greater control over their work, thus lowering their levels of stress.

The Social Context for Office Automation

Office automation is a central focus of this book. However, office automation takes place within particular social contexts. The ways in which computer/telecommunications technologies are employed are influenced heavily by the social context. Therefore, it is necessary to discuss the larger social setting in order to understand more fully the choices which confront us. For example, as office automation systems become more sophisticated, routine clerical operations are often completely automated. In many cases, the remaining clerical jobs require a high level of literacy and good problem-solving skills. In a society where poor people—who are disproportionately African American, Hispanic, and Native American—are too often denied an adequate education, the resultant structural unemployment will fall most heavily on those groups which already suffer the greatest social burdens.

When discussing stress as an occupational health hazard for clerical workers, it is imperative to consider the social context in which office automation systems are implemented. Those clerical workers who have children are already at increased risk of coronary heart disease due to stress associated with the double burden of workplace duties and family responsibilities. Similarly, racism and/or sexual harassment are already critical sources of stress for far too many clerical workers. If the heavy use of a video display terminal is an additional stressor in an already high-stress life, the health consequences for the workers could be cumulative and severe.

Human Choices Determine the Consequences for Workers

Throughout much of this book, I concentrate on the potential harmful effects of office automation on the lives of clerical workers. However, I do not mean to imply that computer/telecommunications technologies are inherently dehumanizing technologies—the use of which ought to be prohibited or heavily restricted. Rather, I view office automation technologies as morally neutral tools, and I contend that most of the bad effects of office automation systems are the result of inept or evil human choices in the use of these technological tools.

Human beings are capable of making good choices in the implementation of office automation technologies. Those technologies can be used to minimize the stultifying human effort previously expended in performing highly routine information processing tasks. To the extent that office automation makes clerical workers more productive, the new technologies could be used to free clerical workers to engage in more creative work.

To the extent that office automation increases productivity and eliminates burdensome work, it will benefit the human community.

However, it is important that both the benefits of office automation and the burdens of this technological transition be shared as equitably as possible. From a moral perspective, it is important that we display a special concern for the burdens thrust upon the more vulnerable members of society. Will more women than men bear the burdens of the emerging information age without garnering an appropriate share of its rewards? Will older, poorer, and/or minority workers (and potential workers) pay a heavy price, while other segments of the community reap the benefits? Religious groups are among those social bodies which can press questions of just treatment for workers affected by office automation. Religious groups can insist that the interests of the marginal, more vulnerable members of the community receive special attention.

The Contribution of a Critical Theology to Justice for Clerical Workers

This book offers ethical reflections from a Christian perspective on changes in clerical work. The fundamental thesis is that changes in clerical work resulting from office automation must be evaluated not only in terms of efficiency or profitability, but also in terms of their effects on the well-being of the workers. Values such as respect for human dignity and justice should be brought to bear when making decisions about the technological transformation of clerical work.

I contend that we need a public debate about how office automation can proceed in a fashion consistent with the well-being of workers (and displaced workers). Concerns about the human impacts of office automation are ultimately a part of a larger, more central moral question. What is the moral quality of the various patterns of participation—including patterns of economic participation—in our society? There are sociologists, philosophers, and theologians who are currently very pessimistic about this society's capacity to engage in mutually intelligible public discourse about the ethical dimensions of social questions.[6] If we are going to reinvigorate modes of public discourse concerning moral issues, then we should not ignore the ethical resources which religion provides.

Both our moral understandings and our motivations to act upon those understandings as individuals and as groups are rooted in particular histories of thought, experience, and faith. In Western civilization and in the United States, Christianity is a significant part of the cultural memory. Moral values rooted in Christian beliefs have *sometimes* heightened and continue *sometimes* to heighten awareness of injustice and commitment to end such injustice. Religious groups are a source of wisdom concerning ethical values and, as such, these groups have potentially important voices to add to the public conversation concerning social policy issues. The religious belief that human beings are ultimately accountable before the Divine Power for their individual and communal acts relativizes less universal appeals. Religious faith prods us to widen our horizons to include concerns beyond the demands of personal success or corporate profitability.

In order to be credible when speaking in a pluralistic society, Christian theologians must be self-critical about their own traditions. Christians need to acknowledge that their religious opinions have been pushed to the margins of public debate in modern Western society, in part, as a reaction against the intolerance and destructiveness which characterized some elements of Christian thought and practice. Wars of religion, witch burnings, slavery, and pogroms have led some morally sensitive persons to distrust the power of Christian religion in public life. In light of this history, which is deeply scarred by forms of hatred and domination that fed on "Christian values," contemporary Christians must employ a certain modesty in public discourse.

If Christians are to develop a theology which can speak to social questions about the uses of computer/telecommunications technology, then Christian participants in the debate must learn to speak without imperialistic or triumphalist tones. While Christian ethicists should speak modestly, they should also speak frankly, acknowledging the religious foundations for the positions which they espouse. I do not concur with those who assert that in public debates all the participants have an obligation to limit themselves exclusively to abstract arguments which appear to be equally intelligible to all "rational persons."[7] I contend that such strictures on material for public discourse ironically reflect a personal and social commitment to one particular faith—a belief system about human nature that is rooted in the world view of Enlightenment rationalism and its elaboration in the tradition of philosophic liberalism. As Stanley Hauerwas has pointed out, "moral disagreements involve rival histories of explanation."[8] What philosophic liberals have increasingly done is to rule out *a priori* any recourse to explicitly religious histories of explanation in public policy debates.

It is both honest and appropriate for religious persons to root their value judgments in appeals to religious images, symbols, and stories. I contend that nonbelievers can share in and be moved by the particularities of religious images and stories which evoke a commitment to values such as justice or compassion, even though nonbelievers are not finally convinced that these images and stories are the best vehicles for salvific truth. Along with theologian David Tracy, I assert that every good story, including every good religious story, has an "authentically public character."[9] The public character of the stories and images also means that they are subject to criticism for the ways in which they fail to fully embody the promise of human wholeness as well as affirmation for the saving power which they still manage to convey.

In addition, many arguments in religious ethics are rooted in particular descriptions of human experience, and, hence, they are open to comprehension and judgment by persons who are not fellow believers. A central concept in this book is the notion of justice as participation. Appreciation of that concept is frequently rooted in some personal experience of its corollary—injustice as marginalization or exclusion. The image of justice as participation has potential persuasive power, especially for those who have at some time been made to feel that they don't belong—they don't count. Thus, assertions about justice as participation should be accessible, up to a point, for many who are not Christian. They are comprehensible to those who do not agree with faith statements about a Divine Being who is at work in our time to bring about justice, peace, and plenty for all. Some persons who are Jews, believers in other religions, or persons of good will who espouse no religion will concur with many or all the ethical judgments made in this book, though they would give somewhat different warrants for their judgments. It should come as

HILTON M. BRIGGS LIBRARY
South Dakota State University
Brookings, SD 57007-1098

no surprise to Christians that the goal of justice for all is shared by morally sensitive non-Christians, for many Christians believe the Creator formed all human beings with the capacity to discern what is right, to love what is good, and (within limits) to do what is just.

If Christian ethicists are going to enter into a public debate about office automation, they need to be self-critical concerning the shortcomings of certain Christian traditions about both women and work— shortcomings which contribute to social blindness to the injustices suffered by clerical workers. Christian views of work have been shaped by a religious history which contains strands of thought which draw a sharp distinction between the material world of daily experience and the eternal, heavenly realm of spiritual fulfillment— between salvation based on inward personal holiness and social questions. From such perspectives, the activities of this world, including ordinary work experiences, are matters of little concern to religion. Christians who hold such points of view have little impetus to strive to transform work experiences in order to achieve greater human fulfillment through work.

There is also a strong strand of gender dualism in Christian thought. The male thinkers who publicly articulated Christian traditions often associated women with gender-defined duties in the household. Throughout much of western Christian history, women were performing important productive functions in the household. With industrialization, socially acknowledged economic activity shifted to the office and the factory. However, many Christian theologians accepted and contributed to a continued connection of women with the home—a home now dissociated from the workplace. In the United States, the increased labor force participation of women throughout the twentieth century undermined the credibility of the man/workplace—woman/home dualism. However, the legacy of that dichotomy in "liberal" Christian ethics is presently manifest not as explicit norms about women's household responsibilities, but as a blind spot. Liberal Christian ethics fails to focus *in a sustained way* on the injustices suffered by women in the workplace.

The difficulty in appealing to Christian traditions in a public debate about justice for women goes deeper than overt religious justifications for female subordination. Many of the saving symbols of the Christian tradition are cast in terms which seem to exclude women. For example, the image of "the Kingdom of God" has had the capacity to sensitize persons to the positive transformative possibilities in their own social situation. Yet, an appeal to that notion is problematic when women's issues are in question. The phrase was created in a patriarchal culture, and it is expressed in androcentric language. The words *Kingdom* and *God* can obscure, not illuminate, justice for women. The word *God* subtly perpetuates the notion that Divine Power is somehow masculine. "He" rules in heaven, therefore, it is appropriate for men to rule on earth. The word *God* is part of a complex cultural system that legitimates the very female subordination which is a central dynamic in the injustice experienced by clerical workers.

In addition, the image of Divine Being as a male sovereign, as a King, has connotations of hierarchy and "power over." The dominance implicit in the words *king* and *kingdom* is inconsistent with the values of solidarity and justice as participation which are stressed throughout this work. From a contemporary feminist perspective, there is a real tension between the promise of a redeemed creation which was announced by Jesus and the connotations of maleness and dominance in the phrase traditionally used to name that reality. In this book, I am struggling to preserve continuity with a centuries-old eschatological vision of a time of freedom, justice and wholeness promised to humanity. Yet, loyalty to the truth of that promise, *as addressed to women*, compels me to challenge the androcentrism of the traditional term. Therefore, in this book, I shall use the term *Reign of God/dess*.[10] *God/dess* is an awkward construct. Still, it forces us to acknowledge that, for Christians, Divine Being is neither male nor female. Rather, God/dess is the Power of Relation in which both men and women participate. While the word *reign* is gender neutral, it still has connotations of *power over* which are in tension with the value of justice as participation. Still I have decided to use the term *Reign of God/dess* in the hopes that it both challenges the androcentrism of *Kingdom of God* and also affirms the hope shared by Christians throughout history for that justice and peace which God/dess holds out to women and men.

In this time of fundamental economic transition to a postindustrial era, society needs moral guidance. Christianity at its best continues to offer moral wisdom and vision. If critically appropriated, some of its stories and images have the capacity to sharpen our moral perceptions and deepen our commitment to do what is right. The achievement of justice for office workers will not come about easily. Therefore, we cannot afford to ignore the resources which Christian faith offer for this social battle.

Justice as Participation,
Sin as the Denial of Justice

Central in the evaluation offered here is the image of justice as participation. Human dignity is realized and sustained in a situation of social solidarity. All persons need to be treated in a fashion which makes plain that they count as valued members of the community. Therefore, human beings flourish when they are able to be *active* participants—producers as well as consumers—in the economic life of early postindustrial society. Given the value assigned to wage labor in this culture, those women who are involuntarily restricted to, or pushed further towards, the margins of the economy will be unjustly be denied both a sense of self-worth and a voice in economic decisions of the society.

Active participation is not enough. The terms for participation must be equitable ones. In this book, I expand upon the the concept of justice as participation by exploring elements for a substantive theory of "good" work. I examine contemporary theological evalua-tions of work, testing them in terms of their appropriateness to the experiences of clerical workers faced with the technological and economic transitions of the early postindustrial age. According to the normative theory of work offered here: Work is essential for human survival, because paid employment is, at present, a major social mechanism through which workers get access to those material goods and human services necessary for survival (and perhaps some mea-sure of comfort) for themselves and dependent loved ones. Wage labor can also provide a measure of financial independence which can be an important underpinning for personal autonomy. Work, even routine clerical work, may provide workers with an opportunity to develop and exercise competencies in which they take pride. Further, the workplace is an arena in which workers may form rewarding personal relationships and come to recognize their interdependence as human beings in ventures to satisfy mutual material needs.

However, too many clerical workers find that aspects of their jobs undercut their dignity and threaten their well-being. It is, therefore, important to examine the impact of sin on clerical women's experiences of work. Sin points to the perennial human tendency to make evil choices, both individually and corporately. Sin may be experienced as a conscious and deliberate personal choice to do something morally wrong. Sin also occurs when we cooperate with and perpetuate patterns of evil in our communal life. Such social sin often has the character of a collective, willful social blindness—we refuse to "see" the patterns of oppression and domination embedded in our cultural beliefs and forms of social organization. The subordination and exploitation of clerical workers has just such an aspect of invisibility and, thus, is allowed to continue without sustained social protest.

As social beings, managers, professionals, and clerical workers all find themselves entrapped in and perpetuating interstructured patterns of sin. Clerical workers are subordinated *both* because of their position at the bottom of the office hierarchy and because of their sex, and the two forms of subordination reinforce each other. Moreover, gender is not the only characteristic which intersects with organizational position in a way which may intensify oppression. Race, ethnic identity, and/or social class all influence persons' opportunities to experience fulfillment through their work. In addition, those characteristics do not operate serially, but interact simultaneously in the lives of many workers. Such sinful patterns of exploitation and domination are difficult to transform, particularly when precarious economic conditions stir anxiety and self-protective greed.

Yet, sin should not be the final word in Christian ethics, for some Christians have also struggled to keep alive hopeful visions of the Reign of God/dess—of restoration of right relationship between God/dess and humankind and among human beings. This is a vision of abundance, human wholeness, and justice. The Reign is to be characterized by new patterns of relationship in which the socially marginal find themselves drawn toward the center, where their needs can be satisfied. While the Reign of God/dess should not be identified entirely with a transformation of exploitative economic patterns or patriarchal relationships, struggles to achieve greater justice for women in the workplace contribute to its triumph.

In the final chapter of this book, I probe strategies to promote right relationships among clerical workers and others in the workplace. What is offered is not a comprehensive policy designed to be *the* solution for clerical workers and potential clerical workers, but rather some proposals for an urgently needed *sustained public debate* about the human consequences of the automation of clerical work. The emphasis is upon how clerical workers can become powerful advocates for their own interests through gaining greater understanding of the transformations of work processes which they are experiencing, through maintaining solidarity in their daily contacts with coworkers, and through forming strong "rank-and-file" unions. Clerical workers, assisted by groups such as international religious bodies, need to find means to create international associations of workers capable of pursuing their legitimate interests in cooperation with— but also, when necessary, in conflict with—the management of multinational business operations.

I explore several policies designed to preserve and extend opportunities for clerical workers (and potential clerical workers) to be active participants in the labor force. These include educational and training programs which equip all persons with the skills necessary in automated workplaces and effective equal employment opportunity efforts. In addition, I examine policies which would promote participation on equitable terms, such as pay equity schemes and provisions for safe and healthful working environments. Of special concern is worker participation in job design, especially in the establishment and monitoring of performance statistics. In particular, we need to consider whether an emphasis on individual, quantitative measures of job performance undermines worker solidarity.

A comprehensive policy designed to enable clerical workers to participate actively in the economic realm presses at the limits of social change possible under postindustrial capitalism. Thus, this work finally raises the explosively open-ended question: what sort of transformation in our economic lives will be necessary in order that there be justice for the women in the workplace?

Those who are concerned about justice for clerical workers need to realize that office automation does not necessarily have to be a zero sum game where some people win, while other people lose. In a more just society, office automation could be implemented in ways which benefit everyone. Workers could find their jobs less tedious and more challenging. Management could have access to more reliable, more timely information at lower cost. Consumers would benefit from new information-based services and from lower costs for goods and services, reflecting lower office overhead costs. Special effort could be expended throughout society to insure that persons from socially vulnerable groups had a genuinely equal opportunity to qualify for jobs in the postindustrial era. Office automation could be used to facilitate economic relationships which demonstrated respect for the dignity of individuals while providing enhanced material well-being for the entire community. Such harmonious results will not be an inevitable outcome of the technology itself. Neither will they be the outcome of an easily achieved human solidarity. Greater harmony, solidarity, and shared material well-being will only result from a long and difficult struggle to overcome the dehumanizing effects of historic injustices and contemporary evil in our common life.

Chapter One

·················

Office Automation

·················

and Clerical

·················

Employment

Throughout this century, as business enterprises have grown in size, they have hired an ever-increasing number of women to process the paperwork necessary to coordinate their complex economic activities. The advent of sophisticated integrated office automation systems, which employ the latest computer/telecommunications technology, may reverse employment trends in clerical fields. By the end of this century, we may see a decline in the relative importance of the clerical sector as a source of employment opportunities. Such a shift in employment patterns would have important implications for women's well-being and, hence, for the common good.

The Feminization of Clerical Work

Although clerical work today is largely women's work, this was not always true. There was a time when employees in offices were almost all men, but as office work was reorganized, during the end of the nineteenth century, the gender composition of the clerical work force began to change. Before the Civil War, in the United States, offices of merchants or other entrepreneurs were small. Under "individual enterprise capitalism,"[1] the office work force often consisted of an employer, a bookkeeper who kept the financial records, one or more clerks who performed varied duties, perhaps one or more copyists who hand copied the few documents which the employer required, and an office boy who served as a messenger and errand

Office Automation and Clerical Employment

boy. Usually, the employer and employees were male. Women were rarely employed in the pre–Civil War office.

The office staff was small because there was little paperwork. Businessmen made many deals face-to-face; therefore, they required minimal documentary records. Financial records were similarly rudimentary. The employer knew the office staff personally and supervised their conduct and the quality of their work directly.

During this period, the job of clerk could be a stepping-stone to management or ownership. Some clerks were economically privileged, young men who were learning how to manage a business by working as a clerical assistant to a relative or family friend. Of course, there were also other male clerks who did not come from the upper classes and who spent their lives as clerical workers.

In the final third of the nineteenth century, the scale of some offices in the United States began to change. Spurred by the Civil War, some factories grew much larger. Improved transportation meant that some manufacturers and distributors could expand to serve regional, national, and even international markets. As businesses grew larger, they needed more records and a larger office staff to track corporate interests. As the number of workers in offices grew, work was reorganized with a greater specialization of duties. The clerk who had performed a wide variety of administrative functions was replaced by new categories of workers performing specialized functions such as typing or preparing invoices. This new specialization of function was (and to some extent still is) most pronounced in larger organizations.

As the office work force grew, the owner or a single manager could no longer supervise each employee personally. A hierarchical authority structure evolved with a larger number of clerical workers at the base—each doing a specific, routine task. These clerical workers were supervised by a managerial corps which reported to senior executives and the owners.

The privileged male career path from clerk to manager or owner was transformed with the development of specialized clerical jobs. As a result of the vast expansion of the clerical work force, far more clerks were hired than could be promoted into professional or managerial positions. Moreover, the new, more specialized clerical jobs did not provide adequate on-the-job, managerial training. The new clerical workers had few opportunities to familiarize themselves with all aspects of the business. They usually understood only one function, such as payroll, receivables, or correspondence.

In a self-reinforcing pattern, as clerical work lost its character as a training ground for management, employers began to hire a new type of employee for the newly routinized clerical jobs. These were unmarried, white women who were viewed as good clerical material, but not perceived as potential professionals or managers. Once clerical work became (white, native-born) women's work, the career links between many clerical positions and professional or managerial positions were almost completely severed.

Women were hired for the new type of clerical positions because they had those socially-ascribed attributes which seemed to suit them especially well for such work. Many women were literate. In addition, women were perceived as dexterous, docile, and willing to work for low pay. The first American manager to hire women clerks was the Secretary of the Treasury during the Civil War. In reporting on the success of this experiment, Secretary Spinner declared, "Some of the females doing more and better work for $900 per annum than many male clerks who were paid double that amount."[2]

By the final decades of the nineteenth century, many unmarried, middle-class, white women had less productive work to do in the home. Thus, they were eager to take the many new clerical positions. This was apparently the group from which employers wished to draw their clerical workers. Employers were unwilling, for the most part, to hire African American women in clerical positions. For example, the African American reformer and lecturer Fannie Barrier Williams told an audience in 1893 that she had tried to help a highly qualified African American woman find a job as a stenographer and typist. Through Williams' connections, the young woman was recommended as a secretary to the president of a Chicago bank. However, the bank's board of directors rejected the young woman because she was African American.[3] In 1900, in the United States "91.3 percent of all female clerical workers were native-born whites, 8.3 percent were foreign-born whites, and . . . only 0.4 percent were nonwhite."[4] As these figures show, there was prejudice against immigrant women as well as African American women. Immigrant women worked in factory or domestic service jobs, the doors of offices were virtually shut to them.

By the close of the nineteenth century, clerical employment for women had increased more than sixfold. In 1890, there were 75,000 female clerical workers; in 1900, there were 503,000. Certain segments of the clerical work force were progressively "feminized." For example, in 1880, 40 percent of the stenographers and typists were women; in 1930, more than 95 percent were women.[5]

As the case of the typewriter shows, organizational changes already underway can call forth new technological solutions. Technology may be employed in response to organizational forces which exist independent of the new technology. Change in the character of office work is not necessarily technology driven.

The entrance of large numbers of white, native-born women into the office work force was facilitated by, but not caused by, the availability of typewriters. Historian Margery Davies points out that the success of the typewriter coincided with *and depended upon the rapid expansion of monopoly capitalism* in the closing decades of the nineteenth century. Expanding business enterprises required more paperwork and, hence, created a demand for the new typewriters. In turn, the increased speed with which a typist could produce an office document made it technically feasible to produce the voluminous records which larger, more complex business firms required.

Since the job category of typist was new, it was, in a sense, sex role neutral. Employers had no preconceived notion that operating the typewriter was man's work, so those young women seeking clerical positions were readily considered for typist openings. The belief that women had a special fine manual dexterity made it seem "natural" that women should be employed to operate typewriters. Moreover, their low salaries, compared to male workers, meant that female typists could produce the burgeoning paperwork at lower cost.

Technological Displacement of Clerical Jobs

From the 1880s through the 1970s, a growing demand for information to coordinate the activities of ever larger-scale organizations

Good Work at the Video Display Terminal

drew a steadily growing number of women into the office work force. In sheer numbers that growth was particularly strong from the 1940s through the 1980s. In those four decades so many women were drawn into the clerical work force that "the proportion of clerical workers to total employment . . . *doubled*."[6] Beginning in the 1950s, considerably more minority women found employment as office workers. As one government study reports: "the movement of black and Hispanic women into office occupations has thus occurred almost entirely within the last 30 years and has aided many of them to move into the middle class."[7]

However, the almost continuous trend, throughout this century, of substantial expansion of employment for women as clerical workers may now be about to shift. The rate of growth of clerical jobs has started to slow, while the volume of information processed continues to grow. By the turn of the century, there may well be a relative, and perhaps even absolute, decline in clerical employment.

A large number of clerical jobs could be eliminated through office automation. A number of office jobs have already been eliminated through the use of computer/telecommunications technologies, but the extent of job loss has been hard to grasp. In the steel or auto industries, large layoffs draw public attention to the impact of automation on manufacturing jobs. However, many companies automating their *offices* have been able, until recently, to eliminate jobs without laying off large numbers of people. Many companies alleviated worker resistance to office automation by making staff cuts through attrition. Since there is high turnover in many clerical jobs, employers did not have to wait long for the staff to shrink. In other cases, employees no longer needed in the departments which were the first to be automated were transferred to vacancies in other divisions which had not yet been automated. When clerical jobs were eliminated by office automation, attrition, early retirement, and lateral transfer alleviated the pain for many individual workers. Now we may be approaching the point at which many organizations no longer choose to—or can—find jobs for all the clerical workers whose functions have been automated. Moreover, jobs which have been eliminated after the present workers leave the company voluntarily are jobs which are not available for other clerical job seekers.

Although few workers have been laid off thus far, there has already been a significant shrinkage in the amount of labor required to perform many clerical functions. The resultant loss of opportunities for work has been difficult to perceive. Such job loss is subtle. A worker who leaves is not replaced. Full-time jobs are redesigned as part-time work. Work is redesigned in a fashion which requires fewer permanent employees; temporary workers are used to handle any peak workloads.

As a result of office automation, certain types of jobs have been virtually eliminated and other clerical positions have been sharply curtailed. Jobs operating various sorts of calculating and tabulating machines have been almost completely abolished. Key punch operating positions were created as a result of computer technologies which employed punch cards, but the occupation is now declining. Automated switching equipment has caused a decline in employment among telephone operators.

Several sources suggest that data entry jobs in the developed nations are increasingly vulnerable to elimination. Alan Westin and his colleagues note that data entry positions in the United States are at risk as a result of new systems designed to minimize the need for workers to recopy information from other formats into computer readable form and as a result of competition from cheaper overseas data entry operations.[8] Many companies already use optical character scanners to "translate" typed or printed material directly into electronic impulses. A scanner minimizes the need for word processing operators or data entry clerks to "rekey" data so that it can be processed by computer. Scanners can recognize and record at 75 to 120 characters per second, while the best human clerks handle 7 characters per second. However, human operators must interpret certain nonstandard material which the scanner cannot recognize. Still, a system which uses scanner technology allows a few clerks to handle a volume of data which would previously have required many more employees.

The need for clerical services is also eliminated when work previously done by clerical workers is shifted to other workers or consumers/clients. Many bank customers use automatic teller machines to transact business which would previously have required the help of a teller. Some travelers use automated systems available through on-line computer database networks to select flights, hotel accommodations, and rental cars and to make confirmed reservations all without the intervention of a reservations agent. Many companies have portable computer systems which allow sales personnel to record all purchase information electronically as an order is placed, thereby eliminating some manual, clerical operations. Businesses as diverse as auto manufacturers, chemical companies, and grocery chains are planning "electronic data interchange" systems which will allow them to transmit orders in electronic format directly to their suppliers via telecommunications networks. Such systems will further automate certain clerical operations for both purchaser and supplier. Some professionals and managers are now doing certain clerical functions themselves as they use computer terminals to create, retrieve, or transmit information. Therefore, fewer clerical workers are needed to assist them. This may be one reason technical, professional, and managerial employment continued to grow rapidly during the early 1980s, while clerical employment leveled off. Several manufacturers are now preparing to release new computer-based devices called voice-activated typewriters. These devices allow a person to speak a message aloud; then to have the message recorded and displayed on the computer screen. Creating instructions to allow a computer to recognize human language as enunciated by a variety of speakers is a very difficult technical feat. Current machines recognize only a very limited vocabulary; the equipment must be "trained" to respond to a specific user's speech patterns; and users must speak slowly. However, some experts foresee the availability of vastly improved voice-activated typewriters by the mid-1990s.[9] A breakthrough in this technology would have a massive impact on clerical employment.

The Magnitude of Job Loss

Expert Predictions. Throughout the 1970s, growing demands for information exceeded the productivity gains yielded by office automation and thus the clerical work force continued to expand. Some clerical jobs were abolished, but new clerical positions were created in other areas. This expansionary trend in clerical employment may be ending. There are some expert predictions that suggest a decline in the relative importance of the clerical sector as a source of employment. Furthermore, that decline may be severe.

The potential magnitude of the impact of office automation on clerical jobs can be seen in the pioneering office automation project undertaken in some divisions of Citibank during the 1970s. In three years, the bank reduced its back office staff by 2,447—a 30 percent reduction. At the same time, the division cleared a serious backlog of work and handled a substantially increased workload. While 2,447 jobs were eliminated, *only 179 people were fired.* All the others were transferred to other positions in the bank, left to take other jobs, or took early retirement.[10]

Citibank's 30 percent reduction is in line with the more pessimistic estimates of the overall impact of office automation on clerical jobs. Potential job loss due to office automation is a matter of controversy not just in the United States, but in many of the other industrialized nations of the West as well. In a famous report, Siemens, a major German computer manufacturer, predicted that 25 to 30 percent of West German office jobs could be eliminated by thorough use of automation.[11] The British Equal Opportunities Commission has predicted that up to 40 percent of all clerical jobs in Britain are at risk due to office automation.[12]

In a major report commissioned by the French government, researchers Alain Minc and Simon Nora predicted that French banks and insurance companies could achieve a 30 percent reduction in labor required to produce their services. Since clerical workers are spread across so many kinds of businesses, it was impossible for Minc and Nora to analyze with any precision the impact of new office technologies on employment of clerical workers throughout the French economy. However, they predict "the effects on employment will certainly be massive."[13]

Several recent studies have shown that the rate of growth in clerical occupations in the United States is already slowing. A 1985 study by the United States Bureau of Labor Statistics shows that the rapid growth in clerical employment which characterized most of the post–World War II period has tapered off. Economists at the Bureau have

Good Work at the Video Display Terminal

revised previous forecasts, now predicting that growth in clerical employment will be below the general rate of job growth.[14] Samuel Ehrenhalt, the New York regional commissioner of the Bureau of Labor Statistics, concurs "the bloom is off the job growth among clerical workers. In relative importance, they have begun to decline."[15]

Another report by 9to5, the National Association of Working Women, confirms that, after four decades of rapid growth, employment in clerical categories began to level off in the period between 1980 and 1984. The number of persons employed as secretaries, stenographers, and typists declined from 1981 to 1982 and hovered very close to the depressed 1982 level through 1984.[16] Even more ominous were the findings for the Industrial Midwest, an area which did not benefit from the tepid, uneven economic recovery of the mid 1980s. In the Industrial Midwest, clerical employment declined in absolute numbers from 1980 to 1983—largely because of heavy cuts in the clerical work force employed by local, state, and federal government.[17] Erosion of clerical employment opportunities was especially pronounced in the inner city areas of Chicago and Detroit. The 9to5 report concluded that this stagnation of clerical employment provides "a powerful early warning signal"[18] that the clerical jobs which have provided employment for many women, a growing proportion of whom are minority women, may dwindle.

A study done by J. David Roessner and colleagues at the Georgia Institute of Technology projected the impact of office automation on clerical employment to the year 2000. The study team predicted that the impact of office automation on routine clerical operations would develop slowly until 1990, but after that time the decline in clerical labor required to perform standard office functions would accelerate significantly. They forecast that by 2000, clerical employment in the banking and insurance industries would fall below 1980 levels. They predicted a decline of over 30 percent in the absolute number of clerical jobs available in those two key economic sectors.[19] Their best estimate of changes in employment in the insurance industry was a loss of 40 percent of clerical jobs between 1980 and 2000. In the banking industry, their best estimate was a decline in jobs from 1.15 million to 824,000 by 2000.[20] It should be noted that insurance and

Office Automation and Clerical Employment

banking are both clerical-intensive industries with a high demand for routine information processing services. Other industries, like agriculture or construction, which employ a smaller proportion of clerical workers and which have a higher percentage of less repetitive clerical tasks, may not be likely to reduce their clerical staffs by comparable percentages.

Another study by Wassily Leontief and Faye Duchin also predicted major declines in the amount of clerical labor required to produce a given volume of office work by the year 2000. Loontief and Duchin projected labor impacts of computer-based technology on the office work force under two sets of conditions. One presumed rapid deployment of integrated office systems throughout medium-sized and large businesses. The other scenario presupposed a slower penetration the new computer/telecommunications technologies. Duchin now says that it is her opinion that the slower scenario may be more likely, since senior management is more aware of the difficulties involved in implementing the most technologically sophisticated systems.[21] According to their slower deployment findings, certain clerical jobs such as bank teller or office machine operator will be significantly curtailed over the next 15 years. The study indicates that 20 percent fewer tellers will be needed to handle the present volume of transactions by 1990 and 40 percent fewer by 2000. In the category of office machine operator, they suggest 45 percent of the present work force could handle the present volume of work by 1990 and 15 percent could handle the work by 2000. In other major categories of clerical workers, they project significant labor savings by 2000. They forecast that 76 percent of typists and secretaries and 74 percent of other clerical workers could handle the present volume of work.[22] Leontief and Duchin suggest that clerical work will become a less important employment sector. Under their slower deployment scenario, clerical workers will fall from 17.8 percent of the work force to 14.9 percent by 2000.[23] The Leontief and Duchin study implies that a very large increase in the volume of routine information to be processed would mitigate the impact of computer-based technology on clerical employment. However, the Georgia team points out that their results indicate that after 1990 the volume of information processing will increase while clerical employment declines, "a situation different from any faced in recent decades."[24] If the Georgia study proves correct, the link between increased demand for information and increased clerical employment which has been an important factor in the growth of women's labor force participation may be severed. Organizations may be able to collect, process, transmit, and store much more information while requiring the services of fewer clerical workers. Roessner and his colleagues predict: "*The historical, positive correlation between workload and clerical employment . . . [will] be shattered in banking and insurance, in the 1990s.*"[25] In an earlier draft of this report, the Georgia researchers warned: "If our forecasts are approximately correct, traditional methods firms use to handle clerical workers displaced by new technology such as attrition, reassignment and retraining will fall substantially short of meeting the need."[26]

Variable Factors Influencing Clerical Employment. Many experts on employment would dispute such forecasts of substantial job losses in the clerical sector. These experts might point out that widespread unemployment was predicted in the 1950s and 60s, when electronic computers first came into use. Such massive unemployment never occurred. However, at least two crucial factors were different then: (1) early computers were so expensive that only large, expanding corporations could afford them, and (2) the United States' economy was growing rapidly. These trends have been reversed in the 1980s.

Technological changes make today's microprocessors potentially far more potent in their social impact than were the early computers. The development of the silicon chip (or microprocessor) has permitted design of computerized equipment which is much smaller, faster, and more reliable. With the development of the silicon chip, computer power increased dramatically while price declined rapidly. Nora and Minc note that if the price of a Rolls Royce had declined in a fashion comparable to the decline in computer costs, by 1978 the most expensive Rolls would have cost only one franc.[27]

During the 1950s and 1960s when computers remained very expensive, only large, expanding companies could afford to purchase them. Increased clerical productivity made possible by computer systems merely allowed major corporations to expand output greatly without being totally swamped by the accompanying paper work. Computers only slowed the level of job growth in ways imperceptible to all but a few personnel officers, who realized that without the computers much greater increases in personnel would have been necessary.[28]

At first, the impacts of computers on employment were restricted to large corporations. Today, however, it is possible for virtually every small and medium-sized business to afford one or more computers or for major companies to contemplate a computer terminal on every desk. Several studies of small business firms have shown that such businesses have already reduced or plan to reduce staff because of the use of microcomputers.[29] The cost of a computer system able to duplicate the productivity of a full-time clerical employee is often less than one year's salary for that employee. Given the declining cost of computer power, businesses of every size have a strong economic incentive to replace office labor through modest capital investments.

When the first computers were introduced, America dominated a world economy still recovering from World War II. In an environment of rapid economic expansion, the volume of clerical work to be done outstripped the productivity increases produced by new computers. Hence, the number of clerical jobs continued to grow. U. S. corporations which held dominant places in the world economy had little incentive to monitor office labor costs carefully.

In the last decades of this century, however, the global economy has been transformed. United States businesses face stiff international competition from European and Japanese competitors, as well as from firms in the more industrially advanced, developing nations. Major corporations such as IBM, General Motors, Manufacturers Hanover, Prudential, Exxon, and AT&T have responded to severe competitive pressures by making large cuts in their work forces, including their clerical staffs. Current management philosophy stresses the importance of efficiency—of keeping organizations "lean and mean." Recently, politicians and government officials have reinforced this trend. For example, in 1986, the then Under Secretary of the Treasury Richard Darman denounced "corpocracy," i.e., "excessive" layers of corporate bureaucracy.[30] Many corporations are eager to abolish what they now view as unnecessary professional and managerial positions. A wave of corporate "downsizing" and mergers has resulted in cutbacks in clerical "support" jobs, as well as elimination of professional and managerial positions. There is also pressure for increased efficiency in local, state, and federal government agencies which have been a major employer of clerical workers. Budget deficits and resistance to higher taxes will constrain employment in the crucial government sector. Office automation systems are being used by management in these "leaner" organizations to help smaller staffs get essential information processing tasks done efficiently.

The rate of growth in the economy is a critical factor which heavily influences the availability of jobs. As a National Research Council panel comments:

> If economic growth is rapid and demand for labor is high, all those whose jobs become outmoded by technological change will almost certainly be able to find new ones. But if overall economic performance is sluggish, replacement jobs will be hard to find, and the costs of adjusting to job loss that is due to technological change will be high in both economic and human terms.[31]

The panel goes on to explain that economic growth is hard to predict. In an increasingly interdependent global economy, predictions must take into account complex political and economic factors. Recognizing the risks inherent in such predictions, I would suggest that the global economy is in a difficult transition period when strong and stable economic growth can by no means be assumed. In the current, highly competitive, uncertain economic environment, there is severe pressure to reduce corporate costs, especially labor costs. The Nora and Minc report makes clear that in a fiercely competitive international environment, entire industries and even whole nations face intense pressure to automate. They write: "France is being forced by the imperative of foreign trade to compete in a race over which it has no control."[32] What is true of France is true of all the other advanced capitalist nations. None can afford to forego opportunities to lower labor costs, unless their foreign competitors agree to follow similar policies.

It is difficult to predict accurately the full impact of office automation, because it is hard to judge the pace at which automation will proceed. In spite of competitive pressures, office automation may be slowed by worker resistance, especially resistance from more power-ful managerial workers. A lack of workers with the skills necessary to operate the more complex automated equipment efficiently could slow the diffusion of some systems.[33] Corporate managers are now beginning to realize that the costs of *operating* office automation systems represent a substantial and continuing expense. Many senior managers have become reluctant to approve office automation expen-ditures, unless the financial benefits can be clearly documented. Such cost justification has, in turn, often proved difficult.

Availability of capital for investment in high-priced, integrated office automation systems is subject to a wide variety of influences, from corporate profits to the national deficit. Changes in tax policy, especially in regulations about depreciation of equipment, may slow or hasten installation of new office equipment. If office automation lowers overhead and, therefore, the price of goods and services, de-mand and output might rise. This would create new jobs; yet, because of large productivity increases resulting from office automation, there would be a smaller number of new jobs, even with increased demand.

If growth in the labor force slows, then the creation of fewer new jobs may not result in serious unemployment problems. The labor force is expected to grow more slowly during the next decade. Since the clerical sector is so heavily female, it is the growth in the female labor force which is the relevant point. A Department of Labor study predicts a continuing increase in the percentage of adult women in the labor force. "Almost two-thirds of the new entrants into the work force between now and the year 2000 will be women. . . ."[34] Therefore, any significant loss of clerical jobs, which have been a major source of employment for women, may require social policy responses, even if the overall labor force growth is well aligned with the total availability of jobs.

In the second and third decades of the twenty-first century, when the World War II baby boom generation reaches retirement age, the greatly enhanced productivity resulting from use of the microproces-sor may be a social boon. It might allow fewer younger workers to produce the goods and services needed by a growing elderly popula-tion. However, it is possible that in the more immediate future (the next two or three decades), office automation may eliminate jobs more quickly than the pool of potential workers contracts, thus causing serious, though temporary, structural unemployment.

In my judgment, there is a real possibility that office automation will proceed with increasing speed as outside competitive pressures overcome internal resistance. It is also possible that increases in productivity yielded through office automation will be of such a large magnitude that corresponding increases in demand will be hard to achieve. Shrinking employment opportunities in the clerical sector would be the result.

Geographic Displacement of Jobs

At a time when corporate leaders are using office automation to hold down labor costs by curtailing the growth of clerical jobs, they are also using telecommunications technology to transfer routine clerical work away from locations in major cities in the United States to rural or suburban areas in this country or to foreign locations. Advances in telecommunications technology make it possible for workers in lower-cost suburban, rural, or foreign locations to process information generated by major corporations which maintain prestigious administrative headquarters in high-cost urban centers. Studies in New York, Chicago, Detroit, and San Francisco all show that jobs are being moved away from the inner city to outlying suburban areas in these cities. Government researchers have drawn attention to the disturbing implications for African American job seekers of this shift in the location of office work: "Because 55 percent of black Americans live in central cities, as compared to 24 percent of whites, . . . the movement of offices from central cities to suburbs decreases their opportunity for office employment."[35]

Some companies are seeking new sites for their routine clerical operations, because they lack confidence in the ability of urban school systems to supply workers with the skills necessary for these computerized jobs. One computer expert has predicted that telecommunications technology may allow managers to shift work away from socially disadvantaged groups in the cities to other better educated, but still socially vulnerable, workers elsewhere. He sarcastically envisions: "If the company does not like the incompetent Blacks or the

Office Automation and Clerical Employment

inept Chicanos turned out by urban school systems, the business will, in the name of the organization's needs, seek literate, pliable white working women in the suburbs to work at home."[36]

American workers may also find their jobs—at least the routine clerical jobs—transferred overseas to countries where workers are paid much lower wages. At present some companies fly "hard-copy" paperwork overseas to be processed. Then, they return the magnetic media "product," i.e., computer disks or tapes, by plane or transmit the electronic data via telecommunications links. With future improvements in satellite technology, companies may be able routinely to transmit facsimiles of documents overseas, pay lower-wage workers to process them, and transmit the data back to the United States—all at significant financial savings. High satellite transmission costs make such ventures cost justifiable for only a few firms now, but costs are dropping as more commercial satellites go into orbit.[37]

According to a report in *Office Administration and Automation,* "low-cost labor in places like the Caribbean can make farmed-out projects very attractive for domestic firms."[38] For example, one major airline replaced Oklahoma data-entry clerks who made $9.00 an hour with Barbadian clerks who were paid between $1.44 (minimum wage) and $3.00 an hour. A service company in Dallas accepts orders for text entry of material from other corporations. Then, they turn over the text to word processing operators in the People's Republic of China who transfer it to electronic media by rote. The clerks do not read English; they simply enter a string of letters without any understanding of the words which the letters form. Some legal clients consider the Chinese clerks' inability to read litigation material an advantage because it insures confidentiality. These Chinese word processing operators are paid $1.00 a day.[39] Other countries where information processing tasks are now being done for U. S. companies include Korea, India, Mexico, and Haiti. Many of the off-shore data entry clerks are women of color.

As of 1985, off-shore data entry operations were few, and, hence, had little impact on clerical employment in the United States. However, some experts predict rapid growth in such facilities by 2000. After that time, improvements in optical scanners may greatly reduce the need for data-entry labor either here or abroad. A U.S. government report concludes: "It is thus reasonable to expect that off-shore keying may have an effective lifetime of only 15 to 20 years, but during that period it could grow rapidly and have a significant effect on U.S. clerical employment."[40]

Loss of Crucial Rungs in the Clerical Career Ladder

Office automation may be used to eliminate routine clerical jobs. It may also be used to eliminate certain lower level professional and managerial positions which have, up to this point, served as important transitional positions—jobs which allowed certain talented, experienced clerical workers to advance into professional or managerial positions. Thus, office automation could further restrict the limited opportunities for promotion open to clerical workers.

The lack of promotional opportunities for clerical workers is a problem with a long history. As the clerical work force was increasingly feminized, most women workers were drawn into jobs which offered almost no opportunity for career advancement. For example, when sociologist Rosabeth Moss Kanter studied one large corporation in the mid-1970s, she found only 12 percent of the secretaries who worked for the company had held more than three jobs, even though one-fourth of the women had worked for the company for more than 15 years.[41] Even with longevity on the job, most female clerical workers had few opportunities for promotion. Indeed, one of the reasons that turnover is high in the clerical field is that workers who see little hope for advancement with one firm leave that company, hoping to find better opportunities with another firm. Those hopes are often disappointed.

There was a time, prior to the late sixties, when a *white man* with a high school education could get an entry-level clerical job in industries such as banking or insurance. Relying upon on-the-job-training and seniority, he could advance slowly into a professional position or into middle management. Discrimination and job segregation closed those upward paths to white women and minority workers. In the late sixties and early seventies, federally enforced equal employment opportunity programs required that qualified white women and minority workers be considered for promotion on the

Office Automation and Clerical Employment

same basis as their white male peers. But by that time, promotion patterns had changed. According to an analysis by researcher Thierry Noyelle, the higher-level clerical job categories, which had been dominated by white men, were uncoupled from professional and management career tracks. Those internal career ladders "designed to move the ablest workers from nonexempt positions into supervisory and middle managerial positions" were badly weakened.[42] In the banking industry, for example, employers offered more limited on-the-job training to bank tellers, and internal career ladders for tellers became severely truncated.

Instead of promoting lower-level employees within the corporation, many employers increasingly hired persons with specialized academic credentials to fill entry-level technical, professional, and managerial positions. The expansion of higher education facilities after World War II permitted organizations to rely on community colleges, colleges, and universities to provide trained applicants for such openings. In many companies, applicants for these positions must have specific educational qualifications which few clerical workers can match. Thus, it is an irony of history that the civil rights movement and equal opportunity programs opened internal promotion channels to white women and minorities just about the time that those channels became less useful.

There are exceptions to the rule that professional and managerial workers are required to have educational credentials shared by few clerical workers. There are stories about talented clerical workers who displayed such intelligence and initiative on the job that they rose from secretary to upper management. In addition, there are some companies which make it a point to promote lower-level employees from within the company to professional, sales or managerial openings when possible. The Westin study describes a company, fictitiously named "The Graphic," where clerical workers with high school or community college education are given company-supported opportunities to get more training. Workers with good records, good interpersonal skills, and appropriate training are given priority for any higher-level vacancies. Clerical workers at this firm are confident that they have real opportunities for advancement.[43] Unfortunately, such companies are rare.[44] The Westin team investigated whether senior management set clear affirmative action goals for the clerical workers who were performing VDT tasks *and* whether staffs and line managers were *actually implementing these policies.* Only about 10 percent of the organizations which they visited had such effective promotion programs.[45]

Thus, today, clerical career ladders are often short, but different for distinct types of clerical workers. Moreover, office automation may further constrict the already narrow, upward paths for clerical workers. In the past, a secretary's career advancement was often determined by the career advancement of her boss. This was because a secretary's job status was often derived from the job status of her boss. Her job classification reflected the boss' position in the corporate hierarchy, not her own duties or skills.[46]

The traditional route to advancement for a secretary—the boss took the secretary along as the boss moved up—is being changed in large organizations by office automation. In these large organizations, junior-level executives and professionals are not each assigned their own secretaries; rather, several persons share the services of one administrative assistant whose output is supplemented by work done in the word processing center. This can be a more efficient, cost-effective way to arrange clerical support. However, when one of these managers is promoted, the administrative assistant and word processing operators who provided clerical support do not necessarily have an opportunity to move up along with the successful manager.

There is a separate, but similarly short, career ladder for the women clerical workers who are employed in word processing or information processing departments. They can move up through several grades of clerical work to "top out" at clerical supervisor. Even in manual operations, there are few such clerical supervisor positions.[47]

Office automation may also decrease the number of clerical supervisory positions available. Facets of office automation, such as automatic monitoring, may make it possible for one supervisor to oversee the performance of a larger or more spatially disparate group of employees. In settings as diverse as Canadian insurance companies and Australian banks, such supervisory positions have become "a less certain career path to management."[48] Automatic monitoring of rationalized work—and in some cases computer-aided instruction to teach standardized clerical operations—may reduce the need for first line clerical supervisors.

However, as of 1981, aggregate data from the United States Census did not show a decline in clerical supervisor jobs. On the contrary, the number of supervisory positions had grown steadily from 1960 through 1981. Not only were there more jobs in absolute numbers, but there were more supervisors relative to the total number of clerical workers. However, part of this apparent growth in the supervisory ranks may be a result of a change in the way the Census Bureau records the data, rather than a reflection of rapidly swelling supervisory ranks. In 1980, the Census Bureau made particular efforts to enumerate clerical supervisors separately from the general clerical work force. As a result, many more supervisors were counted than in previous years. Hunt and Hunt indicate that, once appropriate corrections are made, clerical supervisory positions grew only slightly more rapidly than clerical work as a whole during the period 1972–82.[49]

Feldberg and Glenn offer some explanations for continuing growth in supervisory categories. They hypothesize that a larger capital investment per worker and a concomitant desire to increase productivity may lead corporate decision-makers to intensify clerical supervision in order to gain greater managerial control of the clerical work process. These researchers also quote one administrator who reported that, as routine clerical work was displaced by automation, a portion of the remaining work which was "more qualitative and less quantitative" was shifted to administrative personnel who were allowed to exercise more discretionary judgment.[50]

While there is as yet little evidence of decline in the number of supervisory positions open to clerical workers, it is possible that the growth trend for such positions is about to be reversed. If the number of clerical workers begins to decline appreciably in the last decade of this century, then supervisory positions should shrink, too. Automatic monitoring and reporting capacities of advanced office systems could accelerate a decline in supervisory positions, although computer printouts on quantitative output can scarcely replace the human relations skills of a good supervisor.

Current Opportunities to Move Into
Technical, Professional, and Managerial Positions

Many full-time clerical employees look at office automation as a chance to learn valuable new skills. They anticipate that their new knowledge of computers will give them a greater opportunity to move out of clerical positions and into technical, professional or managerial jobs. Seventy-three percent of the respondents in one survey of secretaries believed that computer skills would increase their career mobility.[51] However, these hopes may well be thwarted by new structural barriers to upward mobility for clerical workers and by perpetuation of patterns of discrimination in the workplace.

Some clerical workers may hope that training in certain computer applications will provide a bridge over to the burgeoning number of technical jobs in the computer field. However, qualifying for jobs in the computer field is no panacea for women's upward mobility problems. In the computer field, women are clustered in the lowest paying, least challenging positions such as data entry clerks and computer operators. Men are overrepresented in the higher paying, more challenging positions, such as systems designers, systems analysts, electronic engineers, and managers of data processing departments. Within occupational groups in the computer field, women are clustered in jobs at the bottom end. Among computer programmers, for example, women are often assigned the most routine tasks, while men are more often given the more challenging assignments—assignments which can be crucial for career advancement.[52]

The lower-level jobs in the computer field which have been most accessible to women are vulnerable to elimination as computer technology progresses. Experts are already developing computer programs which automatically generate routine computer code following instructions devised by systems designers. Other advances in computer software make it possible for users of computer systems to give instructions directly to the computer to perform customized data operations. The users, in effect, do their own programming. Thus, automation is being used to transfer routine types of technical computer programming work from computer programers to machines and users.

Other office automation systems eliminate more routine professional jobs. Many large corporations are exploring development of "expert" systems which enable computers to handle a number of decisions now being made by some professionals. In the insurance industry, for example, routine underwriting is handled by computer more and more often. However, sophisticated judgments about highly specialized cases must still be handled by professional underwriters. When there is a vacancy among the remaining "high knowledge" underwriter positions, outsiders with specified credentials are recruited to do the work. The gulf in experience and knowledge between clerical positions and the remaining underwriter posts is so great that intelligence and talent alone can rarely bridge it.[53]

Some managerial jobs may also be abolished as a result of office automation. One function of middle management has been to collect and organize data about corporate operations and to transmit that information up the organizational hierarchy. Now senior managers or their clerical assistants can use data management software to extract such information directly from the company's computer databases. Fewer managers are required to produce management reports.

Most clerical workers who hope to be promoted to the remaining lower-level management positions will probably be disappointed. According to a 1982 survey by Minolta, only 17 percent of the executives sampled reported that they could foresee their secretary moving into management. Only 18 percent predicted that their secretaries would advance in the company.[54] Sexism is one reason that some employers cannot conceive of their clerical workers as potential managers. According to Heather Menzies, "a typical response of management to the suggestion that a secretary performing administrative functions be moved into the executive ranks might well be a remark to the effect that, 'You can't make a doctor out of a nurse.' "[55]

Sexism intersects with the low occupational status of clerical work. An employer who might readily hire a woman with a business administration degree for a management opening, might, nevertheless, ignore a clerical worker already employed by the company who had the talent and skill to do the job.

It is possible that the reorganization of work accompanying office automation will decrease the number of lower-level technical, professional, and managerial positions. Such jobs have previously served as important bridge positions for upwardly mobile clerical workers. To the extent that telecommunications technology is used to separate further the location of clerical work from the location of managerial and professional work, another obstacle is placed in the upward path of clerical workers. Spatial separation of "pool" clerical workers has long been a factor both reflecting and reinforcing their low career ceiling. The typing pool and other clerical departments have often been located in different parts of the building away from executive functions. Good workers who have no direct contact with management have always been less likely to be tapped for more responsible duties. New telecommunications technology which permits routine clerical work to be done in another part of the urban area or in another city altogether exacerbates the problem of spatial segregation from professional or managerial openings.

The redesign of new clerical jobs as part-time, temporary, or homework jobs may well tend to increase the number of clerical workers who are viewed as outside normal (limited) promotion channels. (Homework is a term which is being used to describe the labor of persons who do work for organizations from their own homes. A woman who processes insurance claims in her home is an example of a clerical homeworker.) A report from the United States Women's Bureau cautions that the increase in the use of temporary workers to supplement an organization's normal clerical work force creates a special category of employees who are understood to have no opportunities for corporate advancement. "Temporary workers, by definition, operate outside the mobility structure of an organization."[56] The report suggests that temporary workers are attractive to businesses, not just because of present advantages (no company-sponsored benefits, easy layoffs), but also because temporary workers have no organizational standing upon which to base future claims for advancement.

Part-time workers are also in a precarious position with respect to advancement. Such part-time workers may be seen as less serious about their jobs and less committed to the company. Therefore, they may be less likely to be considered for promotion. Homeworkers are another group of workers who are outside the formal opportunity structure of the organization. Some homeworkers are treated as inde-

Office Automation and Clerical Employment

pendent contractors and, thus, are in a situation similar to that of temporary employees. Others are formal employees of the company whose work they process, but their physical isolation from the corporate workplace is a specific form of the spatial barrier to advancement.[57] Contingent work arrangements further jeopardize clerical workers' limited opportunities for promotion.

As a result of trends described in this section, there is too often a "quantum leap" between the top of the clerical job ladder and the bottom rungs of the technical, professional, and managerial ladders.[58] Obstacles to upward mobility of clerical workers in some insurance companies are now so insurmountable that personnel administrators frankly label the remaining clerical jobs as "career clerical," i.e., dead-end jobs.[59]

Another question needs to be asked: Do racist attitudes or ethnic prejudice further narrow the advancement possibilities for minority clerical workers? African American women are disproportionately clustered in those "back office" operations which are spatially separated from the largely white managerial areas. This may restrict their opportunities for advancement, but we need more information about how they are faring in terms of upward mobility from the clerical ranks.

Socioeconomic status plays an increasing role in determining which persons have an opportunity to move into the technical, professional, or managerial ranks. As office automation further undermines internal job ladders, education becomes critical in qualifying for better jobs. Noyelle notes that socioeconomic status frequently influences the extent and quality of one's formal education in a "society [which] continues to lag behind in providing equal access to quality education."[60] The barriers to upward mobility for clerical workers are complex. Sexism limits women's job opportunities and aspirations, but sexism operates in different ways in the lives of women from different racial and ethnic groups and from different social classes. Barbara Baran warns: "because of the significantly greater opportunities available to college educated women, the female occupational structure is apt to bifurcate more sharply than in the past, diminishing even further the egalitarian thrust of feminist strategies."[61]

Class, Race, Sex and the Competition for Scarce Jobs

The overwhelming majority of those who will suffer, if office automation sharply curtails employment opportunities in the clerical field, will be women, especially poor women. Since African American and other minority women are disproportionately represented among the poor, they are at increased risk to lose their access to the remaining office jobs.

In an increasingly automated society, the poorly educated have fewer opportunities for decently paid work. As many low-skilled manufacturing and office jobs disappear, the remaining work is increasingly being divided into better-paying jobs which require a relatively high level of education and low-paying, menial jobs. There are far too many adults in this country who lack even that basic literacy which is essential for many jobs, including clerical jobs. Estimates of adult illiteracy in this country vary. Results of a recent U.S. Census Bureau study indicates that 13 percent of the adult population is illiterate. This figure is among the lower estimates in a wide spectrum of figures on adult illiteracy. A 1979 Ford Foundation study quoted statistics indicating that 23 million Americans are illiterate and 34 million more are functionally illiterate.[62] The functionally illiterate are those who cannot read as well as the average 10-year-old child. Experts applying the University of Texas Adult Performance Level scale estimated that 30 million men and women are "functionally incompetent" and another 54 million "just get by."[63] While authorities disagree about the exact scope of the adult illiteracy problem, it is very clear that a large a number of American adults cannot understand the instruction manuals which explain how to operate computerized equipment nor read the messages displayed on a computer's video display screen.

Illiteracy, unemployment, and poverty are closely intertwined. In one out of every two households falling below the federal poverty line, the head of the household cannot read an eighth-grade book. Over one-third of the mothers dependent on welfare are functionally illiterate. At least half of the eight million unemployed cannot read and write well enough to be retrained for so-called hi-tech jobs.[64]

The largest number of functionally or marginally illiterate persons in the United States are Caucasian. However, illiteracy rates are disproportionately high among African Americans and Hispanics. Sources at the University of Texas indicate that sixteen percent of whites are functionally or marginally illiterate; the percentage rises to 44 percent among African Americans and 56 percent among Hispanics.[65] According to one report, "Black women . . . are more illiterate as a group than any other in the nation."[66]

Illiteracy is a particularly serious problem among minority youth. Forty-seven percent of African American seventeen-year-olds are functionally illiterate. Moreover, that percentage is rising and is expected hit 50 percent by 1990.[67] The educational system is clearly failing Hispanic young people as well. Across the nation, 37.4 percent of Hispanic students do not graduate from high school. In some cities the dropout rate among Hispanic youth reaches 75 to 80 percent.[68] The high school dropout rates cannot, however, be equated with literacy rates. For one thing, some persons with high school diplomas are, nonetheless, functionally illiterate. These statistics on high school dropouts do suggest that too many Hispanic youth are denied an education adequate for the information age.

Illiteracy as cause for unemployment is not a new phenomenon. Higher minority illiteracy rates are one factor in the present higher rates of minority unemployment. One particularly poignant example of this problem was manifest in the results of a pilot project sponsored by four New York City banks along with a coalition of churches. The banks pledged to hire 250 graduates from five troubled city high schools for entry-level positions as tellers, word processors, and file clerks. Yet, after administering an entry-level test described as "roughly the equivalent of an eighth-grade mathematics test," only 100 graduates were hired.[69] This result underlines the fact that, as computers handle more and more routine tasks, sound basic skills will become even more essential for employment. Too many young people are not being helped to develop those skills.

Sound basic skills are necessary to obtain and to hold entry-level clerical jobs. In addition, a familiarity with and confidence about one's ability to operate computer equipment may be another attribute which will give some persons a competitive edge in the changing clerical job market. There is disturbing evidence that white female students, minority students, and poor students are lagging behind economically privileged, white male students in the development of computer competencies. I have deliberately refrained from using the term, *computer literacy*. There is disagreement about what constitutes computer literacy. To some, it includes the ability to write routine computer programs. I do not believe that most students need to learn how to program a computer.

Economically deprived students are less likely to have opportunities to develop computer competence and confidence. There is a disparity in student access to computers in the wealthier schools, both public and private, in comparison with the access offered in the poorer schools. In 1985, there was one computer available for every 54 students in the wealthiest public schools districts, but only one for every 73 students in the poorest public school districts. One-quarter of the poorer schools had no computers at all. Moreover, the per capita number of computers was rising faster in wealthier school districts. Thus, the gap in access to computers as an educational resource was widening.[70] This discrepancy in access to computers is heightened by the differences in exposure to computers in the home. Those who own computers tend to be the socially advantaged. It is primarily the children of the more affluent who can supplement their school computer learning with experience at home.

Early studies showed that African American students had fewer opportunities to gain experience with computers than did white students. However, Quality Education Data reports "our recent results reveal no significant difference between black and white students" [with respect to exposure to computers.][71] Nonetheless, there is some evidence that African American students who now have improved access to microcomputers in the schools are still receiving an inferior type of computer education. Schools in poor, predominantly minority neighborhoods are less likely to have on their staff a teacher who is knowledgable about computers.[72] Educator Carol Edwards warns: "The greater threat to long-term equity lies in the qualitative differences that are surfacing in educational computing. It is disturbing that the disadvantaged students, especially minority disadvantaged students, spend most, if not all, of their hands-on time executing drill and practice programs."[73] Such an education trains

African American students to do the very sort of routine tasks which are being entirely automated, but not to use the computer as a creative tool to accomplish more challenging tasks.

Even relatively affluent white women may be at a disadvantage in a society where the computer is a basic work tool for an increasing number of jobs. Educators report that many more boys than girls are eager to learn to use computers. One New York City educator reports, "Girls do as well in the mandatory classes, but they don't continue. They perceive it as something boys do, as unfeminine."[74] Educators Marlaine Lockheed and Steven Frakt report: "By male self selection and female default, the computer center becomes defined as 'male turf'—as socially inappropriate to girls as the boys' locker room."[75]

Many parents who are affluent enough to purchase home computers seem to see those computers as toys for boys. In a Stanford University study, "All the students in a mid- to upper-income neighborhood who reported home ownership of a computer were boys."[76] Without computer exposure, some women may be awkward or even frightened when confronted with jobs which require them to operate computerized equipment.

In the past, clerical work has provided an important source of employment for women, including a growing number of minority women. Now, there is disturbing evidence to suggest that the clerical sector will no longer offer as many opportunities for employment. If the women and men who have been (or would have been) clerical workers are able to qualify for more satisfying and challenging jobs in other sectors of the work force, then this economic transformation will be to the good. Ominously, though, the educational institutions of this society are denying to many, especially the poor—who are disproportionately Native American, African American, and Hispanic—the skills necessary for employment in the information age.

Organizations which implement office automation systems may eliminate a significant number of routine clerical jobs. This will further narrow the employment opportunities for those with limited educational credentials. Office automation may also eliminate certain lower-level professional and managerial jobs which have been among the few promotional opportunities allowing some workers to move up and out of the clerical ranks.

Good Work at the Video Display Terminal

The use of office automation will alter the character of the work process in many of the remaining clerical jobs. Some of these changes may enhance the quality of work life for some clerical employees by providing them with greater challenge and autonomy. Other changes threaten to diminish the well-being of other clerical workers.

Workers who use interactive computer systems may find work an increasingly isolating experience. Reduction of social contact with coworkers may undermine worker solidarity. Hence, certain changes may undermine the already limited power which many clerical workers have to participate in decisions concerning the conditions of their labor.

Chapter Two

··················

Good Jobs?

··················

Changing Designs in

··················

Automated Offices

Human choices about office automation will eliminate certain clerical jobs. Human decisions about office automation will change the character of the remaining work. This chapter explores issues associated with the design of the remaining computer-assisted clerical jobs. Will they be good jobs? Will human choices about the use of computer technology enhance or diminish the quality of clerical workers' work lives?

The question of job design of the remaining clerical jobs is a difficult one in part because clerical work is marked by great diversity. It varies according to the specific position which a clerical worker holds. The job design issues for a secretary who assists a single manager or professional are different from the job questions which face a clerk who works in a data entry pool. Job design issues also vary from business to business. Senior managers at some corporations foster a corporate culture which encourages employee participation in job design. Leaders in other organizations demand rigorous supervisory control to wring productivity from workers. Job design also varies according to the size of an organization and the stage in the office automation process which that organization has reached. The types of automated office jobs prevalent when major corporations first automated certain discrete, highly repetitive operations, such as payroll preparation or inventory control, are quite different from the new, "electronically broadened production work" or electronically-assisted customer service positions emerging in large companies.[1]

Job design is socially and economically, not technologically, determined. The design of jobs in the automated office is not dictated primarily by some property inherent in computer or telecommunications technologies. There is nothing inherent in computer/telecommunications technology itself which dehumanizes work; rather, the problem of "bad" work results from poor human choices about how to implement technology. That technology itself is not the root of the problem is suggested by the fact that the worst "electronic assembly line" systems devised for clerical workers only extend a decades-old process of "rationalization" of high-volume clerical operations. In the insurance industry, for example, the rationalization of work "actually occurred much earlier and was in no real sense driven by automation."[2]

Scientific Management of Clerical Work

In the late nineteenth century, clerical work began to be divided into a series of separate tasks performed by specialized workers. Clerks who had performed a wide variety of administrative functions in smaller-scale enterprises were succeeded by stenographers, typists, file clerks, and billing clerks who handled discrete aspects of the paperwork generated and exchanged by growing corporations. This specialization of function was (and to some extent still is) most pronounced in larger organizations.

In "paperwork factory" industries, such as banking and insurance, the trend toward routinized, specialized, more tightly supervised clerical work was significantly hastened by the drive toward scientific management in offices during the second through fourth decades of the twentieth century. The most famous exponent of scientific management was Frederick Taylor. For this reason, scientific management is sometimes called Taylorism. Taylor himself never applied his methods to office work, but others, especially William Henry Leffingwell, did.[3]

Scientific management was a set of associated management methods which sought to achieve the most productive work at the lowest labor cost by using scientific observation techniques to determine the one best way to do any task. Often scientific management experts broke a job down into its smallest physical components, did experiments to determine how each action could be most efficiently done, and then reconstructed an "ideal" method for doing office tasks. Once experts had determined the best way to do any type of work, management demanded that workers carefully follow the prescribed methods. Sometimes, prescribed methods were so detailed that very little was left to the worker's discretion.[4]

Many scientific management experts calculated work standards representing a "reasonable" amount of production by a worker within a given unit of time. Such "scientific" work standards could be used by management to set production goals for clerical workers. The process of setting and promulgating work standards often raised the output of clerical units significantly. Harry Braverman suggests that the process of setting high work standards and enforcing those standards through "close and frightening supervision," was responsible for much of the observed increase in worker productivity, despite "pretense" that higher productivity resulted from scientifically achieved improvement in work methods.[5] While one might question Braverman's use of the adjective "frightening," many scientific management plans did require increased monitoring in order to guarantee employee conformity with approved work methods.

Scientific management theory and practice contained several crucial assumptions about human beings as workers. Proponents of scientific management assumed that human beings varied in levels of "natural" ability, with some persons particularly well suited to routine work. Its advocates often believed that such workers could do monotonous work more quickly and accurately than more creative or intelligent types of workers. Moreover, they thought that workers are happiest when working at their own "natural" level of ability.

Racial, ethnic, and sexual discrimination influenced decisions about which workers were "naturally" suited to fill rationalized jobs. Whole new groups of workers were often brought in to fill newly rationalized jobs. To the extent that the new workers were unfamiliar with prior forms of job organization, they might be more willing to accept the tightly circumscribed, rationalized work processes as given. Moreover, since these rationalized jobs often represented better jobs than other forms of employment available to such socially disadvantaged workers, new workers could readily be recruited for the rationalized positions.

Scientific management techniques were often adopted by managers who saw themselves engaged in an adversarial struggle with workers. Workers were viewed as lazy creatures who wanted to do as little work as possible in return for their wages. Management looked to scientific management experts to design work procedures which would allow management to get a full day's work out of the workers. As soon as the volume of paperwork permitted it, managers broke tasks down into simple, subroutines which could be done by "unskilled" workers, because their organizations reaped financial benefit from assigning tasks to the cheapest labor which could and would adequately perform them.

It would be inaccurate to give the impression that scientific management techniques were rigorously employed in all American offices by the 1930s. The evangelical tone of many management journal articles makes clear that many managers remained unconverted to the benefits of scientific management. Many firms, especially smaller ones, ignored these new techniques. Nonetheless, "scientific management . . . represented a concerted and self-conscious drive by a vanguard among businessmen."[6]

Thus, in offices with a high volume of routine paperwork, rationalization of work was well underway before computerized systems were introduced. The first computerized systems simply reinforced existing work patterns. However, there is a difference with computer technology. Earlier scientific management schemes required human tabulation of performance figures, but the effort and cost involved in calculation of worker performance meant that monitoring was often intermittent. There were systems in which supervisors checked regularly on the number of claims completed by each worker or inches of copy produced by each typist. Nevertheless, "employees [could] usually find ways to pace their own activities and to meet standards at a reasonable rate."[7]

Today, computers can be programmed to gather and tabulate work standards data for an affordable, one-time extra cost. Reports about worker performance can be generated using data already collected for other purposes. The employee may not even realize that such data is being tabulated for review by supervisors.

An interactive computer system can monitor each worker's output continuously. Such continuous computer monitoring is qualitatively different from even the strictest human supervision. Harley Shaiken suggests that a core issue associated with computerized productivity monitoring systems is "the pervasiveness of the system, the way it covers each second of what you do."[8]

Job Design Issues

Monitoring. It is easiest to develop monitoring systems for "short-cycle 'production' jobs," i.e., jobs where a limited number of tasks are performed, resulting in "production" of a standardized unit of work. Those limited tasks are reiterated many times during the work day.[9] Processing standardized insurance claims is an example of a short-cycle production job. Thus, most of the office jobs which are easily monitored are the production-oriented clerical jobs, such as word processing operator, data entry clerk, bank (check) proof clerk, or telephone operator. Although it is easiest to monitor such clerical jobs, computerized work measurement techniques are increasingly being applied to other jobs. Until recently, the power and status of professionals and managers, plus the inherent complexity of their work, have protected most them from the worst features of rigid, tightly monitored systems. However, that may change as more sophisticated computer systems are developed to automate certain professional and managerial functions.

A computer can be programmed to tally keystrokes struck, lines or pages produced, forms or other standardized units completed, or claims processed. The electronic components of an advanced phone system can record the number of times a phone rings before it is answered, the length of each conversation, and the number of calls "lost" (i.e., the caller hangs up before the call is answered). In the classified ad department of one large daily newspaper, if the interval between phone calls at a particular workstation is more than five minutes, the supervisor's terminal automatically flashes a signal.

A computer can be programmed to create a log recording when workers are actually entering data and when they have paused. In some systems, workers are required to enter a code every time they leave the machine. At one airline, flight reservationists are required to indicate when they leave their terminals to use the bathroom. Bathroom time for each worker is tallied, and workers who exceed 12 minutes for bathroom breaks in a seven-and-a-half-hour work day are subject to disciplinary warnings.[10]

When computers are connected by telecommunications links, it is possible for more than one person to have access to information at the same time. Thus, supervisors can review information as it is being used by the worker. The supervisor can check the accuracy of the material which the worker is producing. The supervisor can also confirm that the employee is performing corporate duties. As Mary Murphree points out, such supervision can restrain employees from using company time and equipment to do personal clerical tasks, a practice which she describes as "a long cherished perk of office work."[11] There is no technological reason such supervisory oversight need be apparent to the clerical worker. Workers may be completely ignorant that such checking goes on; or they may know that oversight takes place, but not know exactly when they are being monitored. The latter random, "anonymous" monitoring can be particularly stressful for workers.

Units of work monitored can be used as the basis for per minute, per hour, or per day records of each worker's output. They can also be used to evaluate an individual worker's performance over time or to compare one worker's productivity with that of her peers. Statistics gathered by computer monitoring can be used to set and to enforce detailed standards for clerical worker performance. Interviews with workers in one telephone operating company yielded very precise standards for clerical activities. For example, a worker was expected to spend no more than 8.6 seconds verifying billing for the data center and 37 seconds ordering an account printout.[12] In the classified ad department of a major daily newspaper, solicitors are expected to initiate the next call within 10 seconds of completing the previous call.

Computer-generated reports on performance can be used as an incentive to keep employees working at top speed. In many work standards plans, pay is linked to performance. At Blue Cross–Blue Shield of Massachusetts, for example, performance standards are set for each type of insurance claim processed. If a worker exceeds the standard, her pay is increased. If she falls below the minimum standard, her pay is reduced.[13] Docking pay may be an uncommon management practice. However, it is not unusual in some types of clerical work, notably data entry, to offer "incentive" plans, where there is a firm pay floor, or base rate, for acceptable performance with bonuses for workers who exceed certain standards. Where pay is tied directly to output, motivation to work at a quick pace is high. Sometimes, the fastest data entry clerks can increase their salary by 50 percent or more over base pay.[14] Given the low salaries paid many clerical workers, financial incentives are powerful ones. However, doing repetitive work at a constant fast pace creates stress, which can have high health costs for employees. This will be discussed in greater detail in the next chapter. In addition, some employers set the basic work standard higher and higher as workers' average output increases. Labor leaders denounce this practice as "rate busting," and fear of such speed-ups accounts for some worker resistance to work standards programs imposed unilaterally by employers.

While computer monitoring systems appear to offer the advantage of measuring a worker's productivity according to "objective," uniform standards, there are problems with some systems. Systems in which employees are evaluated based on their performance over a short interval, such as a half-day or day, can be especially stressful. During the one lengthy clerical workers' strike by an affiliate of Office and Professional Employees International, a major issue was the union's demand that worker performance be measured against monthly rather than weekly standards.[15] Longer measurement periods allow some workers more variety and control in pacing their own work. Some persons may choose to work in fast bursts at some times, and to maintain a slower pace at others. If work is averaged over a longer period, such employees are not pressured or penalized, as long as their average work rates remain acceptable.

Other computerized performance evaluation systems combine data on worker performance automatically compiled by computer with "subjective" management evaluations. Numeric values can be assigned for attendance, punctuality, and supervisory evaluations of such factors as "attitude." Just such a system, which included subjective managerial judgments in the formula used to evaluate worker performance, was one of the chief grievances of clerical workers in the bitter Equitable Life Assurance Society labor dispute in Syracuse in 1981.

One result of an intensive, detailed electronic monitoring program can be degradation of the quality of service which workers are able to offer to customers. Workers feel pressured to make quick, standard responses to a customer's request in order to complete the transaction within the allotted time. Telephone directory assistance personnel report that they cannot give good service to children, persons who speak English poorly, or callers who make confusing requests. If the directory assistance worker spends a longer time responding to requests from such persons, their AWT (average work time) suffers. As Harley Shaiken notes, "If you put people in an electronic strait-jacket, then they're not going to go outside of that straitjacket to seek to improve the quality of the service that's being presented."[16]

It is difficult to know how many clerical workers experience some form of computer monitoring on the job. Many businesses consider their office productivity monitoring systems to be proprietary information. Since monitoring systems can cause labor-management friction, companies are not eager to draw public attention to their systems. However, the Department of Labor reports: "it is estimated that nearly two-thirds of the 7 million U.S. workers using VDT's in 1984 were monitored electronically by their employers."[17] However, that does not necessarily mean that all (or even) most of these employees were working in situations where collected data was used for purposes of individual work performance evaluation. Still, when Westin and his colleagues visited 110 organizations, virtually every one of them used computer monitoring capabilities to gather some quantitative data on the performance of their clerical-level employees.[18] The Office of Technology Assessment estimates that, perhaps, 20 to 35 percent of clerical employees, i.e., four to six million workers, are subject to monitoring used as the basis for decisions concerning pay, promotion, discipline, or discharge.[19] Moreover, monitoring appears to be heaviest in the most routine clerical jobs in which minority women are disproportionately clustered.

Pacing. Closely associated with computer monitoring is computer pacing of clerical work. Electronic systems can be devised which present work units to clerical workers at a specific pace or in a predetermined order. There are commercially available software packages which flash visible signs or emit an audible tone to prompt operators to keep working at a predetermined pace.

Computer pacing was an aspect of one poorly designed computer system used by an accounts collection unit. Under the previous system, collections agents were each assigned a group of accounts which they had considerable freedom to handle—as long as each agent recovered an acceptable amount of money. This manual system then was replaced by a computer-paced system oriented toward high volume. Collections agents were required to handle calls placed by a computer-based, automatic dialing system. Calls were assigned randomly to agents who were simultaneously shown the account record on their VDT screens. Agents were eager to do well, since their unit was selected as the first one in the company to use the autodialer system. However, since the system was designed to emphasize the quantity of calls placed, but ignored crucial skills exercised by the agents, the unit's performance slumped. One agent reported: "you feel like a robot. . . . After eight hours on the autodialer you're completely burned out."[20] The people who owed money suffered, too, since they were often contacted by a series of different agents who were not knowledgeable about special circumstances pertaining to the account. Amounts collected by the unit fell dramatically.

Customer service personnel increasingly do work paced by automatic call distributors. Each call is electronically assigned to the next available worker. Where the volume of calls is high, workers receive one call virtually as soon as the previous call is terminated. Pressure on the worker is heavy. A worker has little or no opportunity to "recover" from an abusive call, since the computer automatically assigns the next waiting call to the worker's line and response time is being automatically monitored.

Computer-paced work can include computer-generated schedules for a worker's breaks or lunch period. AT&T had a computer system called FADS [Force Administration Data System] which measured the work pattern in each office, then projected the number of workers required at specific time intervals the next day. These projections were used to assign workers' lunch and break times for the next day. Workers could not make lunch plans more than a few hours in advance, could not necessarily schedule lunch or break time to coincide with that of favorite coworkers, nor could they schedule their lunches and breaks according to their own personal preferences or needs.

Management Cautions. While an increasing number of clerical workers use automated systems with computerized pacing and monitoring capacities, there are cautionary management perspectives on the usefulness of such systems. Paul A. Strassman, a former vice-president of Xerox, notes that Xerox absolutely refused to implement automatic monitoring systems within its operations. He described using such systems as "looking for trouble" in employee relations.[21]

Elizabeth Regan argues that use of rigid work rationalization and work measurement schemes in automated offices can be counterproductive. She argues that "the greatest potential of office automation lies in its ability to deal with multiple alternative and complex situations."[22] Yet, systems which rely on narrow task specialization and intensive monitoring give the workers precisely the wrong message. Workers are rewarded for producing a greater volume of information, not more effective information. One manager warns that it is important to emphasize quality in computerized systems. Undue emphasis on quantity is self-defeating: "If you don't put this [quality] at the fore, employees will always find ways to beat the productivity counts, since in any system, there are ways to make the figures look better but not really achieve better service."[23]

Rigid systems of management control—whether manual or computerized—often give rise to covert worker resistance as workers strive to wrest back some control over their own work or to "punish" the employer for imposing such inhumane systems. For example, when a high volume, rigidly monitored accounts collection system was imposed on personnel who had been accustomed to considerable autonomy, the collectors responded by entering fictitious data into the system in order to meet performance targets. A management expert reports the outcome: the collection agents' superiors "were confronted with high productivity figures that did not match the size of monthly revenue."[24] When employees are required to use systems

which deprive them of opportunities to exercise creativity and autonomy, then devising clever, undetectable ways to undermine or even
crash the system becomes the only available way to "test one's
mastery."[25]

Covert resistance is the last resort of employees who have too little
power to negotiate for more humane systems design. Such powerless
workers are disproportionately female and may also be drawn disproportionately from minority groups. For example, in one 9to5 survey,
a higher percentage of African American women reported that they
were required to meet specific production standards than did white
workers.[26] More powerful managerial and professional workers, who
are disproportionately white and male, are less likely to be subjected
to detailed computer monitoring schemes.

Enlargement of Computerized Clerical Jobs.

Computer pacing and monitoring raise some of the sharpest questions concerning the human impact of office automation systems. It
is more difficult to assess the impact of office automation on the
overall design of clerical jobs. For some clerical workers, automation
results in work which requires continuous keyboarding of meaningless segments of information. For others, automation creates jobs
which provide more variety and responsibility than the ones which
the new automated system replaces.

Some of the earliest large-scale automated clerical systems extended the logic of scientific management. Often, such systems were
introduced in facilities where extreme forms of work specialization
and fragmentation characterized the manual systems which were
now being automated. As researcher Barbara Baran indicates: "Both
the cost and technical requirements of the early machines [batch-
oriented mainframe computers] and the tendency to automate in
conformity with the rationalized structure of traditional administrative bureaucracies resulted in intensification of the long term trend
toward task fragmentation and functional centralization."[27] The clerical work associated with such types of computer use was standardized and routinized. Clerical workers were frequently required to
input or to access data rapidly and continuously; data was often

broken down and coded in a fashion that made it meaningless and thus stultifyingly boring for clerical workers. As we have seen, such jobs lent themselves more easily to computerized monitoring. These heavily "rationalized" operations are still in effect in many locations, especially "centralized 'transaction environments' "[28] associated with financial institutions, insurance companies, utility firms, and information processing operations for local, state, or federal government. Eileen Appelbaum describes several such centralized insurance policy processing centers where part-time workers do routine entry of policy application information under close, key-stoke-per-minute monitoring.[29] Baran deplores aspects of these "electronic sweatshops," such as "heightened levels of stress associated with computer-paced speed-up, closer monitoring of operator performance, and, in the case of data entry, [constant] conformity to . . . [computer] codes."[30]

However, for at least some companies, such operations represented only an early stage in the office automation process. As more computer power became available, telecommunications links improved, and better software developed, much of the most repetitive, routine work was completely automated. The remaining jobs bring together information processing tasks which require individual judgment or which involve direct human interaction. Thus, some large companies, which have moved well into the second phase of office automation, are reintegrating tasks which require human intervention. Moreover, the very elements of flexibility and judgment which distinguish these jobs sometimes make it more difficult to devise appropriate electronic monitoring schemes for them. Therefore, some of these jobs are less likely to be subject to intense computerized supervision.

While new electronically broadened jobs represent an advance over the rigidly rationalized tasks of an earlier stage, some of the new jobs continue to have drawbacks. At one utility firm, the same clerk now handles requests for information, processes service orders, and responds to complaints. However, each task must be handled in a specified way consistent with the complex categories used in the computerized system. In this example, each task is also subject to detailed computer monitoring.[31]

Some electronically broadened jobs, such as customer service representative or claims examiner, may allow the worker a measure of authority to make decisions. Clerical workers in some insurance operations make decisions about whether to accept certain routine risks and issue a policy or whether to pay a standard claim. However, clerical decision-making power is limited. Management sets the parameters for clerical authority; "decision rules" are programmed into the computer systems and hence automatically enforced by the machine.[32] The computer system may be programmed, for example, to allow a claims examiner to approve payment for a specific medical service within a specified range of fees or to permit a customer service representative to arrange for installment payments on an overdue account as long as each monthly installment represents at least a fixed percent of the total due.

In some cases, upper-level clerical workers are now performing some of the tasks previously associated with lower-level professional work. (The lower-level professional jobs have been eliminated.) These new high-level clerical positions are being named paraprofessional, paratechnical, or professional-clerical.[33] Many of these new jobs are characterized by increased managerial control over the pace and content of work and more tightly circumscribed opportunities for the exercise of judgment *as compared with the professional jobs they replace.* However, *compared to the previously available clerical jobs,* they offer more variety and more autonomy.[34]

Secretaries have also experienced both job fragmentation and job enlargement as a result of office automation. When word processing equipment first became available, some firms used the equipment to automate their already existing, highly routinized typing pools. Other companies found a fresh incentive for reorganizing their secretarial support systems. In some large corporations which generated a heavy volume of documents (such as large law firms), word processing pools were set up to handle the bulk of document preparation.

In the worst such centralized operations, operators were assigned to keyboard initial dictation from anonymous persons concerning subjects about which they had little or no knowledge. Other workers did all the proofreading, revisions were assigned randomly, and others monitored all the printing. Word processing equipment could automatically merge certain standardized information with variable information, such as names and addresses. To make maximum use of this word processing function, some operators were assigned to enter disjointed pieces of data which the machine then assembled into a meaningful document. In most centers, in order to guarantee document uniformity, the format for standard documents was rigidly specified. In some cases, word processing packages were programmed to control such features as margin width. Some employees felt this made their work easier and more efficient, but other regretted the loss of opportunities to make aesthetic decisions about the placement of elements on the page. Operator output was usually strictly tallied in terms of keystrokes or lines per minute. Since early word processors were expensive and could perform only word processing functions, such standardized operations sometimes appeared to be the only way that such machines could be used continuously and, hence, their costs justified. According to Mary Murphree, the routinization of work in such centers plus the limited need for workers to be familiar with the particularities of the enterprise made it feasible (and economically attractive) to employ part-time or temporary workers.[35] Where trained operators were available, word processing centers sometimes operated on more than one shift in order to make maximum use of the equipment.[36]

The result of such job design is discussed by a legal secretary whose responsibility it was to keyboard and revise text for two lawyers.

> I really have no idea of what's going on here. . . . Things aren't explained to me. It's just "fill this in," "do this, do that," and "don't ask questions." I don't feel any sense of completeness in my work. . . . and I'm never involved from beginning to end. I'm just stuck in the middle somewhere, so I can't relate to anything I'm doing and I really feel like it doesn't matter to anybody else either.[37]

Sometimes, however, use of word processing centers was resisted. Sometimes, staff refused to submit work to the word processing center because of dissatisfaction with the quality of documents prepared by operators who did not understand what they were transcribing. There was also significant resistance from managers and high-prestige professionals, who viewed the loss of a personal secretary as a blow to their status. Resistance of secretaries who resented loss of task variety and of a personal one-to-one relationship with their bosses played a lesser role, since these secretaries had less organizational power.[38]

Improvements in word processors shifted word processing tasks back to secretaries and also changed the types of tasks which some secretaries performed. As multi-function microcomputers with good word processing software became available at lower prices, individual secretaries began to use computers to relieve themselves of the drudgery of retyping multiple drafts of documents.[39] Increasingly, secretaries are being asked to perform a variety of other functions on these microcomputers, thus broadening their range of responsibilities. In a recent survey of an elite group of secretaries, over 70 percent of the respondents indicated that computers had expanded their corporate role.[40] Some secretaries create spreadsheets, handle budget work, do research, retrieve data from computer databases and prepare graphs on computers. Thirty-five percent of the secretaries who responded to this survey are using microcomputers to handle tasks which were previously the responsibility of professionals or managers.[41] Other important tasks which some secretaries perform are training and troubleshooting—helping other clerical workers, professionals, and managers to learn how to use computer equipment.

The secretaries who participated in this survey reported that using computers made their duties more diversified, complex, creative, and challenging.[42] However, they also reported that the persons for whom they worked often had unrealistic expectations about increased productivity. The secretary's total workload frequently increased, since each single request for clerical assistance seemed so "easy" on the computer. For example, bosses were more likely to request multiple revisions of documents.

Moreover, race, ethnic identity, class, and age may unduly influence the distribution of the new, more challenging clerical jobs. Mary Murphree warns of the insidious implications of the bifurcation of secretarial work.

More and more men and privileged white women, disproportionately from the white upper and middle class will get the so-called professional-technical . . . word processing jobs; the inferior, factorylike jobs in the large centers will go to lower-middle-class and working-class women, especially blacks and minorities or older unskilled women.[43]

Her predictions have implications for the bifurcation of other types of clerical work as well.

The Limitations of Enriched Clerical Work

There are several cautions in order about the human meaning of electronically broadened clerical work. Some individual clerical workers now do work formerly assigned to several workers. Yet, the workers in these "integrated" jobs do not necessarily experience their tasks as more varied and, hence, enriched. Sometimes, *the computer system* has been programmed to do automatically a series of activities formerly done by several different workers. One data entry clerk codes and enters data. *The computer system* automatically produces an insurance policy, calculates and credits the agent's bonus, generates the premium bill, and collects data for an automatically generated management report. As Baran has observed: "ironically task variety [as experienced by the clerk] may actually decline since much of *the work reunification is internal to the computer system.*"[44]

Given the routine nature of many clerical information processing tasks, reintegration of several duties does not necessarily create a challenging, creative job. It may simply provide a wider range of dull, boring duties. Michael Beer's report on research about the attitudes of clerical workers who did more routinized versus more complex work for an insurance company showed little difference in the workers' reported satisfaction with their jobs. He concluded that "jobs which appear to management as higher in responsibility and complexity, and which are commonly viewed as promotions, may not always provide additional satisfactions in self-actualization, autonomy, or esteem."[45] He suggested further investigation about what type of job enlargement meets the psychological needs of clerical workers more adequately.

In fact, the heavy use of the computer can reduce the *physical variety* which some clerks experienced previously, even in routine jobs. Formerly, papers had to be rolled into the typewriter, removed from the typewriter, stacked, counted, stapled, moved from desk A to desk B. Now, one simply views a screen and pushes buttons. Baran has commented upon the implications of a loss of physical task variety for some clerical workers in the insurance industry:

> For a wide variety of insurance clerks, however, the previous work process involved a multiplicity of activities—none of which may have been inherently interesting or complex—but which in combination relieved the boredom of the day. Now all these functions are of the same quality, that is, they center around the machine and the manipulation of its abstract symbols. . . . Whereas formerly work was peacefully uninteresting, it is becoming unbearably tedious.[46]

Finally, not all workers welcome job changes which give them more challenge and responsibility. One woman who was working in a department where a job enrichment program was underway said:

> "I think it's probably a step in the right direction, though it bothers me that they seem to think we all want the same thing. I don't think that's true. I think some women, some *people*, want more responsibility and some don't. Some like to work slow and careful and some quick and forget it. Some want to be with other people. Then there are those like me who prefer to work alone. But they act like we're all alike."[47]

There is a body of literature in industrial psychology which also indicates that not all workers respond positively to broadened job duties. However, a critical issue is how one interprets the data that indicate that some human beings prefer duties which are repetitive and tightly circumscribed. In a review of some of this material, Gerald Salancik and Jeffrey Pfeffer recognize that researchers reveal certain value commitments in their conclusions and recommendations.[48] In other words, many psychologists find it morally repulsive to suggest that companies seek out persons who have low needs for autonomy and creativity in order to find docile workers for work environments deficient in variety, challenge, and autonomy.

It is also important to ask how institutionalized patterns of injustice might influence some people to accept jobs too small for the human spirit. Beverly Burris interviewed both high school and college graduates who worked in highly repetitive clerical jobs for a service corporation. Although the high school graduates had complaints similar to those of their college-educated peers about specific aspects of the job, they expressed less general dissatisfaction with their routine jobs. In addition, they "more often blamed themselves for being in a situation where they could not use their full potential."[49] Research by Salvendy showed that older people and people with less formal education "preferred simplified jobs."[50] We need to ask whether negative social attitudes toward older people and toward persons from "lower" classes who have less education were internalized by these subjects. Did demeaning social attitudes rob them of the confidence to accept the challenge of more complex tasks? Nevertheless, we also need to acknowledge that not all workers are able to respond confidently or comfortably to greater job challenge.

Another urgent issue connected with the new electronically broadened jobs is whether pay is commensurate with the worker's new skills and responsibilities. In a few cases, the new responsibilities are recognized, the job is reevaluated, and pay is upgraded accordingly. A report on the model office automation project in the letter of credit operation at Citibank specifically states that the greater responsibility in the enriched jobs was recognized through raising the "grade" assigned to the positions and hence raising the salary.[51]

However, current information suggests that such action to upgrade pay levels is rarely taken when skill requirements are raised as a result of office automation. Although managers in three insurance companies commented to Baran that some jobs should be reclassified to reflect added responsibility, there had been no upgrading of the salaries paid these workers.[52] The National Association of Working Women indicates that salaries of clerical workers using computers have not been upgraded to reflect new productivity and responsibility. In fact, regular salary increases for these jobs had not even kept pace with inflation.[53] Almost 60 percent of clerical workers who responded to a poll by The Secretary magazine reported that they received no increase in pay because of their ability to use computers. Of the 30 percent who did gain a salary increase when they mastered computer skills, many volunteered that the pay increase came along with a promotion or job change. They had not received a pay increase while remaining in the same job or job category.[54]

Social Contact

As work is restructured to take advantage of computer and telecommunications technology, the human relationships at work change. Jobs redesigned to require heavy terminal use may isolate workers from direct contact with coworkers. The worker's terminal may be connected with a minicomputer or a mainframe which contains all necessary files. Since required information is available directly through the computer system, workers rarely need to consult one another. Computer/telecommunications systems make it possible for work to be done at different times or in different geographical locations with the results available via computer. The clerical worker using a such a computer system may have access to information entered by a data entry clerk in another state or to the results of information processed during the night shift, but they have no immediate contact with such workers.

With sophisticated computer systems providing access to virtually all the requisite information, an increasing number of clerical workers find that they rarely need to leave their desks. Thus, they are also deprived of the casual human contact which takes place as people move throughout an office. Shoshana Zuboff reports that employees working in a "back office" group which had recently been computerized agreed that the new system resulted in an uncomfortable social isolation. "Because they had few remaining reasons to interact with co-workers, the local social network was fragmented."[55] When officials from the Office of Technology Assessment interviewed workers in electronically monitored office jobs, these workers reported that meeting production standards left them no opportunities for contact with coworkers.[56]

In the customer service jobs, an important segment of automated clerical jobs, social contact with fellow workers is minimal. The remaining social contact is comprised of a series of conversations with customers who need assistance or have a complaint. The quality of these social interactions is heavily dependent on the design of the computer system. If the system assigns the call to next available worker in a large pool of workers and if the system permits service representatives little or no discretion in handling a transaction, then the quality of human interaction is often low.

Changes in the physical arrangement of work, sometimes coinciding with introduction or modification of automated office systems, can also have an impact on social contact. There has been a trend toward arranging clerical work spaces in so-called "open plan" offices—with movable panels defining the boundaries of a workstation. While open plan offices are touted as promoting *greater* contact among office workers, this is primarily true for professionals and managers who formerly worked in private offices with four permanent walls. Clerical workers in paperwork processing divisions were usually assigned desks grouped together in a larger open space.

Thus, the use of panels to screen workstations provides some clerical workers with greater privacy and minimizes visual distractions, but it also eliminates visual contact with coworkers. Indeed, one management consultant was frank enough to say explicitly that such workstations were desirable, *because* they minimized contact between workers. He extolled workstations surrounded by suitable partitions which "reduce the incidence of eye contact which compels social interaction" and thus minimize "informal chit-chat and time-wasting."[57]

Some clerical workers who have been moved from open spaces where they could see coworkers to paneled workstations complain of an unpleasant experience of isolation. A legal secretary reported:

> Now they have a new set-up called the "open office." There are panels six feet high around all the operators. . . . In many cases, we don't see another person all day except for a 10-minute coffee break and lunchtime. All we see is the walls around us and sometimes the supervisor. The isolation is terrible.[58]

One "back office" employee expressed bitter resentment about loss of contact with fellow workers. The worker fantasized about cutting a peep hole in the workstation panel just to see that someone else was actually on the other side.[59]

Zuboff makes clear that the loss of contact with coworkers means deprivation of a critical human reward associated with work: "The quality of social life—opportunities to chat, form friendships, and offer mutual support—has traditionally been the way that employees humanize their daily environment. The informal workplace community can create commitment to the organization even when tasks are tedious and repetitive."[60]

It is possible that social isolation of workers from one another will also weaken workers' ability to band together to demand some control of work processes and conditions of work. Sociologists Feldberg and Glenn reviewed three job sites where clerical workers had been able to gain some measure of control over their work processes. In all three cases, worker contact on (and off) the job allowed women who shared certain common characteristics to develop a group cohesiveness which served as an important basis for their ability to make changes in their work. Other alterations in work organization which made workers more isolated throughout the work day might undercut the group cohesiveness. Thus, the two researchers warn that "workers would be vulnerable to changes, deliberate or not, that reduced possibilities for interaction on . . . the job."[61]

The ultimate form of isolation from fellow workers could be homework. Cynthia Costello's study of one clerical homework program showed that the health insurance firm involved used the homework program, in part, because it undermined the power of the union representing the in-office employees. Labor relations at the firm were acrimonious. The management planned to operate during any future strike by sending an increased number of claims out to the homeworkers, who were not union members.[62]

It is important not to exaggerate the role of computer technology in creating social isolation for clerical workers. Restricted social contact was already a feature of some highly routinized, manual, clerical jobs which required strict concentration. Office efficiency experts devised *manual* schemes in which all necessary reference tools were within arm's reach and in which forms to be processed were delivered direct to the desk. Clerical workers working in such standardized processing operations rarely left their desks or spoke to their fellow workers. In a journalistic account written in the early 1970s, before widespread office automation, Barbara Garson reports:

> The arrangement of these industrial offices isolates the women from each other. Unlike factory hands, clerical workers usually can't talk while they work. And there is nothing co-operative about their tasks. Though their desks are as close together as possible, the women sit separately, typing, calculating, punching to different drummers.[63]

However, certain forms of intense computer work can heighten that isolation even further. Workers who are isolated from one another while at work may find that as solitary individuals they have even fewer opportunities to participate in decisions which critically affect the quality of their work lives.

Concluding Comments

Human beings are currently making critical choices which determine the *human shape* of computer-assisted clerical jobs. Some managers, systems designers, and office efficiency experts are using some capabilities of computer technology to bolster rigid institutional control over the clerical work processes. The pacing and monitoring features of some computerized information systems permit intensive, continuous managerial control over the activities of clerical workers. Such practices often augment the managerial control over routine clerical work which was already well established in the earlier reign of scientific management techniques. The implementation of advanced office automation systems results in the creation of diverse sorts of clerical jobs. Clerical workers too often toil in electronic sweatshops where they are required to process meaningless, but exacting, bits of electronic data, while also subject to computer-paced speedups and oppressively close computer monitoring. However, other workers are performing electronically broadened paraprofessional/paratechnical jobs which offer greater challenge and autonomy than previous kinds of clerical work. Yet, these jobs often offer fewer challenges, fewer financial rewards, and less autonomy than the professional or technical jobs which they replace. Disturbing, albeit limited, evidence suggests a polarization of clerical workers. The better, more challenging jobs go to better educated, culturally "acceptable" white women and men. The worst jobs are reserved for more poorly educated and socially disadvantaged women, including minority and/or older women. Increasing social isolation on the job may dangerously undermine the solidarity of clerical workers. Isolation may further restrict clerical workers' opportunities to band together to achieve an equitable measure of participation in crucial decisions about their work lives.

If many clerical workers continue to be deprived of power to control the conditions of their work, they may be robbed of physical well-being, too. There is legitimate concern about a variety of health hazards associated with intensive use of video display terminals. In the next chapter, I will examine some of these hazards, giving special attention to stress as an occupational health issue. Evidence now shows that the way in which video display terminals are used makes a difference to workers' health. A crucial issue is the extent to which clerical workers can participate meaningfully in determining their own work processes.

Chapter Three

The VDT:

····················

A Threat to Clerical

····················

Workers' Health?

C lerical work is being redesigned in a manner which often involves long periods of work at a VDT (video display terminal). These new working conditions may take a toll on the health of clerical workers. This chapter will investigate health problems, especially occupational stress, associated with heavy VDT use. Ultimately, women's lives are of one piece. Stress created by other factors—such as racism, sexual harassment, and the double burden of responsibilities at work and in the home—may interact with occupational stress. The health implications of stress produced by certain types of VDT work cannot be fully appreciated unless one considers the cumulative impact of multiple stresses on the quality and, perhaps, even the length of clerical workers' lives.

Health Hazards Associated with VDT Use

There is mounting evidence that a variety of bodily discomforts and health problems are associated with prolonged, intensive use of VDTs. These discomforts are often associated with poor physical design of both equipment and office facilities and are exacerbated by poor job design. Occupational health experts are concerned about eye strain and musculoskeletal problems. Such discomforts, especially ones experienced on a frequent basis, diminish the quality of a worker's life. For example, a New York word processor who is unable focus her eyes to read when she gets home from work experiences bitter disappointment because she loves to read.[1] Such "temporary" discomforts rob some workers of some of the joy in life.

Reports of eye strain or itching, tearing, or burning eyes are among

The VDT: A Threat to Clerical Workers' Health?

the most pervasive complaints voiced by heavy VDT users. Head-aches which may be associated with eyestrain are reported often. There is, at present, no solid scientific evidence that VDT use causes any permanent eye damage or impairment. A recent study probing a possible link between VDT use and cataract formation proved nega-tive. However, researchers cautioned that since VDTs have been used for a relatively short period of time, no conclusions about long-term effects could be drawn.

Many VDT users report back, neck, or shoulder pain. Recently, some health experts have expressed concern about a greater incidence so-called repetitive strain injuries, especially carpal tunnel syn-drome, among persons whose jobs require prolonged operation of a keyboard. Carpal tunnel syndrome is characterized by a loss of feeling and control in portions of the hand. It occurs when the median nerve that runs through a channel in the wrist called the carpal tunnel becomes compressed or injured. Feeling and control in the hand is affected because the median nerve is the main nerve in the hand. It appears that some people develop carpal tunnel syndrome from repeatedly bending their wrists in certain positions, such as the posi-tion required to operate a keyboard. It may be that workers who operate awkwardly-placed keyboards because their office furniture is inappropriately designed are at increased risk.

A study by the Women's Occupational Health Resource Center shows that VDT operators who used the equipment less than four hours per day did not experience the eye strain and musculoskeletal aches reported by full-time users.[2] Well-designed equipment and furniture plus appropriate lighting conditions alleviate many of the problems. Rest breaks are also helpful in maintaining worker comfort (and hence consistent productivity). Unfortunately, companies are sometimes unwilling to spend the money required to create an ade-quate working environment for lower-status clerical workers. How-ever, in an automated office, it is often those lower-level workers whose jobs require them to remain at a terminal for long periods of time. Thus, it is precisely such workers who need an ergonomically sound environment most urgently. (Ergonomics is a study which produces guidelines for the design of safe, comfortable, and efficient workplace environments.)

Those workers who use a terminal intensively to perform routine tasks and who have severely limited ability to control their own activities report the greatest number of physical problems. "Workers in jobs in which a single task (e.g., data entry) dominates the workday, the pay is relatively low, and a worker's responsibility is almost entirely limited to working continually and avoiding errors" voice more complaints of eye discomfort.[3] The Westin report notes that the focus is shifting away "from the VDT itself as a source of health problems, to *employers* who apply the new technology. Critics are moving from technological concerns to implicate other sources of health problems and physical discomfort in the office such as job design and management practices."[4] The director of the Office of Safety and Health for the Communications Workers of America emphasizes the importance of good job design for worker comfort and health: "How much control do people have over their work—that's a key factor."[5]

VDT Use and Reproductive Health

A particularly serious health concern is the fear that heavy VDT use may be associated with problems in pregnancy outcome. Some are worried that prolonged work at a VDT may lead to increased risk of miscarriage or birth of a child with a congenital defect. Such worries were sparked initially by reports of sites throughout the United States, Canada, and Europe where women doing intensive VDT work had suffered an unusually high number of reproductive problems. However, it is entirely possible that these clusters of reproductive problems represent "statistical anomalies." That is, it may have been a coincidence that women working at the same site had a series of pregnancy problems about the same time. The likelihood of coincidence is suggested by the fact that the types of birth defects in several clusters were not similar. In addition, many of the defects were not ones known to be associated with radiation exposure. An expert on birth defects points out: "Many women of childbearing age work at or near VDTs today. In such a large population, some clusters of problem pregnancies would be a normal occurrence."[6]

Nevertheless, there has been some scientific speculation that reproductive difficulties could be caused by exposure to certain types of non-ionizing radiation emitted by VDTs, especially exposure to very low frequency (VLF) or extra low frequency (ELF) radiation.[7] Several studies done on chicken embryos have found that embryos exposed to weak, low-level, pulsed magnetic fields of the type emitted from VDTs show developmental abnormalities. However, it is not clear that chicken embryos provide a good model for human reproduction. Types of non-ionizing radiation which harm chicken embryos might have no effect on human embryos.

The radiation which is emitted from VDTs is discharged primarily from the sides, and especially from the back, not the front of the display tube. If this radiation does pose a hazard to human fertility, the women who are most at risk may be women who are exposed to radiation from coworkers' machines. Risks may be especially high in places where a large number of female computer operators work in the same large room.

Even if VDTs pose no radiation hazard to reproduction, factors associated with their use might contribute to a poor outcome of pregnancy. Heavy users who remain at the terminal throughout most of the workday might suffer ill effects from their stationary posture. Poorly designed equipment and office furniture could exacerbate posture problems which contribute to pregnancy difficulties. Job stress could be a contributing factor in miscarriages and birth defects.

A recent study of reproductive outcome among women affiliated with the Kaiser Permanente Medical Care Program shows that heavy VDT use by administrative support and clerical workers is associated with increased risk of miscarriage. In this study, women who used VDTs more than 20 hours per week had almost twice as many miscarriages as women who did not use VDTs at all. Administrative and clerical workers who made heavy use of VDTs had a much higher miscarriage rate than did managerial and professional women who also used computer equipment extensively. Researchers concluded that comparison to other studies suggests a small, but real, increased risk for miscarriage associated with intensive VDT use.[8] However, the Kaiser Permanente researchers do not consider their own study definitive; rather, they claim to have uncovered a "statistically significant association" between heavy VDT use and miscarriage.[9]

Adequate scientific studies thoroughly investigating possible connections between heavy VDT use and pregnancy problems are urgently needed. In 1982, the National Institute for Occupational Safety and Health began to plan a study aimed at investigating the reproductive effects of exposure to VDTs. However, the study design has been plagued by controversy, and funds were not approved by the Office of Budget and Management until July 1986. Another study scheduled by staff of the Mount Sinai Medical Center in New York was still awaiting funding in fall 1988. Meanwhile, we lack sufficient scientific information to establish or to refute a link between heavy VDT use and reproductive problems.

We also need to investigate the impact of prolonged exposure to VDTs on *male* reproductive function. Are men who use VDTs intensively suffering infertility problems or begetting children with birth defects? There has been virtually no research on male reproductive impacts. Thus, we desperately need more information about the impact of VDT use on both male and female reproductive function.

Job-Related Stress in Clerical Occupations

Occupational stress is, perhaps, the most serious job-related threat to the health of clerical workers. "If loss of limb and back strain are the characteristic occupational hazards of the industrial age, then job stress is *the* characteristic hazard of the computer age."[10] Prolonged occupational stress increases a person's risk of coronary disease, stroke, and mental illness. It diminishes the quality of the worker's daily life. Occupational stress correlates to symptoms such as indigestion, neck, shoulder or back pain, headache, chronic exhaustion, insomnia, anxiety, and depression.

Several studies have shown that clerical workers report high levels of stress-related symptoms and manifest a high incidence of stress-related disease. One National Institute for Occupational Safety and Health [NIOSH] study listed secretary and office manager among the dozen occupations with the highest incidence of stress-related disorders.[11] A group of researchers working in Tennessee found that secretaries had the second-highest rate of hospitalization or death related to coronary heart and artery disease, hypertension, and ulcers. The same study showed that telephone operators, bank tellers, and secretaries sought treatment for mental health problems in higher than expected numbers.[12] The Framingham study on coronary heart disease found that female clerical workers showed an increased incidence of heart disease. Women who were clerical workers were almost twice as likely as housewives, blue-collar or other white-collar women to develop coronary heart disease.[13]

Despite some controversy over preliminary results from a study of telephone workers in North Carolina, both the primary researchers and staff members from NIOSH agree that this data indicates that VDT operators report a significantly greater incidence of chest pain. Research subjects were responding to a questionnaire designed to elicit information about angina, a type of chest pain which is symptomatic of coronary heart disease. However, it is difficult to distinguish angina from several other types of chest pain, when the responses are based solely on the subject's recall. Nevertheless, the frequency of chest pain was much higher among heavy VDT users. The frequency of chest *pain increased as* the workers' *control* over their work *decreased.* (Worker control was assessed based on the subjects' own reports.) The somewhat more cautious NIOSH reviewers warned: "If the findings are real, they could represent a large source of unrecognized occupational morbidity."[14]

Other NIOSH investigators surveying three automated offices indicated that clerical workers operating VDTs reported a higher number of gastroenteritis problems and a greater incidence of emotional distress than did other clerical workers. Their results showed VDT operators to have one of the highest stress ratings NIOSH had ever recorded. However, professionals using VDTs at these same sites had lower levels of stress than the clerical control group not using VDTs. Factors such as challenging work, job autonomy, greater use of personal skills, and the type of supervision which the professionals experienced may have mitigated any stressors related to VDT use.[15]

The National Survey on Women and Stress also investigated the impact of office automation on the stress experienced by women workers. These results included responses from managers and professionals as well as clerical workers. A majority of workers surveyed (54.3 percent) reported that office automation made their jobs seem less stressful. However, almost one in five (17.8 percent) viewed office automation as adding to job stress. These results suggest that most workers do not perceive office automation technology itself as stressful. Rather, factors such as how the work is structured and the environment in which it is done make a critical difference in how stressful using office automation is.

Results from this survey show that stress is especially high for workers who have shifted to automated systems within the year before the study was done (1983). Almost two in five (38.5 percent) clerical workers whose workplace was automated within the previous year say that it made the work more stressful. Slightly more than one in four (27.5 percent) say it made the work less stressful.[16] These results suggest that the initial stages in the implementation of new computer systems are a particularly stressful period. Moreover, since office automation is an continuing process, the same clerical worker may face multiple transitions during her work life. Strain will be especially high, if the "logistics" of the transition have been poorly planned or if the human aspects of the change have been underestimated or ignored. Transition pressures are also more severe if workers are not given adequate training to operate new systems. In fact, many clerical workers report that they are inadequately trained in the operation of new computer systems.

The impact of office automation on the clerical workers' perceived levels of stress varies according to job categories. Sixty percent of customer service representatives and 44.4 percent of claims examiners called their jobs very stressful. All these respondents were using automated equipment. General clerks who used automated equipment were more likely to label their jobs highly stressful than were general clerks who used non-automated systems (29 percent vs. 19 percent). However, more administrative assistants who did not have access to automated systems described their jobs as highly stressful than did administrative assistants who used such equipment (29.8 percent vs. 18.6 percent). Slightly more secretaries without office automation equipment called their jobs highly stressful (19.0 percent vs. 16.7 percent).[17] Thus, for some workers, office automation eases the pressures of the job; for others, using automated equipment increases job stress. In still other cases, such as many customer service jobs, computerized equipment is now standard equipment used in the performance of duties which are highly stressful in and of themselves.

Job Characteristics Which Exacerbate Stress

Some of the stress associated with heavy VDT use may be associated with a stressful physical work environment. Electronic office equipment can raise the noise level in the office—especially noisy, unshielded printers. The noise can be intense in offices where several secretaries or word processing operators share a single printer, because the printer is in operation more often. Some computer units emit a hum which some operators find annoying. Poor lighting conditions and improper furniture are additional stressors.

Remaining in the same physical position for long periods of time is a physiological stressor. Body posture influences the body's production of noradrenaline, which in turn contributes to blood pressure fluctuation. Research shows that workers who can move about freely have a desirable, low noradrenaline level, while those forced to maintain a fixed position show elevated levels.[18] Thus, VDT operators who are required to spend several hours seated directly in front of the terminal with little opportunity to change position may experience increased stress solely from the enforced stationary posture.

Machine-paced computerized office systems might well be a stressor for VDT operators. In one Scandinavian study, both adrenaline and noradrenaline levels were higher in workers who did machine-paced work than in those who did self-paced work.[19] Chronic high levels of these hormones are a potential health threat. In another study, workers who used office automation systems which included automatic machine-monitoring features reported a higher rate of headaches, nausea, exhaustion, digestive problems, chest pain, anxiety, anger, and depression than did other VDT users.[20]

Working at a job which is much too simple for the worker's skills is another source of stress. Monotonous, repetitive work is actually stressful work. In one survey the highest rates of exhaustion or fatigue correlated with that work which was judged most monotonous. Moreover, women whose work was uninteresting suffered from digestive problems and/or depression. More than one-third of such women had been treated by a physician for one or more stress-related medical problems.[21]

Karasek's study of manufacturing plants has shown that there is a serious underutilization of workers' skills at the lower levels of manufacturing operations and an overutilization of workers' skills at higher decision-making levels. He asserts that "there is an exaggerated inequality of skill usage and control opportunities in the workforce that cannot be justified by individual differences in capabilities."[22] I suggest that this same pattern exists in large office operations. The clerical workers at the lower levels, particularly those in the back office data entry operations or in the word processing centers, may have skills which they cannot use. Office automation systems designed deliberately to limit the range of skills used by the operators are stressful and, accordingly, can contribute to the development of stress-related illnesses.

Both American and Scandinavian studies show that control over one's work decreases both physiological and psychological measures of stress.[23] Workers who face high job demands but have little decision-making power show adverse health effects. Workers in such situations report exhaustion, insomnia, disturbed sleep, trouble waking up in the morning, depression, nervousness, and anxiety.[24] By contrast, workers who have high job demands but who also have high decision latitude do not suffer adverse health effects. (Decision latitude involves intellectual discretion [whether the workers could use judgement and assert control over their use of skill within the work process] and personal schedule freedom.)[25] As one journalist succinctly puts it: "stress is the disease of the highly pressured and the unempowered."[26]

Lack of career development opportunities also puts increased pressure on clerical workers. Cooper and Marshall's review of the literature indicates that lack of opportunities for promotion and lack of job security can be significant job stressors.[27] In a survey by the American Academy of Family Physicians, secretaries (who had the highest level of health complaints of any occupational group studied) listed poor advancement opportunities as their number one job complaint.[28] In another survey, clerical workers in Cleveland and Boston also ranked lack of promotions or raises as their number one source of job stress.[29] Clerical VDT operators in the NIOSH San Francisco Bay study also said they had few opportunities for promotion. Moreover, almost 50 percent said that their jobs were likely to be replaced by totally automated computer systems sometime in the future."[30]

Low pay for clerical workers may be an often-overlooked source of stress for these women. Gregory points out that much of the research on job stress has used male workers as the worker model. Male workers do not often report that low pay is a source of job stress. Therefore, standardized job stress questionnaires usually do not include questions about pay. However, women workers are poorly paid in comparison with men. Since women workers make 65 cents for every dollar made by male workers, they might well experience low pay as a more significant source of stress. When Gregory constructed a stress questionnaire which listed low pay as a significant source of stress on the job, respondents reported that low pay was second only to lack of promotion or raises as a stressor.

Thus, there are many aspects of some clerical jobs which may— alone or in interaction—lead to increased stress. These include boring, monotonous work; underutilization of ability; close, unsupportive supervision; high production demands; machine pacing; low decision-making power; and high uncertainty about job future. It is important to note that such job pressures frequently occur in conjunction with one another.[31]

Cumulative Stress in Clerical Workers' Lives

Some female clerical workers are faced with a high level of occupational stress. There is some disturbing evidence to indicate that clerical workers whose jobs require prolonged use of VDTs run an even higher risk of developing stress-related disorders. There are growing indications that many of these occupational health risks are associated with high performance demands coupled with limited worker autonomy. In order to understand more fully why stress on the job poses such a serious threat to female clerical workers' health, it is essential to investigate several other sources of stress in the lives of certain clerical workers. The stress of heavy household responsibili-

ties, the strains from racism, or the tension created by sexual harassment can combine with stress associated with certain kinds of prolonged used of VDTs to endanger a clerical worker's health. Unless
this cumulative burden is acknowledged, the health risks will be
underestimated.

Stress on the Job and at Home. Stressors on the job combine with
other life stressors to increase a person's risk of emotional illness,
disease, or death. On the one hand, symptoms of occupational stress
continue into workers' time off the job, where they have an impact
on loved ones as well as the workers themselves. On the other hand,
stress which workers experience in their "personal" lives combines
with job-related stress in ways which put a still greater strain on their
health.

A study of female insurance company workers who were working
mandatory overtime showed that both physiological and psychological symptoms of stress [elevated adrenaline level, elevated heart rate,
irritability] continued during the subjects' hours away from work.
Moreover, the negative response to the job stressor (overtime) accu-
mulated gradually. The full impact on the body manifested itself
weeks after the overtime. The overtime peaked in the middle of the
two-month study, but adrenaline excretion was highest at the time
the study ended. Thus, when a worker is stressed at work, the effects
can spill over into time off the job, perhaps for weeks afterwards.[32]

Piotrkowski probes the impact of bad job design on the well-being
on a worker's children. For example, workers whose own skills are
underutilized on the job are less likely to encourage their children to
acquire skills. In particular, *women* whose skills are underutilized
on the job have children with lower math achievement in school.[33]
Moreover, "the small, but consistent, body of research on job satisfaction and mother-child relations suggest [sic] that the social costs of
unsatisfying and stressful jobs are broader than we usually think.
That is, they may affect those people—such as children—who are
not directly involved."[34] There is a need for more social science
research into the impact of stressful or unsatisfying jobs on the inti-
mate relationships of workers. However, it may well be that poorly

designed clerical work is hurting the children of clerical workers as well as the workers themselves.

Paid employment, in itself, is not inordinately stressful for women. Women who work for wages score better on measures of both physical and mental health than do women who are not employed outside the home. However, certain combinations of household responsibilities and workplace duties do pose health risks for women.

Women who have parental obligations and who also work in stressful occupations are at increased health risk. The Framingham study found that it was clerical workers with children who were more likely to develop coronary heart disease [CHD]. Childless clerical workers had no higher incidence of CHD than did non-clerical working women.[35] The combined stresses of clerical work and child rearing seemed to exact a toll on the health of these workers.

In a survey of Boston and Cleveland clerical workers, however, few clerical workers (12.8 percent) reported that juggling work schedules with family responsibilities was a serious source of stress. Nevertheless, the 117 respondents who did rank combined work and family pressures as a major source of stress reported more health problems and more time lost from work than other respondents.[36] Perhaps, most women manage to juggle home and work demands successfully. Still, the health consequences of the double burden are serious for those women for whom the juggling act is most difficult.

A 1978 health survey of white women from Detroit may provide another clue about how some clerical women manage the home/work burden. Married clerical women were more likely to work part-time than other working women. They also had fewer children and their children were older. Thus, many of these clerical workers had avoided the conflict of simultaneous heavy job demands and heavy family responsibilities. However, these clerical workers did not seem happy with their life choices. As Lois Verbrugge reports: "The most striking characteristic of clerical women is their dissatisfaction with job and family roles. Of all occupational groups, they rank lowest or next to lowest for job satisfaction, housework satisfaction, and life satisfaction."[37]

While the strategy of working part-time may have some immediate benefits for white women with heavy domestic responsibilities, it does not seem to offer the same positive opportunity for African American women. In the National Survey on Women and Stress, *white* part-time workers were *less* likely to describe their job as stressful. *African American women* who worked part-time were *more* likely to describe their jobs as very stressful.[38] These African American women may report higher levels of stress because they work part-time involuntarily. Perhaps, they would prefer to have full-time jobs. This finding might be related to the pressures on the disproportionately high number of African American women who are heads of households. It might also be possible that African American women are disproportionately concentrated in certain high-stress jobs, such as certain customer service work, which may be both part-time and highly stressful.

Economic pressures at home may combine with pressures on the job to exacerbate the stress experienced by female clerical workers. In the Framingham study, marriage to a man in a blue-collar job also correlated to increased risk of CHD for clerical women. A woman who had a clerical job, had children, and was married to a man in a blue-collar position was three times more likely to manifest CHD than non-clerical mothers. However, clerical workers who had children and who were married to white-collar men had no excess risk of CHD. Researchers suggested that blue-collar husbands may have made less money and that as a result they may have experienced greater financial pressures in the family.[39] The Framingham data suggests that economic status and responsibility for the financial well-being of children combine with features of clerical work to increase the risk of heart disease.

Racism and Stress

Stress created by intensive operation of video display terminals may combine with family burdens to increase a woman's risk of experiencing stress-related disease. It is also possible that stressful clerical duties may combine with the strains of dealing with racism to imperil the health of African American clerical workers. There is some limited evidence which suggests that a disproportionate number of African American women are employed in more stressful clerical jobs, including high-stress types of VDT use. When stress from the workplace interacts with stress created by racism on and off the job and both combine with women's double duty in the home and on the job, the results on African American women's health are potentially devastating.

Unfortunately, we do not know much about whether the stresses which African American women experience in a racist society interact with job-related stress to threaten their lives, because there has been little research on occupational stress as experienced by African American women. However, African American women's health statistics seem to reflect the multiple burdens which they carry. African American women have higher rates of hypertension than white women, and as a result, suffer a higher rate of kidney failure and stroke.[40] African American women die from heart disease in disproportionate numbers.[41] One in three African American women responding to a survey in *Essence* had been treated in the past five years for stress-related medical problems, such as hypertension, gastritis, heart disease, ulcers, and colitis.[42] African American women also report higher levels of mental distress than white women.[43]

African American women clerical workers are overrepresented in clerical categories such as mail handler, telephone clerk, and key punch operator. These jobs frequently involve machine pacing, intensive performance monitoring, and low autonomy.[44] African American women who are employed as claims examiners, data processors, and accounting clerks are among those African American women who report high levels of job stress.[45] In the National Survey on Women and Stress, African American women who used VDTs reported using the machines more intensively than their white counterparts. Only 31.5 percent of all clerical women used VDTs three-quarters of the week or more; 40.6 percent of African American clerical women used terminals that heavily. Reflecting on these results, researchers speculate that African American women are concentrated in back office data or word processing positions which require heavy computer use, while white women predominate in the more varied secretarial or "front office" positions.[46]

Moreover, African American women who use automated equipment are more likely than white women to have to meet productivity goals. Researchers working for the National Association of Working Women indicate that "within specific job categories where production quotas are common, African American women are even more likely to face constant productivity measures." The disparity is most astonishing among women who describe themselves as word processing specialists: 31.8 percent of the African American women have to meet hourly or daily standards as compared with 5.6 percent of the white specialists. Almost twice as many African American electronic data processing clerks have to meet productivity quotas (56.5 percent African American, 30 percent white).[47] Caution should be used when relying on statistics concerning specific job categories covered in this study, since the number of respondents in particular job categories was small. The margin for error is, thus, greater. However, these results indicate a potential problem in the distribution of stressful work by race; more data should be gathered.

According to the National Survey on Women and Stress, African American clerical workers were the least likely among African American women to describe their jobs as stressful.[48] However, in this study a worker's perception of work as stressful did not always correlate with stress-related health effects. That is, some women who reported one or more stress-related health symptoms, still did not describe their jobs as highly stressful. Those African American women who reported the most serious stress-related symptoms and illnesses were the women who felt their jobs were not secure, who had jobs with little challenge, and/or who were allowed to make few job decisions on their own. Those African American women who work in highly routinized jobs in "back office" operations hold jobs which have such characteristics. Interpreting data on stress experienced by African American women workers, Malveaux suggests: "perhaps some of us with no clout experience health problems as our body's protest against our powerless position on the job."[49]

Sexual Harassment

In order to appreciate fully the health risks which stressful automated work poses for clerical workers, it is important to understand the cumulative nature of stress in these workers' lives. Sexual harassment can be another factor which increases the cumulative stress experienced by clerical workers. Women in all types of occupations experience sexual harassment. Persistent, pervasive, unwanted sexual looks, gestures, or comments, intrusive physical touch, and even attempted or completed rape create constant strain for the victims. Thus, sexual harassment can represent a serious threat to a worker's physical and mental well-being.

When a woman who is being harassed refuses to comply she may face retaliation. Her work may be unfairly criticized; she may be given too little or too much to do; she may be denied training or promotion; she may be fired. Often, the victim finds that the emotional tension carries over after work, and she is unable to relax off the job. Physical and psychological symptoms of stress reported by women subjected to sexual harassment include: sexual dysfunction, alcohol or drug abuse, gastroenteritis problems, insomnia, headaches, exhaustion, drastic weight change, excessive nervousness, depression, and destructive rage [rage directed at inappropriate persons, not the harasser].

There may be a dynamic implicit in clerical work as women's work which creates conditions conducive to sexual harassment. Certain gender expectations about women's subordination to men as sexual partners and as workplace assistants intersect destructively in practices of sexual harassment. Some types of clerical workers, such as secretaries or receptionists, have been viewed as virtual "office wives." Clerical workers in "front office" jobs are often selected based on appearance and manner as well as clerical skills. According to one telling description: "The private secretary must master all the small gestures that make her appear submissive, and yet 'professional,' and must present a classy image by careful behavior and a careful selection of clothing and make-up."[50] When a "nice girl" sexual allure is an unspoken part of the job description, a situation conducive to overt sexual demands is set up. As MacKinnon puts it: "Specifically, if part of the reason the woman is hired is to be pleasing to a male boss, whose notion of a qualified worker merges with a sexist notion of the proper role of women, it is hardly surprising that sexual intimacy, forced when necessary, would be considered part of her duties and his privileges."[51]

When a subliminal sexual come-on is expected from some clerical workers as an unspoken condition of employment, they may become the targets of an insidious kind of harassment. The Working Women's Institute, a group which pioneered in research on sexual harassment, reports that "women in clerical/secretarial jobs are ordinarily subjected to the type of harassment that at first seems like harmless flirting or propositions but begins to cause difficulty because it is unremitting or connected with some sort of threat."[52] Since women have been socialized to be grateful for male flattery about women's sexuality, the clerical worker who is made uncomfortable by *unwanted* sexual attentions may feel confused or guilty. How can she be angry about "compliments?" Is the harassing treatment her fault; did she "invite" it? The Working Women's Institute comments: "In short, the ambiguity of the situation may be even more stressful than a clearly negative situation [in which harassing behavior is unmistakably demeaning and/or physically threatening]."[53]

While both white and African American women are sexually harassed, African American women's experience is somewhat different. Many African American women who are sexually harassed experience a kind of abuse which includes elements of *both sexual and racial domination.* Demeaning social myths depict African American women as especially passionate and promiscuous, hence as sexually available to any male. Such racist lies about African American women inflame sexual harassment. According to one national survey, African American women who worked in institutions which were more than 50 percent white were sexually harassed more often than white women. In the same study, 34 percent of the white women and 29 percent of the African American women reported unwelcome sexual remarks or demands.[54] The lower figure for African American women may be because these African American women are more likely to work in predominantly female workplaces or because they interpreted unwelcome remarks and demands in racial, not sexual, terms. Women of color who have been counseled by the Working Women's Institute say that it took them some time to recognize that besides racial harassment, with which they were very familiar, they were also facing sexual exploitation and domination.[55] When racism and sexism intersect in an African American woman's experience of sexual harassment, the toll on her body may be particularly severe.

Diverse Individual Responses to Workplace Stress

If employers and office systems designers create automated clerical systems which require workers continuously to process meaningless bits of data at a rapid, machine-controlled pace and under oppressive computer monitoring, they may be threatening the health of some of the workers. However, the severity of the threat to a given worker's health will vary, since there is significant individual variation in response to stressors. Workers vary physiologically, psychologically, and intellectually. Some workers have bodies which are stronger and more resilient under pressure. This may, in part, be attributable to genetic differences or previous history of illness.

There is some evidence that women workers respond somewhat differently to stress than do men. In one laboratory experiment which used epinephrine excretion as an indicator of physiological response to stressful situations, researchers found that females had a slower physiological response to stress. Women's epinephrine level did not rise until more stressful conditions were reached.[56] Female workers may have less pronounced physiological but more pronounced psychological responses to stress.[57]

Other research suggests that the personality traits of workers influence their response to machine-paced work. Workers who are more intelligent, assertive, imaginative, shrewd, and self-sufficient prefer self-paced work. Workers who are less intelligent, more humble, practical, forthright, and group-dependent are more tolerant of machine-paced work.[58] Again, however, we need to ask to what extent such variations in temperament and response to machine-paced work are innate and to what extent they are culturally constructed.

Younger workers may be able to tolerate a stressful job more easily than older workers. For example, there is an unusually high turnover rate among United States Postal Service multiple-position letter-sorting-machine operators. That already high turnover rate increases substantially for operators over 40 years of age. Union officials say that workers over 40 cannot keep up with the rapid work pace in this machine-paced position, nor are they able to tolerate the work pressure.[59] On the other hand, Salvendy sees some positive aspects of machine-paced work for older workers. One laboratory study showed older subjects were more efficient in machine-paced work.[60] *Over the short run* of this laboratory experiment, machine pacing stimulated older workers to greater efficiency, but what are the results *over the long run*, if older workers in real world workplaces are "stimulated" by demands for rapid, machine-paced production?

Workers can also safeguard their own health from the impact of job-related stress by practicing good health habits and avoiding poor health practices. One of the reasons that job stress can be so destructive to health is that some people try to cope with stress by using personal "strategies" which are even more destructive to their health. Some people who are under stress smoke too much, eat too much (or too little), drink too much alcohol, or take other drugs in excessive amounts.

Too many women who are under stress keep it to themselves. Women who keep their stress "bottled up" are even more likely to engage in other behaviors which are detrimental to their health. In contrast, individuals can mitigate the stressful effects of their jobs through positive "coping" strategies. Examples include eating the appropriate foods or getting regular exercise. Forming positive relationships off the job also protects a worker against some of the dangerous effects of stress. Persons who are active in union, political, community, or religious groups are less likely to suffer from stress-related disease.

When it comes to finding constructive individual strategies to cope with occupational stress, white women would do well to imitate some positive behaviors of African American women. According to the National Women and Stress Survey, 56 percent of the African American women said they took action to keep tension-producing situations from happening again. Only 49 percent of the white women reported the same behavior. African American women were also less likely to apologize in situations where they believed they had done nothing wrong.[61] White women were more apt to smooth over tensions by apologizing, even when they were not at fault. False apologies were particularly self-destructive, correlating with the most negative (stress-related) health effects.

While it is true that individual workers can take action to mitigate the health hazards associated with stressful work, it is unfair to put the major burden of alleviating the physical and psychological damage of "bad" jobs on individual workers. Workers might choose to use positive techniques for coping with stress as survival skills. Still, it is the responsibility of those who design and implement office systems to create jobs and work environments which minimize unhealthy stressors.

Social Support for Stressed Workers and Its Costs

Social support both on and off the job alleviates the negative health impact of stress. Social support means one or more close relationships with (an)other person(s) who is perceived as willing and able to offer aid and/or emotional support. In order to be effective, there must be relatively frequent interaction between the person under stress and her/his supporter(s).

Women workers have traditionally mitigated the stress of monotonous work by talking with coworkers as they performed routine duties. Redesign of jobs and physical facilities in a fashion which lessens the employees' opportunities to chat with one another may interfere with one "normal and healthy human reaction to stressful boredom."[62] Job changes which isolate workers from one another jeopardize the social support networks which the workers have formed. Thus, more isolated jobs decrease the workers' ability to cope with stress. For example, in the San Francisco NIOSH study, the clerical VDT operators perceived human relationships on the job as less supportive than did other clerical workers. The clerical VDT users felt less cohesion among their peers.[63] They also reported more stress-related health problems.

Supervisors can be an important source of social support on the job. Conversely, unsupportive supervision increases stress. The VDT operators in the San Francisco NIOSH study described their supervisors as offering little support. Perhaps this perception occurred be-

Good Work at the Video Display Terminal

cause the computerized monitoring system made the VDT operators feel their supervisors were keeping a constant, critical eye on them.[64] In a survey of clerical workers in Boston and Cleveland, one-third of the respondents listed an unsupportive boss or supervisory problems as one of five top sources of stress on their jobs.[65] In the Framingham study, having an unsupportive boss increased a clerical worker's risk of CHD.[66]

Racism can undermine social support for African American women in the workplace. Forty-four percent of the readers of *Essence* who responded to a survey reported that they were subjected to racial or ethnic slurs, jokes, or harassment on the job. African American women also perceived "well integrated" workplaces as more hostile environments. African American women who were tokens working in predominantly white workplaces and African American women who worked in majority African American facilities experienced less hostility and greater fairness. It was the African American woman who worked in a group 35 to 50 percent African American who experienced the greatest amount of hostility on the job. In this survey, more African American women reported problems with their bosses. Only 25 percent of the African American women felt management was always respectful to workers at their job, compared to 33 percent of the white women. Fifty-three percent of the African American respondents said that they felt extra pressure to prove themselves on the job because of both their sex and their race.[67] Thus a combination of racism and sexism may damage some of those human relationships on the job which could otherwise alleviate the detrimental effects of stress on African American women's health.

Social support outside of work can also serve as a buffer between job stress and detrimental effects on physical and mental health. Supportive family members or close friends can help prevent stress on the job from damaging a worker's health. However, such personal support offered to a family member, lover, or friend who is suffering from occupational stress has its costs. These can include "expenditures" such as money, time, and emotional energy.[68] Health researchers House and Wells warn that there has been too little attention paid to the pressures which occupational stress transfers to families:

To routinely expect that spouses will buffer workers against the deleterious effects of occupational stress is to displace onto the spouse and/or family responsibilities which are more rightfully those of the organization and/or individual worker. In American society at least, family and marital relationships have too often been assumed to operate in the service of individual or organizational work achievement, with little attention paid to the deleterious effects that work organizations and involvements may have on the family.[69]

It should be mentioned that the cultural stereotype in America has been that the family is subordinated to the individual work achievement of the *man*, but (at least until recently) not the individual work achievement of the *woman*. Moreover, workers who do not live in traditional nuclear families are often supported by loved ones and friends. The costs to those supporters receive virtually no attention.

Good relationships with coworkers, supervisors, loved ones, and friends can protect workers from some of the physical and psychological damage which can be caused by occupational stress. Yet, in justice, "work organizations have no right to expect supervisors and coworkers, much less the spouses, friends, and relatives of workers, to buffer employees against stresses which the organization could reasonably reduce or prevent entirely."[70]

Heavy work at video display terminals is taking its toll on too many clerical workers and their loved ones. For some workers, the price is frequent eyestrain, headaches, muscle strain, and backaches, which diminish their physical well-being on and off the job. For other workers, there is anxiety associated with the uncertain impact of heavy VDT use on pregnancy. For far too many clerical workers, occupational stress diminishes the quality of their daily lives and imperils their psychological and physiological welfare. It is becoming increasingly clear that health problems from eyestrain to stress are particularly severe for workers who are required to do boring jobs under oppressive supervision, who receive low salaries, and who have few opportunities for advancement.

In too many cases, poorly designed office automation systems threaten the physical welfare of clerical workers. So far, however, there has been no outcry raised by religious leaders on behalf of these workers. Thus far, religious groups have not pressed the justice claims of clerical workers on labor unions, business, and government. Neither have religious institutions announced any public reassessment of their own treatment of clerical workers. There are complex, intertwining strands in the Christian religious tradition that make it hard for Christian scholars or leaders to articulate a cry for justice owed to clerical workers. Deeply embedded in the fabric of Christian thought are elements of dualism which devalue ordinary work relationships and, thus, give little attention to changing oppressive work patterns. In addition, male Christian leaders often so emphasize the familial aspects of women's lives that they totally ignore such realities as the changing conditions of wage labor for a large segment of the female labor force—clerical workers.

It is important to give renewed attention to those elements of the Christian tradition which provide a vision of social transformation—those elements which promise wholeness and justice for all. It is also time to refine mediating concepts which serve as bridges between the ideal of the Reign of God/dess and social responses to office automation. One such concept is the notion of justice as active and equitable participation. In the next chapter, I investigate elements for a substantive notion of good work. This substantive concept of good work is tested against the workplace experiences of clerical workers. The notion of good work specifies terms for equitable participation by clerical workers in the automated workplace. It can assist us in getting our moral bearings straight as we confront the human impacts of office automation.

Chapter Four
·················
What Is "Good" Work?
·················
Theological Reflections
·················
on Clerical Work

An ethical assessment of the work place experience of a specific kind of worker is new for late twentieth-century Christian ethics. Over the last twenty-five years, sustained attention to issues of economic justice has become so rare that in a 1975 work John C. Bennett felt it necessary to remind himself and his colleagues that economic issues have central importance for Christian ethics.[1] Beverly Harrison, lamenting the present state of the discussion, comments that "the silence of religious ethicists on economic justice issues [is] deafening and economic reality [is] invisible in our discourse."[2]

There are several proximate reasons for the relative paucity of attention to human labor in recent American Christian ethics.[3] In the second third of the twentieth century, the rise of Nazi totalitarianism, World War II, and the Cold War made questions of political justice especially pressing. During the sixties concrete political questions, particularly concerning the civil rights movement and the Vietnam war, were compelling. In addition, the sustained period of economic prosperity which followed World War II may have made economic questions seem less urgent to Christian social ethicists. When that long period of economic growth ended in the seventies, it was followed by a period of economic turbulence which has been difficult to analyze.

There has been some work done by Christian ethicists on economic questions, much of it clustered around a few specific issues. In response to the publication of Michael Harrington's powerful expose, *The Other America*[4] and to The War on Poverty, there were a series of analyses of social welfare proposals.[5] The oil crises and serious food shortages in other parts of the world provoked a reevaluation of Christian responsibility to conserve natural resources.[6] Some ethicists have analyzed the social responsibilities of stockholders and of burgeoning multinational corporations.[7] Nevertheless, there has been little sustained debate about concrete issues of economic justice and well-being.

However, this comparative neglect of concrete economic issues in contemporary Christian ethics is not solely the result of specific conditions in contemporary history. Rather, it has additional roots in those strands of Christian tradition which are ambivalent about or hostile toward worldly existence and its concerns. Moreover, it is not just a coincidence that changes in the work experience of *clerical workers* have been all but ignored, for, in some influential streams of the Christian heritage, a spirit/world dualism intersects with a dualistic understanding of gender. Those educated males who have had the opportunity to give systematic expression to Christian experience have often identified women primarily with the home, while men (at least privileged men) were assigned a larger sphere of public responsibility.

Until the Industrial Revolution, male theologians did not set women apart from economic activity, for most economic production took place within households in which women performed clearly discernible productive functions. Once the link between the home and "work place" was severed as a result of industrialization, the continuing tendency among Christian theologians to associate woman with the home obscured the real injustices which women workers faced in the workplaces of industrial and postindustrial society. Unacknowledged remnants of Christian gender dualism continue to obscure our view of patterns of injustice which emerge in the experience of female clerical workers. A serious moral assessment of the terms of women's participation in the economy has rarely been attempted. Thus, dualistic elements in Christianity are among those cultural factors contributing to a situation in which the subordination of women workers continues to be "invisible, a natural pattern and thus a non issue."[8]

Work, Women and the World in the
Christian Tradition

Christian traditions regarding work have evolved throughout the centuries. Diverse Christian notions of work were created in response to the economic systems of various ages. Christian notions of men and women's roles in life, including roles in economic life, were elaborated in response to the gender role patterns of differing times. Implicit in religious notions of both work and gender roles are varying understandings of the Christian community's relationship to the world—of the possibility (if any) and desirability of transformation of the world, including its gender relations and its economic ones.

Much of Christian tradition says little about transforming the conditions of women's work, because *any* notion of an obligation to transform the social conditions of work was slow to develop in Christian history. For many centuries, work was passively accepted as necessary for material survival, as a means to obtain goods with which to aid the less fortunate, as a safeguard against the moral hazards of idleness, and as an opportunity for discipline of the body and character development. Still, there was no sense that Christians might have a duty radically to reshape worldly patterns of labor.

For some Christians, there was no thought of such an obligation because all the affairs of this world, including its economic relationships, were of little consequence as they will soon pass away. New patterns of human relationships will soon emerge, but these new patterns will be a result of the apocalyptic intervention of God, who will suddenly break into human history in order to initiate an era of righteousness which is in radical discontinuity with any human efforts to change the world. Such was the apocalyptic perspective of Jesus and Paul in the New Testament and of various millenarian sects throughout Christian history.

Other Christians have refrained from any attempt to transform patterns of work because they have believed that the economic order of their own time satisfactorily harmonized material and spiritual values in one smooth, stable whole. In medieval Christendom, for example, it seemed possible to reconcile human economic activity with religious aims in an elaborate social system which was said to have religious values as its keystone. In spite of the social tensions reflected in the activities of the sectarian movements, Jacob Viner captures a medieval sense of social stability when he declares:

> They [the scholastics, principally Thomas Aquinas] recognized in some measure that virtue had social implications, but in the main they confined their discussion of these implications to repeated emphasis on the priority of the common good over the individual and to scattered and occasional insights on almsgiving and questions of commutative justice arising from transactions between individuals in the ordinary course of their worldly life. They said almost nothing about . . . the possibilities of deliberate or spontaneous remoulding of existing institutions."[9]

Still other Christians have been without any religious notion of a duty to transform the economic structures of their society, because they viewed all worldly involvement as a dangerous distraction from the pursuit of the highest good—spiritual insight and purity. These Christians viewed ordinary social life as requiring inevitable and unacceptable moral compromises; therefore, they sought to withdraw from the world. This has been the stance of many monastic orders and certain sectarian groups.

The monastic system represented a two-tiered moral system within which ordinary work in the world was devalued. Lay men and women who lived in the world were accountable to lower, minimal standards of moral behavior, such as observance of the Ten Commandments, as they labored to produce goods which allowed their families to live in a manner appropriate to their station in a hierarchical social order. Members of religious orders were seen as living a more morally demanding lifestyle, one characterized by observance of the counsel of poverty as well as chastity and obedience.

Various sectarian Christian groups also lived a life of radical material simplicity which contrasted sharply with the worldly, luxurious lifestyle enjoyed by upper-class laity and some "degenerate" members of the upper clergy. Some sectarian adherents tried to establish a "communistic" practice of shared consumer goods based on their interpretation of early church practice. In a few instances, such as the Beguine movement or Hutterite communities, there were models for shared productive activity. Still, such sectarian groups existed as "islands of righteousness in an ocean of iniquity"; they had limited impact on the economic practices of the larger society.[10] As one study on the economic teachings and practices of the Anabaptist movement concludes, their economic goal—the use of material goods to promote the well-being of all members of the community—remained "an expression of the love ethic for a spiritually-united group, and was never intended for society as a whole."[11] Thus, monastic and sectarian groups used distinctive group mores to preserve their moral integrity while participating, at least marginally, in larger economic systems which they did not envision transforming.

It was the Protestant reformers—the Lutherans and especially the Calvinists—who finally gave more serious attention to labor in the world through the theological notion of vocation or calling. Luther challenged the legitimacy of the two-tiered system of morality by scathingly denouncing the legitimacy of monastic life. According to Luther, *all Christians are called to serve God in their ordinary activities in the world.* All work diligently done is pleasing to God. Indeed, obedient service in one's calling is the best way to show love of neighbor. Despite Luther's serious attention to daily labor in the world, there was a static quality to his concept of vocation. Luther thought that God arranges the different callings in a manner which promotes the good order of society. Since one's position in society is assigned by God, it is a sin against God to try to rise above one's station in a stable, hereditary social order.

Calvin shared Luther's belief that all persons were called by God to do certain work *in the world.* However, in contrast to Luther, Calvin stressed the end or purpose of Christian work—the glorification of God and the creation of a Holy Community. Calvinism had a world transformative thrust. The world was a sinful realm, but, according to Calvin, sin required active opposition. While Calvin's theology retained some traces of the notion of individual acquiescence to the role to which one had been assigned by God,[12] work also involved initiative to create the redeemed community through coordinated human effort.

Calvinism promoted worldly asceticism, aiming to achieve "victory over the world while remaining within it."[13] One should work hard, but not overindulge in the sensual pleasure that such hard work could make possible. In the Calvinist tradition, the virtues of love and stewardship were the control mechanisms preventing the misuse of the material plenty which hard work coupled with abstinence from material luxuries generated. As Winthrop Hudson explains, "It was precisely the conviction that one's calling was God's gift for which, as a good steward, the Christian must render an accounting that served as a check to covetousness."[14] Labor and profit were not purely for personal aggrandizement, but rather were gifts from God to be used for the sake of the neighbor and the community.

The Calvinist tradition elevated work to the status of a central religious duty. Work ceased to be merely a means of providing for material survival and a method of bodily discipline. Work became a primary opportunity to exercise faith through labor within one's "calling." This Calvinist blend of worldly, vocational asceticism "produced as an important by-product, that ideal of hard work, of the prosecution of work for its own sake, as a duty in itself."[15] Thus, one root for the modern sense of work as a means of self-realization and as a crucial form of social participation is the Calvinist emphasis on work as a central human obligation.

In some highly dedicated Calvinist communities, such as Geneva in the second half of the sixteenth century or the early Puritan colonial settlements in Massachusetts, religious leaders made strenuous efforts to bring economic relationships under the sway of religious values. Repeated attempts were made to regulate prices, interest rates, and profits in order to promote the temporal and spiritual well-being of the community.[16] These efforts were dependent on the tight religious consensus of the community (of believers). Such attempts to fashion holy commonweals became impossible in the growing number of communities in which religious pluralism forced a religious tolerance inconsistent with vigorous Calvinist communal discipline.

After the creation of the American nation in a religiously pluralistic context, the Calvinist impulse to transform society was channeled into voluntary associations. In the opening decades of the nineteenth century, a wave of religious revivals swept across the United States.

Revival preachers made clear that a genuine conversion experience should bear fruit in an active effort to give expression to God's love in the world. Those preachers, such as Charles Grandison Finney, who proclaimed the possibility of achieving Christian perfection or sanctification during this life, unleashed powerful ethical energies. For some evangelicals, Christian perfection consisted in the development of inward, personal holiness. For others, however, it had a social thrust as well. These latter evangelicals hoped that Christian believers whose hearts had been transformed by Christ could transform society. Thus, an evangelical religious impulse found expression in involvement in all the major humanitarian reform movements of the antebellum era. Evangelicals worked for temperance, women's rights, and the abolition of slavery, to name only a few of the more important causes. (Of course, the latter two movements were highly controversial and were opposed by yet other fervent evangelicals.)

At the turn of the twentieth century, some Christian leaders called for a renewed effort to transform society, and this time they focused on the need for *a structural transformation of the industrial system.* One of the most prominent Social Gospel thinkers, Walter Rauschenbusch, insisted that the notion of the Kingdom of God was central to a proper understanding of Christian ethics. However, unlike the earliest Christians, he did not have in mind an apocalyptic break which ushered in God's reign—a cataclysm which would signal the end of this world and its institutions. Rather, influenced in part by the theory of evolution, he stressed the ways in which human beings could cooperate with God to bring about the Kingdom by working to transform evil social institutions.

The Social Gospel movement broke with those elements in American Protestantism which placed very heavy emphasis on personal conversion and individual salvation. This movement stressed the evil impact of unjust social institutions, emphasized social well-being, and insisted on the importance of a just material base for spiritual values. While not denying the importance of personal conversion, exponents of the Social Gospel stressed the social dimension of both sin and salvation. Social Gospel writers and preachers insisted that the churches should become involved in a concerted effort to end the economic injustices of their day through the application of the social teachings of Jesus to social problems. Social Gospel leaders were disturbed by the conflict between the selfishness, competition, and drive for profits fostered by the capitalist system and the Christian values of love and brotherhood. Proponents of the movement, such as Washington Gladden and Rauschenbusch were further distressed by the gap between political democracy, which gave all citizens a voice in government, and economic oligarchy, which centralized economic decision-making in the hands of a dwindling number of wealthy, powerful people who controlled large corporations.

Rauschenbusch analyzed how the industrial system had distorted the nature of human work. The unequal position of worker and owner meant that the more desperate the material needs of the worker and his family, the more vulnerable the worker was to an exploitative wage. The Social Gospel leader was especially concerned about the insecurity of turn-of-the-century factory work. A worker might be unemployed in one of the many recessions, maimed in an industrial accident, or left destitute when he became too old to work. Rauschenbusch proclaimed that workers were not participating on an equitable basis in the material prosperity made possible by industrialization—an abundance which Rauschenbusch clearly acknowledged as good. "Our blessings have failed to bless us because they were not based on justice and solidarity."[17]

Woman's God-given Role

Throughout much of Christian history, there has been little thought about a systemic transformation of the structures of human labor in this world. There has been even less thought of the possibility or desirability of a fundamental transformation of the social division of labor based upon gender. Many Christian theologians have assumed that gender relationships are based on natural differences between the sexes rooted in the will of the Creator and thus ought to be respected and perpetuated. Other thinkers viewed some aspects of gender relations as a burden placed on women as punishment for the first woman's role in the Fall. Many theologians who held the latter view believed that Christian women should patiently endure a harsh male yoke as the lot God had assigned them in this life. In certain

Christian groups which were critical of the prevailing culture, women have found some elements of freedom denied them in the larger society, but these "prophetic" groups made a limited impact on the gender relations in the larger social world.

Feminist scripture scholars, such as Elisabeth Schüssler Fiorenza, have made a strong argument that there were elements in the earliest Christian experience which pressed Christian households and groups in the direction of a discipleship of equals. However, those egalitarian impulses were suppressed as Christian orthodoxy developed. At first, relationships among the disciples of Jesus—relationships rooted in religious commitment—implicitly challenged the power of the husband in the patriarchal family. Dedication to the immanent Reign of God was stressed even at the expense of normal family ties and responsibilities. The closest followers of Jesus left behind house and kin to prepare the way for the Reign of God. Matthew 10:34-36 (paralleled by Luke 12:51-53) describes a commitment to the Reign preached by Jesus as a sword which destroys family bonds, setting family member against family member. Thus, discipleship had liberating potential for some women whose life possibilities were otherwise tightly circumscribed in a society organized on the basis of patriarchal family relationships.

There is also evidence that women played a prominent role in some of the house churches in the missions to the Gentiles. However, elements pressing toward sexual equality in the life of the earliest Christian communities created social tensions which were resolved before the close of the New Testament period through a capitulation to the prevailing patriarchal family ethic of the Greco-Roman world. Around the turn of the first century, influential elements in the Christian Church accepted and legitimated the prevailing patriarchal family structure. Some leaders of small, politically vulnerable Christian communities, such as the one in Asia Minor, sought to reduce tensions with the surrounding culture by muting the social implications of spiritual equality between the sexes. They chose instead to conform to the customs and ethos of the "pagan," patriarchal household. Therefore, some Christian leaders promulgated household codes which enjoined submission of wife, child, and slave to the *paterfamilias*.[18]

Once male leaders of the Christian community capitulated to conventional mores governing gender relations, a conjunction between woman and the domestic or private sphere became a staple in the treatises of major Christian thinkers. While the content and boundaries of the private realm shifted throughout Christian history, women remained identified with the home in the minds of most male theologians. In the second through the sixth centuries, for example, the Church Fathers favored a role for married women which was in accord with "pagan antiquity's [upper-class] ideal of the chaste and retiring matron."[19] The Greek theologian John Chrysostom expressed a representative viewpoint when he asserted that God had given public responsibilities to men and household duties to women: "to man the important things of social life, like politics, war, the acquisition of property; to woman the small things, like the care of the household, the protection of the patrimony. To man the glorious and public affairs; to woman the private concerns and the hidden chores."[20] In Chrysostom's day, female management of household affairs included much productive activity. Chrysostom believed that God has arranged the division of labor by gender in order that men would not despise the less important, but nonetheless necessary, activities of women. Conversely, God protected women from weightier public burdens, lest they rebel against the divinely ordained authority of their husbands.

Despite his firm assertions that women were fully human, the medieval theologian Thomas Aquinas still assumed a natural division of labor based on gender. Women were created for procreation, in which process they serve as passive vessels. For any purpose other than reproduction, one man will find another man to be a superior companion. Women were innately suited to be the bearers of children and to perform the feminine duties essential to run a household.

Until the Reformation, monastic orders offered some women a religiously sanctioned alternative to marriage, home, and motherhood. From the early centuries of Christian history, some unmarried or widowed Christian women were able take great initiative in charitable, intellectual, and spiritual matters, when they chose a lifestyle of consecrated celibacy. Certain women exercised considerable authority as heads of monastic groups and/or as holy women, i.e., mystics. In point of fact, however, even asceticism did not offer Christian women a stable, certain route to sexual equality in either the social world or the spiritual realm. As Rosemary Ruether reports, "The theoretical principle of spiritual equality [between the sexes] was constantly undermined in practice in the ascetic life."[21] Throughout the history of women's religious groups, male religious authorities have striven repeatedly to control the appearance and activities of women religious in order to guarantee their sexual propriety and obedience.

Nevertheless, the dissolution of women's religious orders in Reformed territories represented a loss for Protestant women. Under Protestantism, the role of wife and mother became virtually the only acknowledged vocation for adult women. The identification of woman with the home became almost total. For Luther, obedience to the will of God for women consisted, not in "papist" rituals of fasting and prayer, but rather in the education of young children, in care for the family, and in the tasks of the kitchen.[22] In his exegesis of Genesis 3:16, Luther declared that as a punishment for the fall, a woman's role is restricted to the affairs of the household; she is "deprived of the ability of administering those affairs that are outside [the home] and that concern the state."[23]

As a result of the fall, wives are subject to their husband's authority in the household,[24] but it is also true that in a genuine Christian marriage a virtuous wife is a partner who shares her husband's bed, table, house, children, and material goods. A husband's authority over his wife is modified by the realization that only God ultimately rules over any human soul. Nonetheless, in all the worldly aspects of life, a husband retains final authority.

While Calvin, too, viewed male dominance as an enduring reality dictated by God as a punishment for human sin and applicable in all areas of human life, he also had a strong belief in loving, mutual service between husband and wife. Moreover, he taught that women should not be dismayed at male supremacy in this passing temporal state, for women have a spiritual equality as creatures in the image of God, as persons redeemed by Christ, and as souls graced by the Spirit. Despite the example of some very powerful women from European royal families, Calvin held that most women should eschew intervention in public affairs. Calvin did concede that God might occasionally call a woman to teach or govern. However, he theorized that most instances of such female authority were examples of divine punishment for social evil. God humiliated sinful men, by allowing *a woman* to exercise power over them.[25] On the whole, Calvin asserted that a virtuous woman should stay always close to her home. In the home she should perform those maternal and household duties to which she is called and for which her very nature is formed.

American evangelical movement of the early nineteenth century was one important source of social empowerment for women. Some evangelical Christian women discovered as a result of their religious experiences the courage to challenge women's exclusion from debate on the great public questions of the day. The evangelical emphasis on personal decision in spiritual matters led some Protestant women to rely on their individual consciences when claiming a larger role in the public sphere. However, such spiritually fueled female assertiveness was controversial. Charles Grandison Finney was severely criticized for his decision to permit women to testify about their conversion experiences during revival meetings where men were present. Bitter debates about women's right to a larger role in public affairs racked both the temperance and anti-slavery movements in the antebellum period.

For all the social gospel's prophetic critique of the evils of industrialization, leaders of the movement continued take for granted the division of labor based on gender. Both Rauschenbusch and Gladden held a view of woman which might, somewhat facetiously, be characterized as separate but equal. Gladden asserted that a good marriage is "the perfect union of two [people] who, though different, are in all respects equal."[26] Consistent with his belief that the thrust of Christian history was to relieve women of that misery which was a punishment for the Fall, he declared: "Authority and subjection are terms of the curse, which ought, after nineteen centuries of Christianity, to disappear from the vocabulary of *wedlock*."[27] He did not explore how female subjection might be dispelled in other social relations.

These two Social Gospel leaders discussed women primarily as wives and homemakers. Both men rarely discussed the experience of wage-earning women. Rauschenbusch thought wage labor for women endangered the family. Therefore, he advocated that male heads of household receive a wage sufficient to support their families. Rauschenbusch believed that the separation of economic production from family life which had taken place during the nineteenth century had capped the positive transformation of family life, because it purified the family of the selfishness which inevitably accompanies productive economic activity. Removing productive functions from the home allowed Christian love to become the sole norm for family life.[28]

The leaders of the Social Gospel movement were often sympathetic proponents of the cult of true womanhood, a complex of social values which extolled the spiritual and moral influence which women could wield from within the sanctity of the home. Rauschenbusch reflects the cultural adulation of the role of mother when he says: "As for the word 'mother'—that carries a mystic breath of religious sweetness to which we all do homage."[29] Church historian Dorothy Bass Fraser points out the social implications of this praise of woman's special virtues: "Granting women a monopoly of 'goodness' rendered impossible their full participation in much of everyday [economic and political] life" which was viewed as inevitably characterized by ruthless competition and moral corruption.[30]

When prominent leaders of the Social Gospel movement accepted and gave religious affirmation to the cult of true womanhood, they were caught in cultural currents which had dangerous implications for religion, women, and work. Throughout the nineteenth century, the cultural understanding of the boundaries between the "public" and the "private" were being redefined. As more and more productive activity moved out of the household and into factories and offices, the workplace became a separate public space. The household, now stripped of many of its former "manufacturing" functions, became the private home. Privileged married, white women who remained at home became the social model for the true woman whose place was limited to the private realm.

At the same time, the public influence of religious groups was dwindling. Religion was increasingly understood as a matter of private conviction. Religious activity was defined as part of the sphere increasingly remote from the public world of business activity. Rose-

mary Ruether has accurately assessed the result for ethics of acquiesc-
ing to this redefinition of public and private spheres: "This split
between the public realm . . . as the sphere of material relations
and functional rationality and the 'home' as the feminine sphere of
morality and sentiment had [and continues to have] a devastating
effect on both women and the quality of public culture."[31] Religious
voices now had a particularly dubious ring when raised in public
debate. Religious leaders who addressed social questions were often
accused to stepping outside their legitimate (personal, spiritual)
realm.

Thus, twentieth-century religion came to be viewed by many as
separated from the business world. In industrial and postindustrial
societies, morality and religion are in danger of being reduced to
matters of idiosyncratic personal choice, without power to influence
the patterns of our economic life. When economics, work, technology,
and functional rationality are on one side of a cultural gulf and
religion is on the other, it is little wonder that Christian ethicists have
almost entirely ignored office automation.

Uncritical acceptance of the split between the public and the private serves, in a special way, to obscure Christian ethicists' perspective on issues of justice for those *women* workers who have poured
into the labor force in ever-increasing numbers throughout the twentieth century. Economic pressures on family units and a feminist challenge to cultural assumptions about "woman's place" have now radically altered views about "women's work." Faced with these changes,
many Christian thinkers have muted their assertions of gender dualism. However, few male Christian leaders have forcefully repudiated
the patriarchal strands in Christian history and even fewer have
articulated a new vision of justice for women, especially women
workers. Feminist criticisms of traditional theological constructs and
initial feminist efforts to create new theological visions of right relationship among human beings, with nature, and with the Power of
Being have not been integrated into most contemporary Christian
theology.

As the world economy moves more deeply into the postindustrial
stage, human experiences of work are being transformed. Transformations in patterns of clerical labor are one important aspect of that

larger process of change. As with the decline of the Roman imperial economy, the rise of mercantile capitalism, or the growth of industrialization, contemporary changes in economic relationships will evoke new religious responses.

A religious passivity which tolerates oppressive forms of work because economic issues are seen as irrelevant distractions from spiritual regeneration does not serve the needs of workers. Neither will a religious complacency which holds that present economic arrangements adequately harmonize material needs and spiritual values for society as a whole. Exhorting the economically powerful to view their wealth as held in trust from God is not a sufficient response to the needs of the more socially vulnerable among wage laborers.

Christian ethicists need to fully repudiate dualistic theologies which devalue mundane activity and which legitimate the subordination of women. I urge that Christians build upon those strands of our tradition which assert a responsibility to participate in shaping the conditions of wage labor. Christian ethicists have a new opportunity to examine and to morally assess gender patterns in the labor force. If Christians are going to participate in reshaping women's work in the clerical sector, then they need guidance about how to help channel change in the direction of human wholeness and well-being. In the section which follows, I will explore the concept of justice as participation, using it as a mediating concept which serves as a bridge between the ideal of the Reign of God/dess and decisions on specific policies about office automation. Justice for women means active and equitable participation in the economic realm. I will offer a substantive theory of good work in order to specify what constitutes equitable labor force participation for women. That substantive notion of good work is developed as a dialogue between clerical workers' experiences of work and the theories of religious ethicists.

Justice as Equitable Participation in Work Processes

The central evaluative concept employed in this section is "justice as participation." In choosing that norm I am expanding upon the concept of justice used in the Catholic bishops' pastoral letter "Economic Justice for All." The Catholic bishops emphasize the importance of human dignity realized and safeguarded in a context of social solidarity. They focus on the experience of marginalization as a sign of the breakdown of social solidarity. Marginalization is the experience which a person or group has when that person or group possesses little or no power in crucial areas of human life. Marginal persons are told, in effect, that they don't simply count as full members of the group. They are treated as if they had little or no moral value as persons in community.

In using this image of justice as participation, I am adopting a very different starting point from that of several culturally influential philosophic theories of justice which initially present us with human persons described as mutually disinterested individuals. Liberal philosophic theories construct basic principles of justice based on an argument about the principles acceptable to individuals in some original position or, in the case of John Rawls, in an initial state which transcends the biases introduced by the moral subject's particular social location. For heuristic purposes, these liberal models begin by examining what principles would be acceptable to a group of selves who seem capable of pursuing their individual aims and goals independently. In contrast, my starting point is with the inevitable sociability of human life. We are always radically interdependent, and whatever personal fulfillment we achieve, we achieve in and through enriching relationships with others. We work out our shared understanding of justice in a specific historical and sociological context which we cannot ever completely transcend.

Once one focuses on the social nature of human beings, employment issues become critical questions because work is a key dimension of human sociality today. At present, access to jobs is a powerful sign of inclusion as a valuable member of the community's joint endeavors. For this reason the bishops' letter emphasizes the importance of access to the workplace and the destructiveness of involuntary restriction to the margins of economic life. According to the bishops, "Increasing active participation in economic life by those who are presently excluded or vulnerable [should be] a high social priority."[32] The bishops tell us that persons have an obligation to be active and productive participants in the life of society, and society has a reciprocal duty to enable them to participate actively. Thus, for the bishops, unemployment is a fundamental issue of justice; the tragedy of unemployment is compounded by the unfair and unequal way in which it is distributed. The major, continuing burden of unemployment in the United States is borne by persons from socially disadvantaged minority groups.

Persons can experience economic marginalization in either or both of the economic dimensions of production and consumption. Persons are marginalized if they are deprived of consumer goods adequate for decent fellowship with their neighbors. They are also marginalized if they are deprived of opportunities to be active participants in production. The bishops make clear that either type of economic marginalization corrodes both human dignity and community. The exclusion and powerlessness of some undermines the moral vitality of the entire social group.

Moral considerations concerning consumption and production are linked by a concern for the dignity of persons. The way in which basic consumer goods and services are obtained is important because the means of obtaining these goods reflects upon the worth which society accords to the recipient. In this society, an (adult) individual's dignity is enhanced, if she or he consumes goods which are the reward for his or her productive activity. Loss of opportunity for labor force participation is a crucial form of economic marginalization, because, in the United States today, it is primarily work in the labor force which is culturally recognized as real labor. The United States is a society in which relationships of production and distribution of goods and services shape our views of the social contribution and corresponding worth of persons. When society treats work for wages as the only real work, many (including full-time homemakers and the unemployed) are demeaned.

Over the long term, the process of recognizing and assigning a value to persons in terms of the wage labor that they do and the level of compensation that their efforts receive must be changed. We need, for example, to recognize the productive contribution of unpaid housework and many forms of volunteer labor—offering social acknowledgment more genuine than the platitudes now occasionally proffered. But, in the short run, given the operational value assigned to wage labor in this culture, those who are involuntarily unemployed

are denied both a sense of self-worth and a voice in economic decision-making. To the extent that persons stand at the margin or outside
the boundaries of the productive sphere, their human dignity is jeop-
ardized and the moral integrity of the community is imperilled.

The concept of justice as participation has genuine, but limited,
usefulness. It is not a universal category—appeals to which solve all
questions of fairness or justice. As philosopher Michael Walzer has
argued, there is no single, formal definition of justice that is appropriate to govern the fair allocation of a wide variety of social goods,
such as jobs, positions of authority, social recognition, and love.
There are persons such as the frail elderly or the severely disabled
who are unable to be active participants in the productive process.
Nevertheless, I argue that justice as participation is an apt term to
describe justice for workers and potential workers.

The bishops helpfully draw our attention to the need of human
beings as social creatures to be active participants in the social group.
However, we need to examine more critically the terms for active
involvement in the economic affairs of society. Are the terms for
participation consistent with the human dignity of all the parties?
Here an examination of the historical experience of women provides
an important caution. Women have been active participants as producers of goods and services essential to meet basic material needs
of every human society. However, women's productive contributions
have often been trivialized or ignored, and, hence, women have been
frequently been relegated to second-class status. As Michael Walzer
acknowledges: "In many societies, women have been the most important group of 'inside' aliens, doing the work that men disdained and
freeing the men not only for more rewarding economic activities but
also for citizenship and politics."[33] For women, participation alone
is not enough, for we have always been crucial contributors to society.
The terms of women's participation must be fair ones.

If women are to participate on an equitable basis, women's economic participation must be recognized, valued and appropriately
rewarded. Recognition of women's contribution is important because
the social invisibility of women's productive labor is an element in
perpetuating the economic injustices which they suffer. When, in
contrast, women's economic contributions are socially acknowl-

edged as valuable, women experience a type of basic respect from fellow members in society.

Clerical workers are entitled to opportunities for equitable, as well as active, participation. Equitable participation entails having an effective voice in institutional decisions which are critical to one's life and to the common good. Persons are denied justice when they are denied the standing and power to define their own needs and desires and to have those needs and desires taken seriously. A person is denied standing when his/her stake in the outcome of a decision is unfairly ignored. In effect, the person is told: "This decision doesn't concern you," or alternately, "you don't have the capabilities necessary to contribute to the resolution of this question."

Workers employed by a business or non-profit enterprise contribute to the joint process of the production of goods and services. Since they are all "members" in a mutual project, they each deserve an opportunity to share in making choices about the specific conditions of their work together. Justice as participation is undermined when some workers have radically unequal chances to take part the decision-making procedures which shape the workers' own work processes. The achievement of justice requires the creation of "structures of participation, mutual accountability and widely distributed power" in the economic realm.[34] In the next chapter, when I discuss worker participation in job design, I will address some the objections to a claim that workers are entitled to a say in decisions which directly affect their own jobs.

In the context of office automation, a notion of justice as participation raises two questions. Will clerical workers continue to be active participants in the economy? Will the terms of their participation be equitable? In the following section, I will expand upon the notion of equitable participation by offering some elements for a substantive notion of good work. I do not claim that this discussion provides a comprehensive normative theory of work. Such a systematic prescriptive statement would be premature for at least two reasons. First, all intellectual assertions about the meaning of work are, in part, conditioned by the economic and cultural environments in which they arise. My reflections in this section must be understood in that light. These are thoughts about human work as it is experienced in what appears to be the early stages of a fundamental economic transition from an industrial age to a postindustrial era. The world economy is undergoing fundamental change; new patterns of work are just beginning to emerge. In such a transition period, analyses of the human meaning of work are appropriately tentative. Second, I am attempting to investigate the human meaning of work in conjunction with an exploration of changing patterns of clerical work. Attention to the labor force experiences of such women workers is so new for ethicists that an affirmation of some traditional ethical categories, criticism of others, and addition of new elements are all appropriately provisional.

Throughout this section, theoretical perspectives on work will be tested in the light of clerical workers' concrete experiences of work. I have drawn upon sociological studies of clerical work and journalists' interviews with women workers in order to describe clerical workers' experiences. I do not claim that these theoretical reflections on work produce distinctive categories—ones which are foreign to the work experiences of other groups of workers. However, in order to create some valid generalizations about human work, it is important to investigate the particularities of work in the lives of diverse groups of workers. In a society where occupations are heavily sex segregated, explicit attention must be paid to the workplace experiences of women, if we are to construct adequate intellectual models of good work.

Work as Means to Material Survival

Wages and the Survival of the Worker. In industrialized societies—and thus far, at least, in postindustrial ones—a paycheck is, for most people, the key means of access to goods necessary for physical survival. Building on a long-established tradition of economic realism about the necessity of wages for survival in such societies, Catholic social teachings speak directly about the importance of work as a means of sustenance. In recent Protestant discussions of work, however, there seems to be a reluctance to dwell on the survival value of wage labor. Protestant theologians and ethicists seem to fear that, in the advanced capitalist nations, work is too readily reduced *only* to its instrumental value as a means to gain material goods. Yet, in avoiding such reductionism, these Protestant thinkers have, perhaps, given too little attention to the crucial subsistence dimension of work in modern society. Work is how most of us (adults) earn the bread we need in order to live.

Catholic social teachings, on the other hand, recognize that, in industrialized societies, wages have become the chief means by which most persons gain access to essential material goods. For example, in *Laborem Exercens*, Pope John Paul II acknowledges that "wages . . . are still a practical means, whereby the vast majority of people can have access to those goods which are intended for common use: both the goods of nature and manufactured goods."[35] From this perspective, persons have a right to employment and wages as the social means through which they get access to the goods of the earth which the Creator has destined for their use.

In the advanced nations of the West, workers have come to rely not solely on wages but also on a complex network of employer-provided fringe benefits and governmental social security programs as crucial sources of financial security. It is through work that workers become part of private and governmental "insurance" plans which pay benefits in the event of illness, disability, old age, and death. Writing in the midst of unprecedented post–World War II prosperity, Pope John XXIII applauded the tranquillity afforded workers as a result of "recent advances in insurance programs and various systems of social security."[36] Turbulent economic conditions throughout the world since the late 1970s led to cutbacks in both government and private insurance plans and other benefits for workers who were fortunate enough to qualify for them. Nonetheless, it is important to include benefit plans as well as wages in an analysis of how work enables human beings to meet essential material needs in the present and in the future.

While Catholic documents recognize that wage labor is the means through which workers provide for their immediate and future financial needs, Protestant writers are less likely to affirm the subsistence value of work. This reluctance to speak about the value of work as means to bodily survival may stem, in part, from a residue of theological dualism. The material needs of the body are recognized, but subordinated to "higher values" of personal fulfillment and social solidarity. As concerned as ethicist Philip Wogaman is to insure that all human beings have secure access to those economic goods and services essential for human existence, he still sees the material world as "primarily to be understood as instrumental to other things."[37] Economic goods and services have instrumental, not intrinsic, value. On the most basic level, certain goods such as food, clothing, and housing are essential for our continued existence, and hence they are to be taken very seriously. Nonetheless, Wogaman is concerned that the (hierarchical) order of human values may be subverted by assigning too high a priority to wages, which are a means to preserve life. According to him, bodily life is a precondition for the realization of such higher values as friendship, communal solidarity, and right relationship with God. He warns that human talents and human relationships are in danger of being regarded primarily as ways of making money.

Protestant ethicists John Raines and Donna Day-Lower are also uneasy with an emphasis on the material gains associated with wages. They speak of the mistake of valuing work as individual effort which is suitably rewarded with the monetary wherewithal to amass private possessions. They contrast the acquisition of things paid for with an individual's earnings to a sense of social cooperation and shared productivity in work, which is not reflected in any one person's pay check. In fact, they go so far as to declare that it is "work as such" and not the "wealth" which it produces which is worthy of serious attention.[38] Still, these two authors are clearly concerned about the financial deprivation suffered by unemployed workers. They are also alarmed that well-paying factory jobs are being replaced by low-wage, service work. Implicit in this lament is a belief that work which pays an adequate wage remains an important good for human beings in early postindustrial societies.

For some Protestant thinkers to affirm that work is a necessary means for survival might be to condemn many people to dehumanizing exploitation for the sake of subsistence. Theologian Dorothee Soelle certainly recognizes that wage labor is the means through which most adults get access to the material goods and the services necessary for survival in modern capitalist societies. However, for

Soelle, this is precisely the problem. She presents capitalism's transformation of labor into a commodity exchanged for wages as a fundamental root of worker oppression. She asserts that wages are no longer
the fitting reward for useful, imaginative work in the service of the
community. Rather, salaries become an end in themselves—a measure of what price one's labor power commands in the market. According to Soelle, dependence on wages makes workers acquiesce to
alienating tasks and to work which sets them in competition with
their neighbors and which plunders our common earth. Soelle warns:
"The destructiveness of bad work cannot be compensated by
payment."[39]

The concern that these Protestant thinkers evince is well taken, up
to a point. A desire for higher wages with which to purchase luxury
goods and services may threaten to subvert the ethical priorities of
some workers. Yet, perhaps, we should ask which workers are most
likely to experience such a distortion of their moral priorities? Is it,
perhaps, a graver danger for some already well-paid professional
and managerial workers and a less immediate danger for lower-paid
workers, such as clerical workers?

Is it necessary, helpful, or appropriate to define material needs met
through wages as lower-order values? After all, human beings are
so deeply immersed in material existence that it falsifies human
experience to give a lower place to provision for our basic physical
needs. Most adults in this society earn the money to purchase food,
shelter, clothing, and medical care through paid employment. Meeting such survival needs has a high, not a secondary, priority.

In effect, Wogaman, Raines, and Day-Lower set up an unnecessary
dichotomy—work has meaning either because it produces individual
wealth (pay) or because it expresses human skill, encourages solidarity, and contributes to the social good. *Good* work allows workers
both to participate in productive human relationships by exercising
skill *and* to take part in the creation of goods and services which
meet their bodily needs. Certainly none of these authors means to
deny this, but their argument wrongly subordinates material needs
to so-called higher-order goods.

Certainly, Soelle is correct that work which is in other ways dehumanizing or socially destructive does not become morally acceptable

because the worker is paid an adequate, or even a high, wage. There is always the potential for dehumanizing exploitation when workers are dependent on their jobs as their only "reliable" means of material survival and comfort. As Walter Muelder warned years ago: "For want of bread a man will sell his freedom. For want of religion, many a man will buy another's freedom for bread."[40] The wage labor system of advanced industrial and postindustrial economies leaves workers vulnerable in specific ways. Most contemporary workers, including clerical workers, are dependent on their jobs for survival. If they lose one job, they must try to find another, for most of them lack the resources to become self-supporting, independent producers. Nonetheless, it would be a mistake to obscure the positive connection between work and material survival, even in an effort to condemn the exploitation of workers.

Wages and Family Survival. The Catholic social tradition has another strong point in its recognition that workers are not isolated individuals who work only to obtain material goods for themselves but, instead, are social beings who work for the benefit of others as well as themselves. The primary image of the workers as social beings in Catholic teachings on economics is that of workers as family members who toil on behalf of their dependents. However, Catholic social teachings have accepted certain sexual stereotypes concerning family roles as representative of the social ideal. The father is seen as the chief breadwinner; the mother is viewed as uniquely capable of nurturing young children in the home. Inspired by this ideal, Pope Pius XI declared: "social justice demands that reforms be introduced without delay which will guarantee every adult working *man* . . . a wage [sufficient to meet ordinary domestic needs]."[41] More recently, Pope John Paul II has stated that the good society is one in which women are not forced to work outside the home, but rather are able to devote themselves to the domestic needs of their families.[42]

Since the time of Pope Pius XII, there has been a growing ambivalence about women's wage labor in Catholic social teachings. For example, the Second Vatican Council affirms the right of women to be free from discrimination in the workplace, but still expresses concern about how female workers can be good mothers. The bishops declare: "this domestic role of hers must be safely preserved, though the legitimate social progress of women should not be underrated on that account."[43] The domestic role of women in contemporary society is far more precarious than official Catholic social teachers have generally acknowledged. In a growing number of families, either both husband and wife or a solitary mother must work in order to provide the family with the material necessities and a few comforts.

Wage Labor as the Basis for Personal Autonomy

Women work not only to earn a wage necessary for survival, but also to achieve that feeling of independence which comes from earning a wage by one's own direct labor and, hence, having money which is one's own. Wages can be an important basis for personal autonomy. Strengthening one's autonomy through paid labor is an aspect of work which is clearly tied to industrial and early postindustrial settings. Prior to the industrial era, most economic production took place in a family context. Productive activity and its rewards were often shared by family members. But with the rise of the industrial system, large numbers of factory and office workers began to receive individual wages as a reward for productive activity.

I do not know of any theological discussions of work which describe wage labor as a foundation for personal autonomy. Contemporary theologians may have failed to discuss the importance of personal autonomy grounded in an income produced by one's own labor, because they are alarmed about anything which smacks of an excessive individualism. Walter Muelder describes autonomy under capitalism as fragmenting social bonds and creating isolation: "Much modern freedom is that of the so-called solitary individual, with freedom *from* serfdom, freedom *from* his own tools, freedom *from* skill, freedom *from* the whole product and freedom *from* the solidarity of the family."[44] Raines and Day-Lower also emphasize the perversion of autonomy as self-centered isolation. They suggest that an exaggerated individualism endemic in American culture leads people to claim their income and their possessions as something each person rightfully earns by individual effort. As a counterbalance, these authors stress the social character of all economic activity. They

see autonomy or self-reliance and social cooperation as opposing
categories and insist that we must opt to stress one or the other in
our vision of good work.[45]

Again, we are presented with a false dichotomy. Human beings are
profoundly social beings. On the one hand, we achieve self-reliance
only in the context of cooperative and supportive relationships with
others. On the other hand, only a person who is capable of exercising
personal autonomy is capable of entering into relationships characterized by reciprocal respect and solidarity. Financial independence
can be an important basis for such confident personal autonomy.
Religious ethicists have been sensitive to the ways in which significant inequalities in the distribution of material goods can imperil
community.[46] However, they have not specifically investigated how
financial dependency can endanger mutuality, even when the dependent has adequate access to material goods. Financial dependency
tends to mute one's voice in economic decisions. Insofar as wage
labor represents financial independence, it gives many women a
valuable sense of their own standing as economic actors and decision-
makers.

One bank teller described the importance of work as a means to
independence like this:

> By afternoon I'm tired, but there's a pride you feel each day when
> you leave work: you've earned your day's pay. That's important,
> not to be a burden to anyone; to me, it has always meant a lot
> that I make a living.[47]

Social science research indicates that a wage-earning woman who
is living with someone else has a greater say in many joint decisions,
particularly economic decisions, than does a non-employed
woman.[48] Moreover, "working-class wives gain more power though
employment than middle-class wives."[49] In one study of African
American families, employed wives were significantly more powerful than the nonemployed.[50]

In another study, wage-earning wives and their husbands were
more likely to report that disagreements were resolved by give-and-
take rather than the capitulation of one partner. Male dominance in
family decision-making was eroded when wives worked for wages.

Wage-earning wives increased their power to influence decisions in important areas such as finances or children.[51] In an interview for yet another project, one working-class husband eloquently expressed his realization that his wife, who now earned her own salary, was more assertive in family decision-making: "She . . . brings home a pay check, so there's no one person above the other. She doesn't want there to be a king in this household."[52]

I am not arguing that all relationships where one party is dependent on the income of the other are characterized by morally offensive inequality or domination. Neither would I want to obscure the reality that the [unpaid] services of a full-time homemaker make an important contribution to the economic well-being of a family. Nonetheless, to the extent that the ability to earn one's own living provides an important type of social standing, autonomy rooted in financial independence is a good which we should acknowledge.

The paradox in the experience of many clerical women is that their paychecks provide them with a measure of independence which they appreciate, even though their wages are often too low to provide a firm foundation for personal autonomy. Insufficient attention to wages as a fragile, vulnerable, yet real root of autonomy impoverishes a theological understanding of work.

Exploring the Connections among Survival, Autonomy, Availability of Jobs and Wages

Most wage-earning women, including the vast number of women who are clerical workers, need jobs because their wages are necessary for their own material survival. Often women's wages are also necessary for the material survival of other persons whom they love. In 1987, 60 percent of all women who worked for wages were single, widowed, divorced, or married to a man who earned less than $15,000 a year. Women need their jobs because they need the money. Sociologist Roberta Goldberg reports the clerical workers whom she surveyed make a major financial contribution to their families. Interviewing a group of Baltimore clerical workers, Goldberg found most of the women "could not rely on a man to provide an adequate income, or in many cases, any income at all."[53] As one clerical worker clearly stated:

> I don't think there's hardly any family where the woman can stay home anymore. Not that you wouldn't like to and that it isn't a job in itself, but you have rent, you have cars, you have children and food.[54]

It is important to recognize that office work affords most clerical workers a *precarious* measure of financial security and independence. The median income for a full time female administrative support worker in the United States in 1986 was $15,509.[55] The growing number of clerical workers who work part-time make even lower wages. The chronic problem of low pay for clerical workers is exacerbated by lack of promotional opportunities. As Goldberg points out: "Lack of promotion ensures that salaries remain inadequate, regardless of years spent on the job or skill level."[56]

Such wages are especially inadequate to the needs of women who head their own households. Over the last two decades, the number of women who *head* households has grown substantially. Marital breakdowns are frequent and more women are having children without marrying. African American women are the most likely to be heading their own households; more Hispanic women head their own households than do other white women. A large and growing number of children depend solely upon women to provide for their economic survival. In 1985, more than 11 million children under the age of 18 lived in a family headed by a woman. Among those female heads of household who are employed the largest proportion are in administrative support jobs, including clerical jobs.[57] The National Association of Working Women estimates that 18 per cent of clerical workers are the sole support of their families.[58] The Association warns that it is likely that many families headed by a female clerical worker live in poverty or near-poverty. In 1983, the median annual income for a full-time clerical worker was only $257 above the poverty line for a family of four.[59]

The economic security of clerical workers and their dependents may be further eroded if more wage earners in the clerical sector work on a part-time, temporary, or home-work basis. The wages of such contingent workers are often low or uncertain. (Temporary and home workers are paid only when work is available, they receive no wages during slack periods.) Moreover, such jobs may not include fringe benefits such as health insurance[60] and company-paid pension contributions.

The most serious threat which office automation poses for the material well-being and financial autonomy of clerical workers is the throat of significant unemployment. Worst-case scenarios suggest that, within the next two decades, women working in clerical occupa tions may face substantial unemployment. If the present trends in the racial and ethnic composition of the clerical worker force continue, women from socially disadvantaged, ethnic or racial groups will be at higher risk of unemployment, because young minority women have been increasing their share of participation in the clerical work force. Even if the most grim predictions about future employment levels among clerical workers prove overly pessimistic, the next two decades will see important changes in the availability and character- istics of specific clerical jobs. Some workers will be at risk of unem- ployment because their job skills are no longer in demand or because their present work has been shifted to new geographic locations.

Crucial entry-level positions may be abolished by office automa- tion. In addition, key transitional positions from upper-level clerical positions to sales, technical, and managerial slots are being elimi- nated through automation. The growth in part-time, temporary, or at- home work for clerical workers also lessens such workers' chances for upward mobility. Thus, too few clerical workers have an opportu- nity to move into better-paying positions which would allow them to meet heavier family responsibilities or to experience greater personal financial security and independence.

Competencies Developed through Work

Theological writings often discuss human creativity manifest in work. This is almost an irresistible theological move, since discussing creativity in work allows the theologian to describe the worker as one who shares some attributes with the Creator. It allows an ethicist to root statements about the just distribution of opportunities for work in the doctrine of creation. However, too much emphasis on creativity—especially creativity analogous to the creativity of a visual artist or master craft worker—may obscure the more modest achievements of those who develop personal competencies while doing more routine work.

In the encyclical, *Laborem Exercens*, Pope John Paul II derives the dignity of work from the call of the human person—as one made in the image of the Creator—to participate in the process of perfecting creation.[61] The human person alone of all the creatures of the earth is capable of imitating God's creative activity.[62] Every worthwhile human activity, even the most mundane task, contributes to the unfolding of Creation. According to John Paul, human persons are beings who *create themselves* in and through their struggle to shape their common world. Work is, thus, both participation in the process of creation and action constitutive of the self. Work expresses and simultaneously increases human dignity. For these reasons, human work (broadly construed) has "fundamental and decisive importance" for social ethics.[63]

Dorothee Soelle is eloquent in expressing the human need to find creative fulfillment in work. She tells us that human beings need the joy which they experience in envisioning a useful object or service, planning and taking responsibility for its production. She asserts: "We need to understand ourselves as co-creators who require constructive and joyful work."[64] In the process of constructive, joyful work, we bring ourselves to self-actualization through exercising our talents and skills. Meaningless, stultifying work is evil because it deprives us of the challenge to become all that we are capable of being. It robs us of opportunities for fuller personhood.

For Soelle, the work of the artist provides a particularly apt model to evoke that sense of mastery for which human beings yearn.

> In understanding what good work means . . . the paradigm of the artist is most relevant. . . . Art, like all good work, enables us to release the power of our imaginations and to become persons as we use this power to come up with an invention, a new solution to a problem, a new way of working.[65]

Thus, the worker-artist uses her talents to collaborate in God's creative activity.

Using artistic work or even craft work as models for good work can be limiting. It encourages a nostalgia for an older kind of work—one in which a single worker planned and executed a finished object. Even in the past, both craft work and artistic work were sometimes a social mode of production, with assistants executing portions of designs planned by the master. It seems that, aside from a small economic sector devoted to the production of hand-crafted objects (often luxury goods), production in advanced industrial and postindustrial societies is irrevocably social. Most workers cooperate in *a social process* resulting in the creation of goods and services which no one worker can claim as the sole fruit of his or her creative act.

I am wary of describing creativity as an essential aspect of work fit for human beings, because creativity seems a rather grand term suited to describe the work of those such as sculptors, musicians, master weavers, and perhaps certain scholars, scientists, and engineers. Does that word really describe even good clerical work? Opportunities to be creative are important to many clerical workers, but so is the exercise of more mundane skills which theologians often ignore.

Competence and mastery are words that more nearly describe the valuable sense of skill which clerical workers develop on the job. Clerical workers have moments of creativity when they produce a particularly pleasing piece of work, devise a new solution to an office problem, or create a new procedure which makes work more accurate, complete, or quick. However, undue emphasis on creativity as a central aspect of work obscures the sense of pride a woman can feel when she does a routine clerical task well.

Clerical workers value work which gives them an opportunity to manifest personal competence and creativity. Psychologist Michael Beer, who surveyed clerical workers at a large American insurance company, found that clerical workers ranked an opportunity for personal growth and fulfillment through work as the most important characteristic of a good job. Beer indicates:

The most important needs listed by a female clerical group are self-actualization, autonomy, and social [relationships], respectively. This is contrary to assumptions widely held by managers. The usual assumption about women employees is that they are not interested in work involvement or intrinsic job satisfactions.[66]

Again, the real situation on the job for clerical workers varies greatly from job to job and work setting to work setting. Some clerical workers report that their jobs give them almost no opportunity to experience personal challenge or competency. Many clerical workers describe their jobs as boring, mindless, meaningless. Goldberg reports that clerical workers want "to have responsibility, to be able to be innovative with their work, to find work a challenge,"[67] but few clerical workers find that their jobs give them adequate scope for their creativity. Workers whose jobs consist entirely of repetitive processing of small, meaningless bits of information may be particularly dissatisfied by their lack of opportunity to exercise creativity. Some census data and sociological reports suggest that African American women are more likely than white women to be trapped in such deadening clerical jobs.

Yet, in spite of the narrow scope of too much clerical work, many clerical workers experience their jobs as requiring skills in which the women can take pride. A journalist who took a job as a customer service representative at the telephone company reported that, in spite of the oppressive way the work was organized, she could sometimes experience a genuine sense of achievement on the job. "A well-handled contact could be satisfying in some way. . . . if you could provide him [the customer] with what he wants, on time and efficiently, you might reasonably feel satisfied about it."[68]

Good work offers human beings opportunities to develop skills; good work also provides *social acknowledgment* of those skills and of their contribution to the well-being of the organization and the larger society. One of the more demeaning aspects of some clerical jobs is the lack of recognition and praise for the competence of clerical workers. Certain crucial human relations skills which many clerical workers exercise are a form of competence particularly likely to go unrecognized. Such clerical workers exercise those traditionally feminine "caring" skills essential for cooperation among coworkers, but frequently taken for granted as merely the "natural" functioning of the female character.

For example, one administrative support person in the computer systems department of a large insurance company explained how she "clowned around" with the staff in the word processing and duplicating centers where she delivered and picked up departmental material. The kidding was fun, but, in addition, "the best way to get things back fast . . . [was] to socialize, be friendly, you'll get better service."[69] Her human relations skills enabled her department to function more efficiently.

African American ward secretaries in a southern hospital also exercised crucial, but unrecognized human relations skills. They coordinated many aspects of patient care in addition to maintaining accurate records of that care.[70] These coordination duties required a very high order of negotiation skills. Ward secretaries had to elicit cooperation from "people whose jobs and places in the hospital's hierarchy of power and prestige often put them in conflict."[71] Moreover, experienced ward secretaries created informal training procedures which helped new hires to develop those same negotiation skills. However, such "invisible skills" were not acknowledged or financially rewarded by the hospital administration.

Thus, while some clerical workers report that their jobs require them to develop competencies which enhance their sense of self-worth, many of the same workers protest that their clerical skills are ignored. Indeed, the mastery exercised by many clerical workers is so little noted that Soelle herself sympathetically comments upon "those who are confined to repetitive, routine, unsatisfying jobs, such as clerks, cashiers, secretaries, housewives, and many industrial workers."[72] Soelle apparently could not imagine the challenging work which some clerical workers report that they do.

Work as a Locus of Community

For many adults today, the workplace is an important area in which to form relationships with other human beings. The process of work requires social cooperation and, hence, reminds us that we are by nature social beings. Work illuminates our interdependence and involves us in joint ventures to satisfy our mutual needs. As Soelle tells us: "Work creates community and imbues people with the pride of belonging to a group dedicated to pursuits both respected and needed by society."[73]

Raines and Day-Lower emphasize the human connections experienced through work when they explore potential *social* meanings of the Christian notion of vocation. They suggest that, in our work lives (broadly defined), we are *jointly called* by God to the task of making life on this planet sustainable, decent, and just. Work is labor together for the sake of the community. They assert: "There is a shared and prior responsibility to the community; individual work is just an expression of that."[74] In a complex economic order, work processes bind people to others whom they never meet face-to-face, but with whom they cooperate in the process of meeting humanity's needs for goods and services. Given our present global economic order, good work is work which ultimately creates a sense of global connectedness and solidarity.

Face-to-Face Relationships. Work as a form of community is known first among the immediate coworkers who perform certain tasks together. Such relationships can be of great personal importance for workers. While it would be naive to ignore the superficiality of some working relationships or the tensions, resentments, jealousies, and grievances which mar others, working together can provide an important opportunity to get to know others, to support them in their difficulties, to be supported by them, and to enjoy one another's company.

Clerical workers value the positive human relationships which they form at work. For some clerical workers, the people they work with "are like your family."[75] Repeatedly, clerical workers have told researchers that relationships with other workers on the job are one of the most important rewards of their work. A temporary worker at the telephone company reports that one of the most humane aspects of her work was the generosity shown by coworkers who used the few quiet moments in their highly stressful day to help a newcomer learn the ropes. The network of personal relationships among African

American ward secretaries at "New South" hospital were among the most rewarding and empowering features of their jobs.

Thus, even work in an oppressive environment can also offer "the warmth of friendships, the mutual support, the opportunities for sharing and for gossip." One clerical worker at a major bank explained the importance of friendships with other workers especially well. "The work was very boring, but at least we could talk a little, take heart in one another."[76] Women clerical workers understand well the importance of taking heart in one another.

The workplace can also be a place for clerical workers to form mutually supportive and respectful relationships with bosses and clients/customers. However, a number of clerical workers report that their supervisors, managers, and others treat them in ways which ignore their contribution to the common well-being and which deny their dignity as persons. Too often, clerical workers are treated by others as if they did not even exist. Karen Nussbaum, the leader of a major union of clerical workers, remembers the time a student entered the office in which she was working and asked several clerks, "Isn't anyone here?"[77] Even a legal secretary—a woman who holds one of the most prestigious jobs available to a clerical worker—deplores:

attorneys' failing to recognize any personal dignity in secretaries. Secretaries are viewed totally as machines. They are ignored. For instance, if an attorney brings a client into his office, he will introduce everybody but the secretary.[78]

One of the African American ward secretaries in "New South" hospital voiced the anger of many of her peers when she complained: "They don't try to learn your name; they call us 'hey you.' Very few say 'good morning.' "[79] Another clerical worker asserted that African American women were particularly likely to be ignored:

Different people that I encounter day in and day out for years never bother to introduce themselves or even to speak. This is especially true if you happen to be Black in my department.[80]

Too many office automation systems deprive clerical workers of opportunities for fulfilling social contact on the job. Some organizations try to obtain the highest possible level of clerical worker produc-

tivity in routine information processing operations by restricting "un-
productive" conversations with fellow workers. In other cases,
isolation is an unintended consequence of new automated office
systems. The technical capacities of integrated office automation systems put virtually all necessary information at a worker's fingertips
and eliminate many opportunities to consult with coworkers. The
solitude of partitioned workstations can exacerbate social isolation.
If systems designers and management develop and authorize systems
which impose a high degree of social isolation upon workers, then
they rob workers of an important source of human fulfillment through
work.

Work at Shared Workbenches. While clerical workers speak about
the value of the face-to-face human relationships which they form
on the job, several recent theological works point up other, more
extended, human connections created by work. Pope John Paul II
insists that work connects human beings *over time.* Work involves
us in a historical process in which generations of human beings
produce goods needed to live and also to work. Human beings fashion
tools to make their work more efficient from natural resources destined by the Creator for the well-being of the human community.
Each subsequent generation uses technological knowledge, which is
social knowledge, to improve some tools and to invent others. Thus,
those tools which are used for current production represent "the
historical heritage of human labor."[81] In particular, technological
devices, such as computers or telecommunications equipment, are a
fruit of humanity's historical drive to create useful tools out of the
shared resources of creation. Using a striking metaphor, John Paul
asserts that workers in the present generation inherit a claim on
the common "workbench" which has been created by the labor of
previous generations.

This view of the social nature of technological innovation is in
sharp disagreement with theories of justice which emphasize the
individual inventor's right to reap the benefits of his or her personal
ingenuity. It would be consistent with the work of philosopher Robert
Nozick, for example, to hold that all claims to the benefits of a technical advance in computers or telecommunications belong to the inven-

tor or to individuals with whom the inventor makes a voluntary contract or to whom the inventor delegates the benefits as a gift. For Nozick, all claims to determine the use of technology and to participate in its benefits are based on proof that the technology was voluntarily acquired and voluntarily transferred by free individuals.[82] Such views are based upon a narrow individualistic perspective which does not take into account the social nature of modern technological development or the history of shared innovation upon which all new developments are based.

I contend that control over technology is not the sole prerogative of those who invent it or, more to the point, those who can afford to acquire such equipment through a voluntary contract. Rather, technology is an "inheritance" which belongs to the whole human community. Labor-saving technology is the result of *collective* human ingenuity and effort. Therefore, uses of technology are rightfully subordinated to the common good.

It is important to acknowledge explicitly that clerical workers are among those groups which cooperate in the work processes through which modern technological tools like computers or telecommunications networks are created, produced, and distributed. Office automation equipment is produced by organizations which could not function without the gathering, processing, and distribution of information done by clerical workers. Therefore, clerical workers as a group are entitled to a voice in how technological advances are used.

An interesting testimony to the importance of clerical services in the design of new office automation tools are comments about the role of Rosemarie Seale, the secretary who worked with the team which designed Data General Corporation's Eclipse MV/8000 superminicomputer. Seale provided key emotional, as well as clerical, support. She took care of many of the practical bureaucratic hassles, thus allowing the engineers and technicians to concentrate on the process of creating a new machine. For example, when the company's mailroom was relocated during the project, Seale went to the mailroom each workday for several weeks and sorted through the mail herself to insure that important documents were not delayed due to mailroom confusion. One vivid symbol of the importance of her work was her role in training new engineers recruited for the team. The new recruits needed to learn how to use a computer system necessary for building the new machine. Their supervisor designed a training game which required the new engineers to find, open, and print a certain computer file. At some point, almost all the new recruits went to Seale for help, which she provided as requested. The supervisor considered approaching Seale a resourceful solution, since, in his words, "if a person knows how to get the right secretary, he can get everything."[83]

Clerical workers have a right to a voice in the use of office automation technology, because some of them and some of their predecessors have participated in the social process through which these new tools are designed and diffused throughout the workplace. Moreover, as human beings, they are the joint heirs in the technological legacy which belongs to all humankind. Office automation systems are a shared workbench which ought to be used in a fashion which enhances rather than diminishes opportunities for good work.

Work and the Body

To be created human is to be created flesh—body. It is to be able to move, grasp, manipulate, shape, and speak in order to satisfy our hungers. Work (broadly conceived) is the exertion of our body-selves in order to satisfy our hunger for bread, beauty, knowledge, and worship. A profound acceptance and celebration of human embodiment are implicit in the Christian doctrines of creation and incarnation (although one cannot deny that other influential strands in Christian thought have denigrated the body).

Body-selves move within a given culture. A part of any culture is the technology available to do work. As body-selves our possibilities are shaped by the system of tools available to us. Our work is limited and defined in part by the objects we have to work with. Yet we also make choices about how to use existing tools and create new tools, thus transforming the workplace around us. In postindustrial society there will soon be fewer and fewer workers who can do their jobs without using microprocessor-based tools. We have barely begun to sense what work with computers will mean for our body-selves.

It is in and through our bodies that we see and reach out to make contact with other persons. To be bodily is to be necessarily connected to other body-selves. It is as body-selves that we recognize our coworkers and coordinate our efforts with theirs. As computer-mediated work grows, we may be in contact with other persons who exist for us, not as flesh and blood, but as strings of letters and numbers across the surface of a video display screen. Thus, a new technology extends the reach of our bodies, allowing us to "make contact" with persons with whom we would never otherwise be in touch. As telecommunications networks expand, new global networks of human relationships are facilitated. However, the character of our human interaction also changes.

Work can strengthen and extend the power of our bodies. It can also put the body at risk or cause it harm. That work involves risk of physical harm is an age-old reality for certain workers. Some hunters are killed by wild animals; some industrial workers are maimed by their machines. Today some computer operators suffer life-diminishing aches and pains; some computer users endure life-threatening stress. Because we are fragile, finite beings, some amount of bodily risk is inevitable and unavoidable. However, other threats to bodily well-being in the workplace could be eliminated. Bodily life is a precious gift which requires active cherishing. Such active cherishing requires organizational and social change to safeguard the physical well-being of clerical workers.

Toil, Sin, and Alienated Work

The aspects of work discussed above are glimpses of what good work can be. Good work enables us to meet our own material needs and those of others dependent on us. It provides a financial base for autonomy. Good work allows us to take pride in our competencies and, perhaps, offers some opportunities for creativity. It connects us to coworkers and makes us active participants in local, national, and global economic life. Good work takes place in an environment free from unnecessary risk to our physiological and psychological well-being. For too many workers, however, some or all of these aspects of good work are missing. Too often work does not enhance a worker's well-being. Instead, it saps the worker's energy and diminishes the worker's dignity.

Some of the enduring negative dimensions of human work are inherent in finite human existence. I will use the word *toil* to name the burdens and frustrations inherent in work as experienced by finite human beings. Some tasks which urgently need doing are inherently repetitious or laborious. Even a worker who has a challenging and well-designed job sometimes finds the work exhausting, frustrating, boring, or burdensome. Even teams dedicated to working together in a style which enhances their mutual respect and creativity find that they can't articulate a common solution—just can't pull it all together.

Toil names some of the unavoidably burdensome aspects of human work. Other burdensome and demeaning aspects of work are the result of sin—i.e., the result of evil human choices *and* the enduring consequences of those choices for our common life. The word *sin* may seem a hackneyed one, evocative primarily of individual misdeeds such as drunkenness or sexual promiscuity. As theologian Bernard Murchland has warned: "our religious formulas, many of them burdened by centuries of usage, stand in special danger of corrosion. 'Sin' . . . is a case in point. It is a weary word. But the reality it signifies is energetic and destructive."[84]

Some contemporary Christian understandings of sin provide a penetrating insight into the power of evil in our common life, including our economic life. Sin is both "our fate and our responsibility" as human beings.[85] Sin is our inherited condition; we perpetually find ourselves in sinful situations which we did not individually create or choose. Evil is already embedded in particular patterns of cultural belief and social organization. Surrounded by evil, we suffer a loss of our moral sensitivity and of our motive power to do what is right.[86]

As theologian Langdon Gilkey frankly admits: "Evil as we experience it does seem a grim, unalterable, and thus tragic condition, . . . and yet *we are also aware of being ourselves continuing perpetuators of this same evil and thus responsible ourselves . . . for it.*"[87] We actively appropriate the heritage of sin and bend it to our own purposes. Thus, sin also names the evil which we do, both personally and corporately. Sin may be experienced as a conscious and deliberate personal choice to do a wrong act. However, an overemphasis on individual wrongdoing may obscure another dimension of human evil, i.e., "social sin." Social sin occurs when we cooperate with and perpetuate patterns of evil in our communal life. Such sinful human activity may have less the character of conscious choice and more the aspect of "collective blindness." We don't "see"—or rather we refuse to see—the harm which results from certain social practices in which we engage.[88]

Sin warps or severs right relationships. It simultaneously distorts the relationships between humanity and the Deity and among human beings. Sin manifest in patterns of exploitation and domination has a crucial historical dimension. Human beings find themselves entrapped in and perpetuating patterns of injustice which continue over time. Ethicist Charles Curran points out that: "sin . . . incarnates itself in the structures, customs and institutions of our environment; and thus the reign of sin grows and increases."[89] Sexism, racism, and class exploitation are among those patterns of injustice which are deeply intertwined within the historical fabric of our social lives and which are thus passed on from generation to generation.

The history of the feminization of clerical work is part of the history of economic exploitation of women workers. The historical continuity of this exploitation makes it hard to recognize, to "name," and to challenge. The social "givenness" of the subordination of clerical workers is an example of social sin as blindness. It seems "natural" and, hence, unalterable that women workers will perform the numerous routine paperwork tasks and human relations efforts necessary to facilitate business operations while receiving little financial reward or social recognition for their contributions.

The economic exploitation of clerical workers is one manifestation of sin. Institutionalized structures of domination which render clerical workers organizationally powerless are another manifestation of sin. Such structures deprive clerical workers of opportunities to exert control over their work and to have a voice in decisions concerning their work processes. Two sociologists who have surveyed a variety of clerical settings warn: "Overall, the *lack* of worker participation in decision-making is simply taken for granted, if workers are women;

subordination is invisible, a natural pattern and thus a non issue."[90] I contend that these sociologists have just provided an important concrete example of social sin.

An adequate analysis of the human impact of office automation requires an acknowledgment of the *interstructuring* of institutional barriers to "good" work. Clerical workers are disadvantaged because of their relatively powerless organizational position. Moreover, their organizational position intersects with various other forms of social vulnerability which workers bring with them to the job. As a group, clerical workers are denied more equitable participation in workplace decisions both because of their position toward the bottom of the office hierarchy and because of their gender composition, and the two forms of subordination reinforce each other.

However, gender is not the only characteristic intersecting with organizational position in ways which intensify oppression. Race, ethnic identity, and/or social class all influence a person's chance to qualify for "good" jobs. Moreover, those characteristics do not operate serially, but interact simultaneously in the lives of many workers. Enduring patterns of racism and ethnic prejudice have resulted in somewhat different forms of oppression of minority women. Initially, African American and immigrant women were barred from office positions. More recently, too many minority women have been shunted into the more burdensome, "back office" clerical jobs. These are the jobs which are less satisfying, pose a greater risk to health, and are most vulnerable to elimination by office automation.

Sinful patterns of economic exploitation and domination are particularly difficult to challenge effectively and to transform. This is because human beings have a propensity toward avarice. Human beings are tempted by a craving for more than their fair share of the world's goods; the economically privileged strive for power to insure their grasp on their hoard. As Walter Rausenbusch recognized many years ago: "Moral suasion is strangely feeble where the sources of . . .[a person's] income are concerned."[91]

When economic conditions are precarious, human greed is amplified by anxiety about the loss of luxuries and even necessities. We are in such a period of economic anxiety today. Intense economic competition creates fierce pressures throughout the world economy.

Theological Reflections on Clerical Work

Individual, corporate, and national debts have risen to levels that imperil the international financial system. In the United States, some the largest, "blue chip" companies—businesses which once provided lifetime security to employees—have announced major layoffs. As Larry Rasmussen and Bruce Birch indicate "human solidarity, never extensive at best, is doubly tenuous when the future is ominous."[92]

Thus, I contend, the ills which may well follow in the wake of extensive office automation will not be merely a result of poor technological design, shortsighted management decisions, or inappropriate social policies. The suffering which will ensue, if office automation is used in ways which are detrimental to the well-being of the less powerful among us, will be a result of sin. Evil choices about office automation will flow from human perversity on the level of choices made by individuals and on the level of structures which institutionalize the dominance of some groups over others.

It is well to face squarely the power of sin, but sin is not the final reality. According to Christian belief, redemption has been irrevocably offered to human beings and a positive transformation of human life *in all its dimensions* is already underway. Deeper than the deformities which sin causes in human life is a yearning for that restored common life which Jesus of Nazareth declared had already begun among us.

Jesus preached the Kingdom of God—a communal transformation which reestablished right relationship between God and humanity and among human beings. The vision of this Reign encompasses both individual holiness and social wholeness, both justice and an abundance of good things. The Reign of God/dess will be characterized by new patterns of relationship in which the socially marginal find themselves drawn toward the center, where their needs can be satisfied.

Movements to obtain justice for exploited workers contribute to the building up of the Reign of God/dess. However, that Reign is not to be identified completely with the success of movements on behalf of workers or even with the triumph of the women's liberation movement. For neither workers nor women alone are the elect. The Reign of God/dess promises a redeemed humanity and cosmos—a new creation, not just an egalitarian "office of the future" or a postpatriar-

chal society. We have only fleeting intimations of the personal wholeness and deep connectedness among humans and with the Earth
which is the "salvation" which the Divine Being holds out before us.

While I would insist that the Reign of God/dess is not to be wholly
identified with either a transformation of exploitative economic patterns or an end to patriarchal relationships, I also insist that the real
danger in religious circles in the United States today is not premature
identification of the Reign with some penultimate liberation movement, but rather apathy in the face of massive injustice.

It is in struggles to achieve greater justice, including economic
justice, that we manifest an authentic love for God/dess. There are
genuine possibilities for greater justice for clerical workers. Realizing
those possibilities requires the commitment of clerical workers to
demand working conditions consistent with their human dignity. It
also requires dedication from others to assist clerical workers in
pressing their claims for justice. Justice for clerical workers will
require that serious social attention be paid to the technological
transformation of their work processes. We need a broad, public
debate about strategies for protecting and enhancing the well-being
of these millions of women. I will examine some specific strategies
to further this goal in the final chapter.

Chapter Five
·················
Strategies to Insure
·················
Participative Justice for
·················
Clerical Workers

Paid employment is crucial to well-being and fulfillment for many adults living in the advanced industrial/postindustrial nations. A combination of technological and economic change is transforming the character of clerical employment. This chapter explores some of the economic and social policies which would safeguard the interests of clerical workers [and potential clerical workers] as office automation proceeds. I explore strategies to insure that clerical workers will receive an adequate wage, operate in a physically safe and comfortable environment, maintain enriching social contacts in the workplace, and, thus, participate on an equitable basis as active members in the economic endeavors of their communities.

In other words, I examine means to ensure greater justice for clerical workers. The primary paradigm of justice here will be the image of justice as participation. In justice, adult persons in our society are due genuine opportunities to take part in the economic endeavors of their communities and are entitled to receive recognition and a fair financial reward for their contributions. What is offered here is not a comprehensive policy designed to be *the* solution for clerical workers and potential clerical workers, but rather proposals to be explored as part of urgently needed public conversation about the conditions necessary for the well-being of these women.

Making Clerical Work Issues Visible

An essential step in achieving justice for clerical workers is developing a *sustained public debate* about the impacts of office automation on clerical work. Up to this point the transformation of clerical work has received limited social attention. Labor unions and government agencies have sponsored conferences and issued reports, but the information which they have disseminated has received only sporadic and brief attention. Legislation on health and safety aspects of video display terminal work has been introduced in several states and localities, but such legislation has remained largely the concern of labor union representatives, user-industry groups, and manufacturers' lobbyists, not the general public. Throughout the 1980s, there has been intermittent media coverage of the human impacts of office automation, particularly of the health and safety debate. This has included occasional articles in major newspapers and magazines and a few discussions on national network television programs.

Still, there has been comparatively little continuing attention to changes taking place in the working lives of clerical workers, who represent the largest segment of the labor force. I contend that such comparative silence reflects the reality that, in a sexist society, women's work is taken less seriously than men's. Therefore, major changes in women's work—especially in low-status occupations such as clerical work—are all but ignored. Again, women are in danger of being treated as "inside aliens," who do work essential to the survival of corporations, but are denied an active role in corporate decision-making.[1] Comparative silence about the human impact of office automation contributes to clerical workers' exploitation. Patterns of exploitation which we refuse to recognize and criticize as a betrayal of human dignity we will not be moved to change.

At this stage, it is important to describe the basic realities of women's lives repeatedly. Today, most women will be in the labor force for much of their adult lives—many of them as clerical workers. Therefore, the conditions of women's labor are a crucial aspect of women's well-being and the well-being of their loved ones and dependents. Human beings are making decisions about office automation which will have important consequences for many women workers. Office automation technology could be used in ways which undermine the welfare of millions of women. It could also be used in ways which would enhance the fulfillment which they experience on the job. Women workers need a more effective voice in these choices, if their interests are to receive adequate attention.

Facilitating Active Participation by Clerical Workers

Knowledge as a Precondition for Participation. If clerical workers are to be active participants in the office automation process and to be effective advocates for themselves, then they need to have a clear understanding of the transformation of work processes which they are experiencing. Clerical workers and their supporters need more information than is now available about a wide range of questions, such as the impact of video display terminal use on pregnancy, new models for organization of clerical work (particularly in the less information-intensive industries), and nationwide patterns of technological change. It is also important to gather more data about trends in contingent employment in clerical fields, including information about how these trends intersect with office automation. Contingent employment includes temporary work, part-time work, or work at home on a contract basis. More data should be gathered about clerical worker characteristics such as race, ethnicity, and age, because we urgently need to know more about whether persons from socially disadvantaged groups are suffering disproportionate negative effects from office automation.[2]

Those labor unions which represent clerical workers are producing materials to inform their members about office automation and its consequences. Such union materials are also often distributed to potential members in unionization drives. In several instances, unions have been instrumental in the initiation of crucial research projects such as the NIOSH [National Institute for Occupational Safety and Health] study on the health impacts of clerical work done at video display terminals. Unions often monitor ongoing studies and educate their members and others about significant findings. Both government agencies and private groups, such as foundations and the media, should continue to gather, analyze, and disseminate information about the human impact on office automation, with special attention to the effects on workers from more socially vulnerable groups.

Workers faced with specific organizational plans to change work patterns substantially or even to eliminate jobs can respond more effectively, if they are notified of the changes or proposed staff reductions in advance. Some unions, such as the Communications Workers of America, have contract provisions which assure them advance notification of any major technological changes. Federal legislation has recently been passed which requires advance notification when larger employers plan to close a facility.[3] However, such legislation mandates a 180-day advance notification. Realistically, there is seldom much workers can do in a period of six months to save their jobs. In programs where unions are guaranteed advance notice of technological changes which substantially alter work processes, the notification frequently comes too late for the workers to have a strong influence on the design of the system. To become active participants in the office automation process, workers need to know about proposed new systems early in the development cycle. They also need access to technological experts who will give them independent advice about the human impacts of the new systems.

Participation: Day-to-Day Social Contact. A crucial form of active participation in economic endeavors is involvement in the daily face-to-face work relationships. This social contact is one of the most valuable aspects of the job for many clerical workers. Yet, heavy use of interactive office automation systems threatens to isolate workers from one another and, in so doing, to undermine the solidarity that they experience in and through work. Up to this point, there has been little attention to the increased social isolation associated with intensive VDT use. However, it is important for workers, their representatives, and their employers to consider ways of organizing automated office work which preserve or restore opportunities for human contact.

When workers spend much of their workday at individual, computerized workstations, then it becomes particularly important to create common areas within office buildings which "invite" people to congregate for breaks, lunches, etc. Pleasant lounge areas and eating facilities encourage the kind of human interaction which may take place be less frequently and spontaneously within the automated office itself. One Japanese report identifies social isolation as a problem and recommends that "as tasks become more mechanical and isolating, more group activities and worker clubs and incentive systems need to be developed to keep up team spirit and morale."[4] While Japanese cultural attitudes toward "team activities" among workers differ from American ones, there might be culturally appropriate ways to encourage American clerical workers to keep up work group spirit and morale in automated offices.

While providing physical facilities and social programs which encourage human interaction is important, even more important is the corporate culture with respect to human relationships at work. *Corporate culture* is a term which draws attention to the patterns of behavior and values promulgated by the management of a corporation and transmitted to succeeding generations of employees. It is "the way we do things around here."[5] In this context, the question is the values which management conveys concerning the importance of sociality in the workplace. Does management have a balanced attitude toward "chit-chat"? Do executives who set the tone for office operations make clear that the company respects and fosters good relationships among its workers? A corporate policy which fosters positive relationships among workers is a sign of respect for the dignity of the worker as a social being. The opportunity (as one worker put it) to "take heart in one another"[6] is one of the most important human dimension of labor. It is wrong to design facilities and systems which deprive workers of such opportunities.

Special questions need to be asked about whether corporate culture and practice control socializing among lower-level female workers more rigidly than forms of male bonding behavior. Feldberg and Glenn observed that supervisors for a clerical division of a utility company were more likely to chastise female workers for too much talking among themselves. Comparable behavior by male employees was tolerated without comment.[7] As the character of much clerical work becomes more isolating, such attitudes of contempt for female relationships could severely diminish the human meaning of work for many women workers.

Positive social contact among workers is a good in itself which should be preserved out of respect for the dignity of workers as social beings. Continued opportunities to develop solidarity on the job are also important, in order that workers have both the opportunity and capacity to band together to influence decisions about their own work processes. In some cases, informal groups of clerical workers, who have positive working relationships, can exert informal control over the conditions of their labor. In other cases, social contacts on the job can serve as a base for union organizing. Unions represent an important vehicle through which clerical workers can gain opportunities for effective participation in automation decisions which have a major impact on their work lives.

Unions as a Vehicle for Participation

Clerical workers should strengthen their power to participate actively in workplace decisions, by creating and supporting strong unions. To advocate strong union representation for clerical workers is to advocate a major social change in the United States, because the percentage of union-represented workers in this country is not only low but declining further. Moreover, outside the government sector, few clerical workers belong to unions. In 1987, only 13.1 percent of United States administrative support[8] workers were members of unions.[9] In some of the key industries, such as banking and insurance, rates of unionization are even lower. In 1980, 1.5 percent of the clerical workers in the insurance industry were unionized.[10] Nevertheless, there may be an opportunity to increase union representation for women, such as clerical workers, for according to some surveys, women are now more interested than men in joining unions.[11]

It must be acknowledged that the present low rate of clerical worker unionization is, in part, a legacy of sexism in the union movement in the United States. Historically, male-dominated unions rarely provided adequate resources to support unionization drives among women workers. Until relatively recently, many union leaders showed little interest in organizing female office workers. However, a combination of factors has changed such attitudes. As their traditional membership base among blue-collar workers in heavy industry has declined, unions have realized that their survival depends upon their ability to recruit new members in the growing service sector, where many workers are female. At the same time, women in the union movement have formed groups, such as the Coalition of Labor Union Women [CLUW] to challenge sexism in the labor movement, and they have had a real impact on the attitudes and policies of union organizations.

Thus, several labor unions are currently exploring new organizing methods to reach out to the vast number of nonunion clerical workers. The organizing drive and subsequent strike (1984–85) by Yale University's Local 34 of the Federation of University Employees was an example of the use of innovative methods to galvanize female clerical workers. Union organizers emphasized health and safety issues, promotion and transfer policies, and wage inequities. (The union contended that female clerical workers' wages were systematically depressed relative to those of blue-collar workers.) Moreover, the union emphasized that clerical workers performed important duties and that their skills deserved more recognition and reward.

Perhaps most important, the local was organized and run by the workers themselves. Thus, the workers were active participants in the process of goal setting and strategy development. One experienced observer of labor unions declared: "Throughout the campaign, a major union goal was to fashion a rank-and-file union, one run by the workers, not union officials. The practice is always talked about in unions but rarely achieved."[12] Thus the Yale organizing campaign is a positive example of the importance of justice as participation as a standard for internal union operations, as well as for union and management relations.

Union leaders need to come to grips creatively with new forms of clerical employment. It is certainly appropriate for union leaders to oppose abuses associated with contingent labor arrangements, especially homework done on a so-called contract worker basis. However, union leaders also need to find ways to reach out to contingent workers—to help them meet their needs for flexibility. As Karen Nussbaum, president of District 925, a clerical workers' union, has recognized: "What we need is to begin to challenge management's version of flexibility in order to create the kind of flexibility workers genuinely need. Where men and women choose to work less than full-time in order to raise children, go to school, or semi-retire, part-time and temporary jobs which dignify workers—not penalize them—must be made available."[13]

Unions and organizations supportive of union aims need to explore ways in which they can use their economic power to support efforts to organize and represent clerical workers. During the Equitable Life Assurance Society labor dispute in Syracuse, the AFL-CIO decided to "boycott" Equitable's pension management services. A cooperative union drive is proposed to organize the clerical work force employed by Blue Cross/Blue Shield health insurance groups. Unions leaders plan to use unionized workers' health coverage as a lever to reduce management resistance to organizing efforts. Supporting organizations which represent clerical workers is essential if these workers are to experience that minimum level of participation in determining their work processes which is their due as human beings.

While it is crucial that clerical workers form and maintain strong unions as a vehicle for participation in decisions which affect their work lives, there are drawbacks and difficulties associated with such a recommendation. A number of female clerical workers are not initially receptive to union activities, because they view unions as disruptive of important, positive management-worker relationships. This is more likely to be true among those clericals, such as secretaries and administrative assistants, who work closely with professionals and managers. Moreover, as general union representation rates fall in the United States, fewer nonunion clerical workers have family members or friends with pro-union attitudes. An union organizer campaigning at a university press reported her peers considered union members "selfish, overpaid blue-collar workers with no regard for people who had to suffer."[14] Such stereotypes, which are derived, in part, from arrogant union behavior, make unions seem less appealing, especially to women who value civility and service to others.

When the clerical job market is tight, some workers are afraid to confront their employers during organizing campaigns. If the more severe job loss estimates in this book should prove to be correct, it may become increasingly difficult to organize clerical workers, as constrictions of the clerical sector intimidate some of the remaining

Participative Justice for Clerical Workers

workers. Moreover, successful union drives—in particular, successful union bids for higher pay and greater worker control of the work
process—could accelerate the automation of more routine clerical
jobs. As wages rise, management has a greater incentive to replace
clerical labor through capital investment or to shift clerical work to
regions of the nation or the world where labor costs are lower and/or
labor union activities are restricted.

Management can use office automation technology to undermine
union strength. Sophisticated office systems make it possible for
supervisors or new hires to process a large volume of information
during a strike. During the bitter labor dispute at the Equitable Life
Assurance Society office in Syracuse, New York, the union never
called a strike. As one organizer explained: "We can't strike. . . . With
this technology, they could flick a switch, and the work could be in
Kansas City."[15] Under such conditions, "to gain enough leverage to
win a good contract, unions are . . . faced with the need to organize
many far-flung facilities at the same time, a far more difficult task
than organizing a single plant."[16]

Since telecommunications technology makes it possible to shift
routine clerical work to other nations, union groups representing the
interests of clerical workers in one country are not enough. In today's
global economy, unions with a national membership face corporations which are multinational. It is imperative that clerical workers
and their representatives and supporters find means to facilitate international cooperation among workers if unions are to play an effective
role in negotiating with multinational corporate employers. Workers
need to create strong, permanent, international agencies which enable workers to be active and effective participants in the global
economy.

There is presently an organization known as *Fédération Internatio-
nale des Employés Techniciens* [FIET],[17] which is an international
umbrella organization for 234 unions representing white-collar workers in 89 countries. In 1984, the organization sponsored an international conference on video display terminal technology. Its general
secretary reported that the conference was the first international
meeting ever to be held on specific bargaining issues, such as limitations on hours per day of VDT use, control over work pace and

content, and provisions for job security and career development. Organizers declared that the meeting represented "an important step forward in coordinating the work of the international union movement in relation to technological change."[18] While such international cooperation among trade unionists is worthwhile, FIET as it presently operates does not provide an adequate mechanism for equitable worker participation in the decision-making of multinational business operations.

Structures to channel clerical worker power on an international scale are badly needed, but they will be difficult to create and sustain. Differences in laws, customs, and culture in varying nations will make worker solidarity hard to achieve. Potentially clashing interests of clerical workers in varying nations will have to recognized and resolved if solidarity is to be realized. Many religious groups have international affiliations, and believers from diverse nations share certain religious value commitments. Therefore, such religious bodies might be in a particularly good position to promote understanding and cooperation among workers from various nations.

Preserving Opportunities for Employment

We have seen that that the concept of justice as participation entails special concern about employment opportunities because jobs allow persons to be active contributors in the economic order. As office automation transforms the nature of clerical work it is necessary to consider policies which will help to insure that displaced clerical workers will be able to qualify for other jobs elsewhere in the economy.

Education and Training for Employment. As more routine clerical tasks are completely automated, transferred to off-shore locations, or absorbed into the activities of other workers or consumers, an increasing proportion of the remaining jobs will be what economist Eileen Appelbaum calls paraclerical/paraprofessional work. Skill requirements for these positions will be relatively high. A commitment to justice as active participation entails a concern that the educational system provide *all* young people with the skills necessary to function as workers in an automated workplace. Providing an adequate education for poorer children as well as more economically privileged children, for African American, Hispanic, and Native American students as well as white students is a complex challenge. Some religious groups have impressive experience in providing quality education for poor and/or minority students. Religious groups are among those private groups which can serve as vocal advocates for high-quality public education for all children.

Displaced clerical workers and women entering or reentering the job market may need access to educational and training programs which prepare them for paraprofessional clerical work or other occupations. Programs for labor force entrants and displaced workers ought to take into account the special needs of the many women whose responsibilities for care of dependent family members make it more difficult for them to participate in retraining programs. Special attention should be paid to needs of older and/or minority women among the displaced workers. It is especially important that programs be devised which expand the skills of women with only a high school education.[19]

Even workers who remain employed will need to acquire new skills as office automation systems evolve. Some employers provide in-house training when automated systems are introduced. In some cases, unions negotiate with employers to guarantee such training. Still, "there are no reliable statistics on how many companies retrain workers for new technology, but most experts feel that such programs are few—or at least underdeveloped—compared with what will soon be required."[20] In far too many companies, workers are left to flounder on their own with the user's manual when new computer applications are introduced.

Clerical workers might benefit most from training programs which help them develop general problem-solving skills, rather than training which concentrates on specific operations of one particular computerized system. Broad-based training would help clerical workers to cope with future changes in their office automation systems and would also allow them to qualify for other jobs more readily if their present positions were later abolished.

However, narrowly conceived training may appear to be more cost-beneficial to employers over the short run. Additionally, employers have been less willing to finance training or educational reimbursement programs for *female* employees.[21] As a result of stereotypes concerning age, older women workers are even more likely to be excluded from training programs.[22] Moreover, many employers are resistant to providing retraining for current employees if adequately trained personnel can be hired from outside the company.[23] This is consistent with economist Thierry Noyelle's assertion that in the post–World War II period, many United States businesses have "externalized" training costs by hiring middle-level workers with two- or four-year-college educations.[24] This brings us full circle to a concern for equal access to educational programs.

In an increasingly computerized society, strong basic literacy skills and access to timely training programs to maintain specific job skills are critical if persons are to be able to find and keep jobs. Without fair access to basic education and retraining, some women—often socially disadvantaged women—will be relegated to the margins of the postindustrial economic order.

Equal Employment Opportunities. Clerical workers who are displaced due to office automation may find it easier to secure other jobs, perhaps even better jobs, in a robust economy. In an economy in which many attractive new jobs are being created and unemployment is low, workers are in a stronger position to bargain for ergonomically optimal working conditions and for corporate facilities and policies which diminish social isolation. Conversely, clerical workers and job seekers will face greater difficulties if the economy remains sluggish or goes into a decline. While the overall "health" of the economy has an important bearing on the job prospects of clerical workers, policy suggestions on sustainable economic growth are far beyond the scope of this book. Moreover, it should be remembered that, depending on how office automation is implemented, it is possible for companies to experience growth in sales and profits without a corresponding growth in their clerical work force. If technologies such as office automation are used primarily to lower labor costs rather than to extend the range and quality of office services, then we face the specter of jobless economic growth in some companies or industries.

A relative [and perhaps absolute] decline in clerical employment poses a serious problem for female job seekers, because occupational segregation by sex is still pervasive. A review of 1980 census data on 514 detailed occupations revealed the following pattern. Sixty-nine percent of women were employed in female-dominated jobs, 21 percent in sex-neutral jobs, and only 9.5 percent in male-dominated jobs.[25] While women have made some progress over the past two decades in moving into what were formerly overwhelmingly male occupations, that progress has been limited and slow. Thus, most female workers are still concentrated in a narrow range of occupations, of which the major clerical occupations are a crucial subset. If clerical jobs are lost through automation and if present patterns of occupational segregation endure, then most displaced clerical workers will find themselves competing for jobs in an even more fiercely competitive female job market. The result could be higher female unemployment rates and even lower wages for many women workers.

Faced with a potentially significant job loss in the clerical sector, it becomes especially urgent to assure equal employment opportunity for women and to recruit more women for traditionally male positions. Otherwise, a growing number of women will be pushed even farther toward the margins of the economy. However, programs which guarantee equality of opportunity for white women and minority women and men are particularly hard to maintain in a sluggish or declining economic environment. Strong government enforcement of equal employment opportunity laws is necessary, but past practice is not encouraging. Economist Barbara Bergmann has bluntly described the lack of vigorous government action to guarantee equal opportunity:

Under Democratic administrations, ostensibly committed to the achievement of fair employment practices, the agencies charged with fighting employment discrimination have not been models of energy and efficiency. Republican administrations have tended to be openly hostile, if not to the ideal of fair employment practices, then to any instrument that might be used by the government to promote that goal.[26]

Religious institutions can play a potentially important role in help-ing to create a moral climate in which equal employment opportunity is viewed as a fundamental requirement of justice—as one of the basic rules of the game in a decent society. However, if religious bodies are to be effective advocates for equal employment opportu-nity, then religious institutions *must follow such principles in their own hiring and promotion policies.* As the 1971 Synod of [Roman Catholic] Bishops declared "Anyone who ventures to speak to people about justice must first be just in their eyes."[27]

Good Work as Equitable Participation

Pay Equity. Quality education for all young people; appropriate training programs for a variety of clerical workers, displaced workers, and new labor force entrants; and vigorous equal employment oppor-tunity policies are all necessary in order that women have adequate opportunities to be active participants in the labor force. However, in order to be just, that participation must be on equitable terms. Women workers deserve a fair economic return for their contribution to the economy. Clerical workers are entitled to good jobs, i.e., jobs which enable them to meet their material needs and those of others dependent upon them—jobs which provide a financial base for per-sonal autonomy. However, pay levels in clerical occupation, like pay levels in many other female-dominated occupations, have been depressed as a result of sex discrimination. In 1986, the median wage for a woman who was a full-time administrative support worker was $15,509 annually.[28] Such wages offer a limited level of material comfort and autonomy. Therefore, serious consideration should be given to adoption of pay equity policies. (The terms comparable worth or equal pay for comparable work are also used by some com-mentators to describe the same proposal.) Such pay equity programs would raise the level of pay for some clerical workers.

In giving serious consideration to pay equity programs, I am dis-senting vigorously from the view of those commentators who contend that there are no substantive criteria according to which the fairness of a given salary for a given type of work may be determined. Such commentators assert instead that fair salaries are best set through the impartial mechanism of the free market. The operation of the market becomes a method of achieving procedural justice in the distribution of wages. Each worker receives the highest wages he or she can command in an open competition. Since the competition is defined as fair, the outcome is fair no matter what disparities in income result. If an individual woman gets lower wages than some man, it is because she has less natural ability or has invested in less training or because she values some other reward—such as time off to meet domestic responsibilities—more highly than a higher wage.

I counter that there is no unitary and impartial labor market in which all men and women compete on equal terms for wages and other rewards. Wages are not set solely on the basis of the employers' rational calculation of the most beneficial balance between quality of labor input and wage costs. Employers are historical and social beings who can be powerfully influenced by a pervasive sexism which leads to systematic devaluation of the worth of women's labor. Women workers' choices about training and conditions of employment are also constrained by sexist cultural patterns and institutional practices. Sexism as a social sin so distorts the operation of the labor market that we cannot assume that labor market outcomes are automatically just.

Therefore, we need to consider proposals such as pay equity which offer methods to redress the impact of discrimination on women's wages. Pay equity schemes involve assessing all job categories within an establishment or company according to "compensable factors," i.e., criteria such as knowledge and skills, mental demands, autonomy and leadership requirements, and working conditions. Job titles are each assigned a numerical score reflecting their demands. That score serves as an indicator of the relative rate of pay appropriate for each job. If—as usually is the case—male jobs with a given numerical value are paid at a higher rate than female jobs with a similar numerical value, then a plan is devised to bring women's salaries into line with men's pay scales.

Since office automation is changing the skill requirements and working conditions of many clerical jobs, it is particularly appropriate to review the compensation offered for such jobs. Indeed, some observers argue that upgrading in job complexity and responsibility must be rewarded with increased pay (regardless of local market supply of women), if unlawful sex discrimination is to be avoided.[29]

Still, questions need to be explored concerning pay equity programs. A large role is accorded human judgment in any job evaluation scheme. Researchers for the Brookings Institution point this out. "Subjective evaluations enter at every step of the way: in determining what attributes to include in the job evaluation, in setting the point weights for each attribute, in deciding how many points each job should get for each attribute, and in calibrating the resulting point scores with pay."[30]

Achieving authentic "equity" requires the development of genuinely fair criteria for job evaluation. However, commonly used criteria are open to criticism. For example, some people have suggested that most pay equity plans perpetuate class privilege by assigning too high a value to advanced educational credentials. Moreover, it is possible to "rig" the criteria in such a way as to justify existing inequities. Bergmann cautions that: "Some job evaluation schemes are 'fixed' to produce low pay for women by discounting the factors that distinguish women's jobs and rewarding highly the factors that distinguish men's. Giving high points for physical strength requirements, and few points for requirements of fine attention to detail or boredom, are examples."[31]

A fair assessment of the skills exercised by clerical workers would make visible and economically valuable those human relations skills necessary in a growing portion of clerical jobs. For example, a customer service representative must handle an inquiry or complaint from customer in a fashion which creates or preserves customer goodwill toward the organization. Often, customer service representatives must exercise extraordinary tact in dealing with customers who are angry about what appears to the customer to be a mishandled transaction. Under an adequate pay equity program, the value of such human relations skills would be reflected in workers' paychecks.

There is also the problem of inaccurate judgment in applying criteria to the evaluation of a particular job title. As a case in point: unless consultants are knowledgeable about the health risks associated with some kinds of VDT use, they are likely to evaluate working conditions based on the social stereotype—i.e., office work is clean, pleasant, and poses few health risks. Some clerical jobs have been automated in a fashion which creates a more stressful work environment. Clerical workers who process high volumes of repetitive information under intensive computer monitoring deserve hardship pay along with employees who work under other types of undesirable conditions. It is no longer accurate to assume that all clerical work poses low risk to health.

Thus far, pay equity schemes have been adopted primarily in the public sector, where political pressure can be brought to bear to narrow the wage gap between men and women workers performing work of comparable worth. Notable examples are the city of San Jose, California, and the states of Washington and Minnesota. A comprehensive national pay equity scheme would require massive government intervention in the salary arrangements of many private companies. Such a plan would be opposed by those who saw it as too expensive and cumbersome, as well as by persons philosophically opposed to large-scale government intervention in the private economic sector. Realistically, pay equity plans in the United States will likely result from government self-regulation or private-sector collective bargaining agreements. Public-sector pay equity schemes could help a large number of women, since a higher percentage of women than men work in government jobs. Nevertheless, not all clerical workers will be covered by pay equity arrangements, except in the unlikely event that such plans are made federally mandatory for all employers.

Demands for pay equity can be an important union organizing tool. As was mentioned above, pay equity was a major issue in the successful campaign to organize clerical and technical workers at Yale University. However, upward adjustments in the pay scales for clerical workers at both Yale and San Jose were won in campaigns which included heavily publicized *strikes*. Yet, in a sluggish economy such concessions may be hard for unions to win. An organizer from San Jose warns: "There's the problem now of the lack of prosperity in the economy. Strikes are not occurring because of the fear of losing job security."[32]

Pay equity is no magic cure-all. The impact of pay equity schemes is muted by the differential distribution of women and men in establishments and companies. Pay equity plans compare the rate of pay received by men and women who work for *the same* establishment or company. However, women are not equally distributed in establishments and companies. Some business places employ more women; others employ predominantly men. Women are more often hired by employers who pay lower salaries. Therefore, pay equity schemes would only raise women's salaries in comparison with the salaries of men who work for the same, usually lower-wage, establishments or businesses.

Opponents of pay equity raise serious questions about how salaries of underpaid workers could be raised without undermining the competitive position of the organizations that were among the first to initiate such programs. Given concern about a possible resurgence of inflation in the late 1980s, criticisms that pay equity programs would add further fuel to inflationary trends become especially powerful ones. Yet, the experience in Australia, where a broad-based program to raise salaries in some traditionally female occupations has been in effect for some time, is encouraging, for there have been no serious inflation problems attributable to the program.

To the extent that widespread pay equity programs did result in higher pay for a number of clerical workers, the rise in pay would increase employers' incentives to replace clerical labor with automated processes, and could thus spur job loss. Economist Jennifer Roback predicts: "A smaller number of more lucrative jobs will go to those with the most experience and best [educational] credentials."[33] For this reason, it is important that pay equity programs be coupled with serious equal employment opportunity efforts and appropriate retraining programs, so that displaced clerical workers can qualify for jobs in other sectors of the economy.

Pay equity may be one strategy useful *along with others* to better the lot of clerical workers. However, it is, by itself, no panacea. In spite of the drawbacks and limitations associated with pay equity, we need serious public debate about mechanisms to redress wage inequities in the female-dominated occupations, for female workers need wages which will provide the necessities of life and some of its material comforts for them and for their dependents. They need wages which are sufficient to serve as a financial base for personal autonomy.

A Safe Work Environment. Active participation in the work force should not exact an unnecessary cost in terms of workers' physical comfort and health. As embodied beings, clerical workers need and deserve physically safe working environments as a minimum condition for their well-being. Workers and the unions which represent them should demand healthy office surroundings.

Employers have a *moral* obligation to remove any *avoidable* health burdens from offices. They should not coerce workers into accepting physical discomfort and health hazards in order to obtain or retain employment. Employers also have a general *legal* obligation to provide a safe and healthy working environment; this obligation is reflected in federal and state occupational health and safety legislation. However, there is no federal legislation and very little state legislation which expressly regulates the conditions for use of video display terminals.

There is an entire field of study, ergonomics, which provides information about working environments conducive to human well-being. Researchers in ergonomics investigate the interrelationships among human beings, tools, and the work environment. The goal of ergonomics is to devise tools and work environments best suited to enhance productivity and workers' physical and psychological well-being.

Ergonomic experts have a good deal of information about how to design and furnish automated office facilities in order to enhance the health and comfort of the workers. Proper work environments can alleviate many of the types of eye and musculoskeletal discomfort experienced by heavy VDT users. In this book, it would be inappropriate to attempt to provide a comprehensive set of standards for an ergonomically sound office environment. But, it is important to indicate that such information is available.

While employers, particularly large businesses in information-intensive industries, are becoming more aware of the need for special work environments appropriate for intensive VDT use, too many video display terminals are still brought into offices without sufficient concern for changes necessary to safeguard workers' physical well-being. Occupational health experts Jeanne Stellman and Mary Sue Henifin comment: "It is all too common to see a VDT simply plunked down into an office that is already crowded and uncomfortable."[34] Such an inadequate working environment is a foolish economy, for poor working conditions interfere with worker efficiency and productivity.

Workers—where possible, through their unions—should demand that adequate working conditions be maintained. Workers also have a role to play in using well-designed equipment in the proper way. For example, one especially crucial piece of a equipment for a properly furnished workstation is an adjustable chair. A well-engineered and properly adjusted chair is essential for maintaining proper posture and avoiding recurrent discomfort, including neck and shoulder pain and especially backaches. Over prolonged periods, improper chair support may even lead to muscle-joint disease. Since workers vary physiologically, adjustable chairs will not provide the physical benefits for which they were designed unless workers are taught how to adjust them properly and *make the effort to do so whenever necessary.*

Properly designed chairs are only one example of the type of equipment which will preserve workers' comfort. Other aspects of the physical environment, such as air quality, noise level, and especially lighting conditions, are also important for comfortable, productive operation of video display terminals.

There have been proposals that state or local governments legislate minimum standards to protect workers' health in automated offices. The first such comprehensive health legislation was passed by the Suffolk County Legislature [New York] in the summer of 1988. The bill requires that companies with 20 or more terminals provide equipment with detachable keyboards, adjustable furniture, and special lighting. It mandates fifteen-minute work breaks every three hours for employees who use the terminals more than 26 hours per week. Employers must pay 80 percent of the cost for annual eye examinations and for eyeglasses which are needed to correct eye problems resulting from VDT use.

Business leaders lobbied aggressively against the Suffolk County legislation, arguing that the costs associated with the bill would put county businesses at a competitive disadvantage. Several companies declared that they would not build new facilities or expand existing operations in the county because of costs incurred through compliance with the legislation. For example, Northwest Airlines announced cancellation of a planned expansion of its Suffolk County facility. An estimated 650 new jobs were lost to the county as a result of the Northwest decision.[35]

Opponents of the legislation argue that there is insufficient scientific data upon which to base such detailed legal prescriptions. They suggest that companies on the cutting edge of ergonomic developments may be hampered in implementing future improvements in design and employment practices by swiftly outdated provisions in the law. Moreover, some employers may be caught between conflicting demands of nationwide collective bargaining agreements and county law. If legislative bodies in other locales pass their own office safety legislation, some companies may be faced with the difficulty of complying with contradictory requirements for operations in different jurisdictions. For example, different specifications for workstation features, such as display screens, might complicate corporate purchasing arrangements and deprive a large company of some of the benefits of uniform volume buying.

Legislation which mandates specific office design features and work practices is a rather heavy-handed approach to safeguarding the comfort and health of workers. However, it does offer some measure of protection to workers whose employers do not provide ergonomically sound working conditions voluntarily. It also protects the many nonunionized office workers, who cannot use collective bargaining agreements to achieve certain office safety goals.

Alleviating Unnecessary Stress. Increased and unnecessary occupational stress poses a particularly serious threat to the physical and mental health of clerical workers. There are many aspects of some clerical jobs which lead to increased stress. These include boring, monotonous work; underutilization of ability; close, unsupportive supervision; high production demands; machine pacing; low decision-making power; and high uncertainty about job future. In many cases, such job pressures occur in conjunction with one another. According to Lee Schore, at the core of the problem "we find that many of the stressors relate directly to workers' lack of opportunities to use their intelligence, creativity, and skills, as well as the degree to which they feel they are not given respect and dignity as human beings."[36] It is imperative that clerical workers maintain or regain a large measure of control over their own work processes, for such worker autonomy is crucial for the physical and psychological well-being of workers.

Regard for the bodily well-being of clerical workers requires that workers and employers jointly develop policies that minimize health-threatening stress. Intensive use of video display terminals appears to be especially stressful. Therefore, some experts suggest that workers with such duties should take frequent breaks. For example, one NIOSH study recommends fifteen minutes away from the VDT for every two hours of moderately heavy use; fifteen minutes away for every hour of very intensive use. There is some evidence that use of VDTs more than four hours per day significantly increases stress. Based upon such findings, proposed legislation in Norway limits VDT work to fours hours. Such guidelines are an aspect of occupational health policies which should be explored further by government officials, labor leaders, and managers in the United States.

Since low pay, lack of advancement opportunities, and anxiety over job loss all increase stress upon clerical workers, the educational and training, equal opportunity enforcement, and pay equity policies discussed above would also contribute to clerical workers' bodily well-being. The stress of heavy household responsibilities, the strains from racism, and/or the tension caused by sexual harassment can combine with stress associated with certain kinds of prolonged used of VDTs to endanger a clerical worker's health. This cumulative burden must be acknowledged in order to formulate adequate strategies for safeguarding workers' health. While specific suggestions in these areas are beyond the scope of this work, problems of racism and sexual harassment have to be addressed seriously in order to minimize stress for *all* women in the workplace. Similarly, the double burden of paid labor and household duties has to be redistributed substantially in order to protect the health of many women workers.[37]

Both individual workers and organizations can emphasize good personal "coping" strategies with which to protect the health of workers from stressful aspects of work that cannot be changed or during periods in which unnecessary stressors still exist. Individuals can become informed about and practice habits of good nutrition and

proper exercise. Persons can learn the increased health risks associated with smoking and excessive use of drugs (including alcohol).
Various relaxation techniques, including meditation, may be useful.
Unions and employers can sponsor "wellness" programs which encourage proper diet, provide opportunities for exercise, and help
workers stop unhealthful habits, such as smoking. Such efforts to
improve workers' health habits supplement, but *do not substitute for,*
measures to insure a safe and healthful work place.

Worker solidarity is an important means to safeguard worker
health. Persons who band together with coworkers to change poor
working conditions simultaneously lower their risks of stress-related
disease through positive, communal action. Organizing offices based
on the fundamental ethical principle of respect for the dignity of each
person is crucial. As occupational health expert Barbara Cohen has
asserted, "fundamental to the creation of a healthy atmosphere in
any organization is the daily overriding *respect* that is shown *for each
employee as a total person* regardless of status or tasks performed."[38]

Participation in Job Design. The concept of justice as participation
is consistent with programs which enlist clerical worker participation
in the redesign of their jobs during the continuing process of office
automation. Some system designers and management consultants
recommend that employees participate in projects to develop new
office automation systems from the beginning of the design process.[39]
Worker participation in design may benefit the entire organization,
since clerical workers may have a more accurate understanding of
the work which they do. Many seemingly standard clerical work
processes actually require clerical workers to deviate from regular
procedure in order to accommodate recurrent variances from normal
modes of operation. If managers and system designers who are unfamiliar with details of the clerical tasks fail to recognize the need for
such variances, the resulting rigid automated system may prevent
workers from exercising that judgment necessary for efficient, timely,
and high-quality service.

Given the diversity of clerical jobs and of job settings, it is not
possible to offer detailed suggestions regarding job redesign here.
Moreover, controversies concerning various alternatives in job design

are rooted, in part, in disagreements about theories of industrial engineering, occupational psychology, and organizational dynamics. The literature on these subjects is vast; only a small part of the literature relates explicitly to clerical jobs. Managers and consultants need to examine how job design issues intersect with the process of office automation. For example, as more and more clerical work is computerized, opportunities for task variety and job rotation may be foreshortened because tasks performed tend to be alike and, hence, to require similar skills. These are issues with important implications for the well-being of workers, but detailed responses are beyond the scope of this discussion.

I do, however, want to draw special attention to the issue of worker participation in setting and monitoring performance standards. One promising example of such worker participation was a program set up by AT&T and the Communications Workers of America in Tempe, a suburb of Phoenix, Arizona. Telephone operators in that program set their own performance standards and supervised their own compliance. AWTs [average work time per call] were compiled for the whole group, but not for individual workers. Results were very positive; operators exceeded average performance levels, and profitability rose 45 percent.[40] Heavy layers of supervision were eliminated; some of the money saved on supervisory salaries was reallocated for employee training. This is a particularly interesting experiment, given AT&T's long-standing tradition of intensive performance monitoring and multiple levels of supervision.

There were similarly positive results from a participatory project to develop work standards for a group of legal case analysts who handled correspondence and traced the progress of legal cases by using a computerized system. The work measurement expert called in to develop performance standards held a lengthy series of seminars in which analysts themselves decided upon the simplest and most effective procedures for each task and helped to set time standards. The productivity of the unit increased immediately.[41]

As Alan Westin and his colleagues point out, questions of fair treatment are involved in determining work standards themselves, in selecting methods to measure output relative to the standards, and in deciding on the weight to assign to quantitative performance statistics in the evaluation and reward or discipline of individual workers. Westin and his colleagues insist that employees should have direct access to their own job performance statistics. They also recommend a due process procedure which guarantees employees the right to challenge or amend disputed job performance reports.[42] Questions of justice are also raised with respect to employee participation in determining work standards and monitoring procedures. Employee participation is rare now. Government researchers have found that "in most classes, employers introduce electronic monitoring unilaterally, only informing employees of the change after all decisions have been made."[43]

Management has a legitimate need for certain information about workers' performance for purposes of planning and to insure adequate service. However, in many cases management objectives could be met by gathering data on the performance of the entire work group, without tallying performance statistics for individual employees. As we have seen, computer monitoring of individual performance, especially if done over short intervals, can increase stress and, therefore, raise workers' risk of stress-related disorders.

Moreover, I am concerned that monitoring *individual* performance may undermine solidarity among coworkers. First, workers may find that monitoring of individual performance puts pressure on them to concentrate intensely upon completion of units of work at their individual workstations. Workers cannot afford to pause for an interchange with a coworker because the "lost" time will worsen their average work time. Several studies confirm that monitoring decreases coworker interaction.[44] Workers might even feel that they have been pitted in direct competition against one another. This is a particular danger in units where individual performance results are posted in the joint work area. The epitome of this threat to solidarity among workers was reached in one computer system programmed to spur flagging productivity by flashing on the screen the message, "You're not working as fast as the person next to you."[45] Laws in West Germany and Sweden forbid the compiling of performance statistics on individual workers. In this country, we should examine corporate policies which utilize (or repudiate reliance on) quantitative performance statistics when evaluating individual workers. We should also assess the need for government regulation of work measurement practices.

Job redesign projects often result in improvement of office procedures, allowing clerical workers to process a greater volume of information on a timely basis. Some job redesign plans recombine office tasks in a fashion that requires workers to exercise greater skill and judgement. If job redesign allows workers to be more productive, the question arises as to whether workers should share in the financial gain which their enhanced productivity makes possible. Of course, the effort and skill of employees are only two factors which may influence increased productivity. Capital investment in more efficient automated equipment plus technical ingenuity in the design of effective new software are also important and deserve be rewarded. I am not suggesting that all the profits from enhanced productivity should be passed through to the clerical workers who operate the system.

Nonetheless, industrial relations specialist John E. Kelly warns that his colleagues underestimate the importance of material rewards to workers.[46] Workers may become understandably disgruntled if they are required to produce a higher output and exercise greater responsibility without a corresponding increase in pay. The failure of a job enrichment plan in one insurance office demonstrates the pitfalls of refusing to address questions of equitable pay for redesigned jobs. In this project, each insurance coder was reassigned to new duties that integrated all the functions necessary to process the work for one or more branch offices. Each coder now performed all the tasks necessary in order to complete action on a set of specific claims. However, the incentive pay plan already in effect in the coders' office was based upon work standards which were not recalibrated to reflect the coders' enlarged duties. As a result, "the coders in enriched jobs [had] to work harder and faster than they had before in order to stay within the wage incentive time standards. Management did not seem to realize that this would negatively affect the coders' attitudes toward enriched work."[47] The coders resented working harder in order to maintain the same pay level. Their consequent resistance to the job redesign program caused it to fail. It is significant that workers were explicitly denied participation in the planning for this job redesign project because the consultant believed: "(1) it was management's prerogative to restructure jobs, (2) it would be awkward for supervisors and subordinates to jointly plan changes in subordinates' jobs, and (3) the expectations of the subordinates might be unrealistic and the actual change therefore disappointing."[48]

Work redesign experts J. Richard Hackman and Greg Oldham point out that when issues of pay are raised in conjunction with job redesign projects, questions need to be asked about the mode of payment, as well as levels of pay. Some job redesign plans make pay increases contingent on exceeding certain performance standards. Hackman and Oldham assert that contingent pay plans are appropriate where management and workers both agree that the work standards are acceptable and allow sufficient latitude for quality service. They continue: "A second factor is the level of *trust* between management and employees. Contingent reward systems may be incompatible with enriched work if employees perceive the systems as attempts by management to control and manipulate their behavior on enriched jobs."[49] Thus, work redesign which enhances clerical workers' productivity and autonomy raises associated questions about fair compensation and connects with my earlier discussion of pay equity for female clerical workers.

There are a variety of mechanisms to increase the participation of clerical workers in the design of their work processes. Sociologists Feldberg and Glenn describe three cases in which clerical workers were able to make significant choices about the conditions of their own work. In all three cases, crucial factors were a social cohesiveness in the clerical work group that enhanced their mutual cooperation plus a relative lack of managerial concern to structure the clerical work process. For example, one work group was the payroll office staff in a small college. The college's administrators did not care how the payroll office workers organized their duties as long as payroll checks were issued in an accurate and timely fashion. Feldberg and Glenn conclude that while there are real opportunities for some individuals and groups to take greater initiative in determining their own clerical work processes, worker participation is likely to be "confined to areas defined as marginal by managers and professionals." They continue: "it seems evident that discretion over activities and decisions that are defined as central to managerial power and even individual career advancement would not be given over to workers" in the absence of fundamental restructuring of organizations.[50]

Another option is a formal joint management and labor task force empowered to address issues of job design. One benefit of programs which bring management and clerical workers together to discuss job design issues can be increased recognition of clerical workers' insight and creativity. As a result of one experiment in joint management and support staff participation in the restructuring of work at a small corporate headquarters, management came to recognize that support staff were "intelligent, interested, and often promotable."[51] Finally, unions can address some issues of job design through collective bargaining. For example, the national offices of several unions representing clerical workers provide locals with sample contract language restricting computer monitoring and guaranteeing due process rights where evaluations are based on individual performance statistics. However, unions have had only limited success in getting such provisions accepted during the bargaining process. Moreover, union contracts are set for several years at a time, but the pace of technological change associated with office automation is so fast that contract provisions may be quickly outdated. Additionally, many office workers are not a part of any bargaining unit.

Employee participation in job redesign is controversial. Such employee participation does involve additional cost. Employees contribute to the redesign project on company time and, therefore, at company expense. Moreover, employees' normal activities may be disrupted. Job design is often understood as a clear management prerogative. The need for management control over all aspects of the work process is an assumption built into scientific management theory. As a result, job redesign programs based upon scientific management techniques tend to stress management and expert consultation, but make limited use of employee input.

Some persons argue that it is inappropriate for workers such as clerical staff to participate in job redesign decisions because lower-level employees have a narrow perspective, limited to their own specific job duties and personal interests. Critics of employee participation contend that lower-level employees do not understand how their particular tasks fit as a part of the overall pattern of corporate activity and contribute to the organization's economic objectives. In response to such objections, Hackman and Oldham recommend "informed participation." They contend that a general request for suggestions from workers may not yield much wisdom, "especially if [the workers'] relationship with management has historically been strained." However, when employees are informed more fully about the purpose of the work redesign program and are treated as "full partners in the redesign process," then workers may venture ideas "whose quality would surprise and please even skeptical managers and consultants."[52]

Philosopher Robert Nozick argues that the right to make decisions and give orders is an entitlement which is based upon just acquisition of property rights in a business. Ownership entails unrestricted managerial discretion on the part of the owners or those to whom they choice to delegate authority. Workers have no claim to a voice in managerial decisions unless they negotiate such rights when entering into the employment contract or unless they are simultaneously owners who have property rights in an economic cooperative. Religious ethicist Robert Benne also raises objections to employee participation in a wide variety of economic decisions. He argues that lower-level employees are not responsible for the results of such corporate decisions and, therefore, they do not have a valid claim to participate in making them. The scope and intensity of the employees' responsibility is low relative to the management's accountability for the success of the entire venture. Benne makes this point by comparing employee participation in corporate decision-making with experiments allowing students "full" participation in university decisions during the 1960s. One could easily quarrel with Benne's pessimistic description of students as unable and unwilling to understand the internal dynamics of a university and, hence, as incompetent to take part in decisions regarding overall educational priorities. In any case, the comparison between students and workers is not an apt one, since students are involved in the affairs of a university for a limited period of time. Workers have an open-ended commitment to their jobs, as do managers.

Benne also asserts "it is unlikely that anyone anywhere has full control over the conditions of his or her productive existence. Interdependence and specialization of function precludes such grandiose hopes."[53] However, what I advocate is not total clerical worker control, but rather shared participation when making decisions which have an immediate and important impact on the employees' own work process.

Benne acknowledges that workers make a contribution in an interdependent work process. However, he believes that such contributions are appropriately rewarded with a paycheck. "A person can be paid for specific services in a complex process without having a claim to control over the process." Benne continues: "If, in addition, the person is free to offer his or her services to other bidders, or to change the service offered, I fail to see the immorality of it all."[54] Nozick's position also rests on an assumption that workers are entirely free to seek other forms of employment which better satisfy their personal values and desires. However, certain cultural assumptions about male supremacy and pervasive sexist institutional patterns result in a situation where there are few opportunities for clerical workers to find employers who will agree to give them shared control over work processes. Moreover, given pervasive sex segregation in employment, women who are clerical workers are free to offer their services primarily within a *limited pink-collar job market*. Finally, Benne argues that additional participative mechanisms are not necessary because "the worker is likely to have union power guarding against unjust treatment."[55] Yet, as we have already seen, at present clerical workers in the private sector are rarely protected by union representation.

I am advocating shared participation between management and clerical workers on issues which have an immediate and substantial impact on the employees' work process. It may be that such participation will have an inner dynamic that drives toward greater participation in broader issues of corporate policy and strategy. One union group envisions: "In the right context, such [office automation] innovations could eliminate routinized labor while allowing each worker to develop general, system-wide skills. These developments could eventually lay the basis for the much more direct employee participation in management."[56] Thus, issues of participation in job redesign press us in the direction a fundamental restructuring of authority within economic organizations.

VDTs, Justice, and the Reign of God/dess

The elements for a vision of justice for clerical workers (and for women who can no longer be absorbed into the clerical sector) which I have presented here press at the limits of social change possible under postindustrial capitalism. The question—"Can justice be achieved for women workers within our present capitalist context?"—remains, for me, an explosively open question. I did not begin this work with that question. Rather, I began by looking at specific changes happening in the daily work lives of a particular category of women workers. As I imagined the conditions under which those women could receive a greater measure of justice, I began to have disturbing doubts about how requisite changes could be brought about within the present economic system. Will postindustrial capitalism allow women secure opportunities for active and equitable participation in the economic life of their communities? Can it provide jobs for all the women who want them? Can it furnish a sufficient number of jobs which pay a wage adequate to support workers and their dependents in moderate comfort, which challenge women to develop satisfying competencies, and which foster enriching relationships on the job?

Some forms of incremental change that would benefit some women are certainly possible under our present economic arrangements. Provision of safer working facilities, which enhance the physical comfort and health of clerical workers, is one illustration. Such a change is easier to make, because it benefits all parties. Providing such an environment serves the interests of both employer and employees, because employees are more productive in ergonomically sound environments. However, it might not be possible to implement other policies designed to produce justice for all women without profound economic transformation. For example, pay equity schemes may be very difficult to implement in the current global economy, because firms—or even nations—which promote such plans raise their labor costs relative to the costs of competitors who continue to reap the benefits of sexist wage policies.

Office automation represents a profound transformation in a crucial employment sector for women. If clerical workers [and potential clerical workers] are to know the joys of good work, society will need to establish policies which enhance their opportunities for active participation in the economic realm.

The pervasiveness of sin will make it difficult to achieve greater justice for office workers. Greed is a perennial and powerful force in the human heart. Difficult economic times, such as those we face for the foreseeable future, create economic anxiety. Persons suffering from such anxiety are easily tempted to participate in the exploitation of others in order to gain a seemingly greater measure of economic security for themselves.

In addition, we will need to acknowledge the weight of complex, interstructured forms of oppression, if we are to have a realistic notion of the difficulties of achieving greater justice for office workers. Clerical workers are subordinated *both* because of their relatively powerless organizational position and because of their sex. The two forms of subordination reinforce each other. Moreover, these two forms of oppression intersect with racial, ethnic, and/or class identity in ways which intensify the exploitation suffered by the most vulnerable members of society.

Sexist elements in the Christian tradition serve as a form of cultural legitimation for continued exploitation of female clerical workers. Dualistic tendencies which are deeply imbedded in western Christian traditions obscure the moral dimensions of the current technological transformation of clerical work. In the history of Christian thought, a long heritage of limited concern for work in the world combines with presumptions that women's duties are centered in the household. These historical trends make it difficult for Christian leaders to recognize that this transformation of women's work is a serious ethical issue. Thus, Christians should come to the global struggle for the dignity and well-being of women workers chastened by the knowledge that "resistance to or witness against the oppression of women is, at best, very muted" in the Christian scriptures and traditions.[57]

However, we need not only to face the realities of sin—including sinful social blindness within Christian traditions—but also to acknowledge the promise of redemption. That Divine Power which which enables just human relationships abides with us in the midst of concrete struggles to improve the work lives of women in clerical jobs. Office workers build up the Reign of God/dess when they organize local, national, and international groups which allow them a greater measure of participation in the decisions that determine the quality of their work lives. The struggle for God/dess's justice is waged in day-to-day battles for adequate education and training programs, for effective equal employment opportunity policies, and for equal pay for work of comparable worth.

In the Reign of God/dess, human beings will experience the fulfillment of those fundamental capacities given to human beings by the Creator. Since human beings are embodied beings, bodily comfort and enjoyment are an important aspect of human flourishing. We honor the good of bodily well-being when we strive to guarantee safe and comfortable workplaces for all employees. We show an appreciation for the our creation and our future "blessedness" as social beings when we develop attitudes and policies which protect social relationships in computerized workplaces. Maintaining opportunities to "take heart in one another" is essential to preserving both our own humanity and that solidarity which is necessary to foster the value of justice as active participation.

The Reign of God/dess will be characterized by new patterns of relationship in which the socially marginal find themselves drawn toward the center, where their needs can be satisfied. This religious vision promises both justice and an abundance of good things for all. While the Reign of God/dess should not be identified simplistically with the success of movements on behalf of workers or with the triumph of any particular liberation movement, such concrete struggles for justice contribute to the Reign. The Spirit is working to bring about greater justice in human history and that deeply religious work of liberation proceeds, in part, through a mundane, bodily struggle to transform the conditions of work at the VDT.

Notes

•••••••••••••••••

•••••••••••••••••

•••••••••••••••••

Introduction

1. Karen Nussbaum, quoted in Karen Sacks, "Work," *The Women's Annual 1982–1983*, ed. Barbara Haber (Boston: G. W. Hale, 1983), 263.

2. In this book the term *minority women* will be used to identify women from socially disadvantaged racial and ethnic groups. As I use the term, it denotes primarily African American, Hispanic, and Native American women. The term *minority women* is problematic because women of color are in the majority from a global perspective. They are also in a majority in certain geographical areas of the United States. I considered use of the term *racial/ethnic* women, but it implies that Caucasian women are not also women bound by a particular racial experience and various ethnic experiences. I have not discovered any vocabulary contrasting the experience of white (non-Hispanic) women with African American, Hispanic, Native American and Asian-Pacific women which does not implicitly make white women's experience normative. Faced with a variety of unsatisfactory terms, I have chosen one whose brevity makes for easier reading.

3. June Nash and Maria Patricia Fernandez-Kelly, "Introduction," *Women, Men and the International Division of Labor* (Albany: State Univ. of New York Press, 1983), xi.

4. In the electronics assembly facilities which remain in the United States, the workers are increasingly women of color. See three case studies found in Nash and Fernandez-Kelly, *Women, Men and the International Division of Labor*, 273–373.

5. U. S. Department of Commerce, Bureau of the Census, *Statistical Abstract of the United States, 1988* (Washington: Government Printing Office, 1988), Table 627.

6. Robert N. Bellah *et. al.*, *Habits of the Heart: Individualism and Commitment in American Life* (New York: Harper and Row, 1985); Alasdair MacIntyre, *After Virtue: a Study in Moral Theory* (Notre Dame, IN: Univ. of Notre Dame Press, 1981), and Richard John Neuhaus, *The Naked Public Square: Religion and Democracy in America* (Grand Rapids, MI: Eerdmans, 1984).

7. For a thoughtful statement of the position from which I dissent, see Kent Greena-

walt, *Religious Convictions and Political Choice* (New York: Oxford Univ. Press, 1988).

8. Stanley Hauerwas, with David Burrell, "From System to Story: An Alternative Pattern for Rationality in Ethics," in *Truthfulness and Tragedy: Further Investigations Into Christian Ethics* (Notre Dame, IN: Univ. of Notre Dame Press, 1977), 15.

9. David Tracy, *The Analogical Imagination: Christian Theology and the Culture of Pluralism* (New York: Crossroad, 1981), 6.

10. In choosing the word *God/dess*, I have followed the example of Rosemary Ruether in *Sexism and God-talk* (Boston: Beacon Press, 1983).

Chapter One

1. David Lockwood, *The Blackcoated Worker: A Study in Class Consciousness* (London: George Allen and Unwin Ltd., 1958), 19.

2. Margery W. Davies, *Woman's Place is at the Typewriter: Office Work and Office Workers 1870–1930* (Philadelphia: Temple Univ. Press, 1982), 51.

3. Fannie Barrier Williams, "The Intellectual Progress of the Colored Women of the United States Since the Emancipation Proclamation," in *Black Women in Nineteenth-Century American Life,* ed. Bert James Loewenberg and Ruth Bogin (University Park: Pennsylvania State Univ. Press, 1976), 276.

4. Davies, *Woman's Place is at the Typewriter,* 74.

5. Barbara Mayer Wertheimer, *We Were There: The Story of Working Women in America* (New York: Pantheon Books, 1977), 233.

6. Heidi Hartmann et al., eds., *Computer Chips and Paper Clips: Technology and Women's Employment* (Washington: National Academy Press, 1986), 1: 86.

7. United States Congress, Office of Technology Assessment [OTA], *Automation of America's Offices: 1985–2000* (Washington: Government Printing Office, 1985), 303.

8. Alan Westin et al., *The Changing Workplace: A Guide to Managing the People, Organizational and Regulatory Aspects of Office Technology* (White Plains, NY: Knowledge Industry Publications, 1985), 13–4.

9. Joseph J. Lazzaro, "Talking Instead of Typing," *High Technology* 6 (Jan. 1986): 59.

10. John A. Seeger, Jay Lorsch, and Cyrus F. Gibson, "First City Bank Operating Group (B)," Harvard Business School Case Services, 1975. Case number 474–166.

11. Unpublished report, cited in Judith Gregory and Karen Nussbaum, "Race Against Time: Automation of the Office," *Office: Technology and People* 1 (1982): 203.

12. Alan Burns, *The Microchip: Appropriate or Inappropriate Technology* (New York: John Wiley, 1981), 91.

13. Simon Nora and Alain Minc, *The Computerization of Society: A Report to the President of France* (Cambridge: MIT Press, 1980), 37.

14. George T. Silvestri and John M. Lukasiewicz, "Occupational Employment Projections: the 1984–95 Outlook," *Monthly Labor Review* 108 (Nov. 1985): 42–59. It

should be noted that there has been a shift in the classification of some specific occupational groups, notably cashiers, from the clerical category to the sales category. Such shifts effect the overall employment projections. For some brief remarks on this data problem, see Hartmann, *Computer Chips and Paper Clips*, 1:106–7.

15. "2 Studies Show Growth in Clerical Jobs Slowing," *New York Times*, 7 Oct. 1985, A26.

16. 9to5, National Association of Working Women, *Hidden Victims: Clerical Workers, Automation, and the Changing Economy* (Cleveland: National Association of Working Women, 1985), Table 7, 51.

17. Ibid., Table 9, 52.

18. Ibid., 5.

19. J. David Roessner et al., *The Impact of Office Automation on Clerical Employment, 1985–2000* (Westport, CT: Quorum Books, 1985), 149.

20. Ibid., 227–28.

21. Roger Draper, "The Impact of Automation on Labor: an Interview with Faye Duchin," *Managing Automation* (May 1986): 71.

22. Wassily Leontief and Faye Duchin, *The Future Impact of Automation on Workers* (New York: Oxford Univ. Press, 1986), Table 3.2, 75.

23. Ibid., 14.

24. Roessner, *Impact of Office Automation*, 228.

25. Ibid., 150. Emphasis in original.

26. J. David Roessner, "Impact of Office Automation on Office Workers: Final Report, Vol. II: Technical Summary," 37.

27. Nora, *The Computerization of Society*, 16.

28. Murray Laver, *Computers and Social Change* (Cambridge: Cambridge Univ. Press, 1980), 38.

29. See OTA, *Automation of America's Offices*, 292.

30. Mark Green and John F. Berry, "Takeovers, a Symptom of 'Corpocracy,' " *New York Times*, 3 Dec. 1986, A31.

31. Hartmann, *Computer Chips and Paper Clips*, 1: 65.

32. Nora and Minc, *Computerization of Society*, 40–41.

33. Diane Werneke, *Microelectronics and Office Jobs: The Impact of the Chip on Women's Employment* (Geneva: International Labour Office, 1983), 22.

34. United States Department of Labor, *Workforce 2000: Work and Workers for the 21st Century: Executive Summary* (n.p, n. d.), xx.

35. Office of Technology Assessment, *Automation of America's Offices*, 304.

36. Joseph F. Coates, "Computers and Business—a Case of Ethical Overload," *Journal of Business Ethics* 1 (Aug. 1982): 243.

37. The slowdown in the United States space program which followed in the wake of the Challenger disaster means that there have been fewer space vehicles available for launching commercial satellites. Thus, there has been a delay in the availability of reasonably priced satellite transmission services.

38. Randi T. Sachs, "Should You Send Your Input Overseas?" *Office Administration and Automation* 44 (March 1983): 70.

39. "Problems of Technology Examined, Solutions Offered at AFL-CIO Conference," *White Collar Report* 59 (23 April 1986): 396.

40. OTA, *Automation of America's Offices*, 214.

41. Rosabeth Moss Kanter, *Men and Women of the Corporation* (New York: Basic Books, 1977), 71.

42. Thierry J. Noyelle, "The New Technology and the New Economy: Some Implications for Equal Employment Opportunity," in *Computer Chips and Paper Clips*, ed. Hartmann, 2: 384.

43. Westin, *Changing Workplace*, 13–7.

44. Paul Osterman also describes some companies with a strong commitment to inside training and promotion for all company employees. He, too, indicates that such companies were in the minority in his study. "White-Collar Internal Labor Markets," in *Internal Labor Markets* (Cambridge: MIT Press, 1984), 163–89.

45. Westin, *Changing Workplace*, 13–5. This is disappointing, especially in view of the fact that this study team had visited relatively "enlightened" employers.

46. This is what Kanter calls "reflected status." *Men and Women of the Corporation,* 74.

47. See Louise Kapp Howe, *Pink Collar Workers: Inside the World of Women's Work,* (New York: Avon Books, 1977), 149–50.

48. Werneke, *Microelectronics and Office Jobs*, p. 89; see also p. 49.

49. H. Allan Hunt and Timothy L. Hunt, *Clerical Employment and Technological Change* (Kalamazoo, MI: W. E. Upjohn Institute for Employment Research, 1986), 44 and 104.

50. Roslyn Feldberg and Evelyn Nakano Glenn, "Technology and Work Degradation: Effects of Office Automation on Women Clerical Workers," in *Machina Ex Dea: Feminist Perspectives on Technology*, ed. Joan Rothschild (New York: Pergamon Press, 1983), 63, 76 n.5.

51. Kay Fusselman, "Do Computer Skills Means Higher Pay, Better Jobs?" *The Secretary* (June/July 1986): 21.

52. Joan M. Greenbaum, *In the Name of Efficiency: Management Theory and Shopfloor Practice in Data-Processing Work* (Philadelphia: Temple Univ. Press, 1979), 99, 145–46.

53. Eileen Appelbaum, "Technology and Work Organization in the Insurance Industry," *ILR Report* [Industrial and Labor Relations Report, Cornell University] (Fall 1985): 25; Barbara Baran, "The Technological Transformation of White-Collar Work," in *Computer Chips and Paper Clips*, ed. Hartmann, 2: 48.

54. Michael Major, "Partners or Pawns?" *Modern Office Technology* (June 1984): 100.

55. Heather Menzies, *Women and the Chip: Case Studies of the Effects of Informatics on Employment in Canada* (Montreal: Institute for Research on Public Policy, 1981), 61.

56. United States Department of Labor, Women's Bureau, *Women and Office Automa-*

tion: *Issues for the Decade Ahead* (Washington: Government Printing Office, 1985), 12.

57. Kathleen E. Christensen, "Impacts of Computer-mediated Home-based Work on Women and Their Families," *Office: Technology and People* 3 (1987): 219.

58. This phrase was used by an insurance company manager. See Baran, "Technological Innovation and Regulation," 137–38.

59. Appelbaum, "Technology and Work Organization," 25.

60. Noyelle, "The New Technology and the New Economy," 373.

61. Baran, "Office Automation and Women's Work," 30.

62. Carman St. John Hunter and David Harman, *Adult Illiteracy in the United States: A Report to the Ford Foundation* (New York: McGraw Hill, 1979), 27.

63. Interview with staff of the APL project, University of Texas, reported in Jonathan Kozol, *Illiterate America* (Garden City, NJ: Doubleday, 1985), 9.

64. Ibid, 5.

65. Ibid, 4.

66. William McGowan, "Iliterasee att Wurk," *New York Times*, 19 Aug. 1982, A27. Emphasis added.

67. Kozol, *Illiterate America*, 4

68. Lydia Chavez, "Encouraging Hispanic Students to Stay in School," *New York Times*, 3 Aug. 1986, E9.

69. Jane Perlez, "Banks' Job Program Fails to Find Enough Qualified Students," *New York Times*, 29 June 1987, B1.

70. Edward B. Fiske, "There's a Computer Gap and It's Growing Wider," *New York Times*, 4 Aug. 1985, section IV, 8.

71. Ronald E. Anderson et al., "Inequities in Opportunities for Computer Literacy," *Computing Teacher* 11 (April 1984): 12.

72. Irving P. McPhail, "Computer Inequities in School Uses of Microcomputers: Policy Implications," *Journal of Negro Education* 54 (Winter 1985): 8.

73. Carol Edwards, "Achieving Equity," *Computing Teacher* 11 (April 1984): 62.

74. "Girls Get Advice on Dealing with Technology," *New York Times*, 15 May 1983, A26.

75. Marlaine E. Lockheed and Steven Frakt, "Sex Equity: Increasing Girls' Use of Computers," *Computing Teacher* 11 (April 1984): 17.

76. Jo Shuchat Sanders, "The Computer: Male, Female, or Androgynous?" *Computing Teacher* 11 (April 1984): 31.

Chapter Two

1. Barbara Baran et al., "Technological Innovation and Deregulation: The Transformation of the Labor Process in the Insurance Industry" (Working Paper, Berkeley Roundtable on International Economy, Jan. 1985), 221.

2. Ibid., 122.

3. William Henry Leffingwell, *Office Management: Principles and Practice* (Chicago: A. W. Shaw, 1925); *Scientific Office Management* (Chicago: A. W. Shaw, 1917); *Making the Office Pay* (Chicago: A. W. Shaw, 1918).

4. Margery Davies, *Woman's Place is at the Typewriter*, 116–18.

5. Harry Braverman, *Labor and Monopoly Capital: The Degradation of Work in the Twentieth Century* (New York: Monthly Review Press, 1974), 309.

6. Davies, *Woman's Place is at the Typewriter*, 107.

7. Shoshana Zuboff, "New Worlds of Computer-mediated Work," in *Catching up with the Computer Revolution*, ed. Lynn M. Salerno (New York: John Wiley, 1983), 458.

8. The MacNeil/Lehrer News Hour, 28 Dec. 1983, transcript #2153, 13.

9. United States Congress, Office of Technology Assessment [OTA], *The Electronic Supervisor: New Technology, New Tensions* (Washington: Government Printing Office, 1987), 28.

10. 9to5, National Association of Working Women, *Computer Monitoring and Other Dirty Tricks* (Cleveland: National Association of Working Women, 1986), 7.

11. Mary Murphree, "Brave New Office: The Changing World of the Legal Secretary," in *My Troubles Are Going to Have Trouble with Me: Everyday Trials and Triumphs of Women Workers*, ed. Karen Brodkin Sacks and Dorothy Remy (New Brunswick, NJ: Rutgers Univ. Press, 1984), 153.

12. 9to5, National Association of Working Women, *Hidden Victims*, 33.

13. The MacNeil/Lehrer News Hour, 8.

14. OTA, *Electronic Supervisor*, 45.

15. "Changing 45 Million Jobs," *Business Week*, 3 Aug. 1981, 66.

16. MacNeil/Lehrer News Hour, 11.

17. Women's Bureau, *Women and Office Automation*, 5.

18. Westin, *Changing Workplace*, 6–2.

19. *Electronic Supervisor*, 32.

20. Westin, *Changing Workplace*, 5–6.

21. "Changing 45 Million Jobs," *Business Week*, 3 Aug. 1981, 67.

22. Elizabeth Regan, "Managing a New Generation of Office Jobs," *Words* (April–May 1983): 26.

23. Westin, *Changing Workplace*, 6–11.

24. Shoshanah Zuboff, "New Worlds of Computer-mediated Work," in *Catching Up with the Computer Revolution*, ed. Lynn M. Salerno (New York: John Wiley, 1983), 463.

25. Ibid.

26. 9to5, National Association of Working Women, *The 9to5 National Survey on Women and Stress, Office Automation: Addendum* (Cleveland: National Association of Working Women, 1984), 7.

27. Barbara Baran, "Office Automation and Women's Work," 7.

28. Women's Bureau, *Women and Office Automation*, 5.

29. Eileen Appelbaum, "Technology and Work Organization in the Insurance Industry," 22.

30. Baran, "Technological Innovation and Deregulation," 123. Baran's comments were made in the context of a discussion of word processing centers, but, as her final line makes clear, they are appropriate to both the centralized data entry operations discussed here and the centralized word processing operations discussed below.
31. Roslyn L. Feldberg and Evelyn Nakano Glenn, "Technology and Work Degradation," 71–75.
32. Baran, "Technological Innovation and Deregulation," 66–69.
33. Ibid., 128.
34. Appelbaum, "Technology and Work," 22.
35. Murphree, "Brave New Office," 156. See also Feldberg and Glenn, "Technology and Work Degradation."
36. Most of the centralized data entry facilities described here also employed part-time or temporary workers and operated on more than one shift when possible.
37. Westin, *Changing Workplace*, 5–7.
38. Anne Machung, "Word Processing: Forward for Business, Backward for Women," in *My Troubles Are Going to Have Trouble with Me*, ed. Sacks and Remy, 128.
39. An intermediate form of organization, which I will not discuss, is a satellite secretarial center located close to the managers' offices, where a small group of clerical workers handles the typing and other support services for a relatively small group of managers. For a description of this form of organization of secretarial services, see Murphree, "Brave New Office," 154–56.
40. Kay Fusselman, "Do Computer Skills Means Higher Pay, Better Jobs?" *The Secretary* (June/July 1986): 15.
41. Ibid., 17.
42. Ibid., 16.
43. Murphree, "Brave New Office," 157.
44. Baran, "Technological Innovation and Deregulation," 4. Emphasis added.
45. Michael Beer, "Needs and Need Satisfaction Among Clerical Workers in Complex and Routine Jobs, *Personnel Psychology* 21 (Summer 1968): 221. Given the date of this research, most or all of these clerical tasks were non-automated.
46. Baran, "Technological Innovation and Deregulation," 135.
47. Louise Kapp Howe, *Pink Collar Workers: Inside the World of Women's Work* (New York: Avon Books, 1977), 159–60.
48. Gerald R. Salancik and Jeffrey Pfeffer, "An Examination of Need-Satisfaction Models of Job Attitudes," *Administrative Science Quarterly* 22 (Sept. 1977): 433.
49. Beverly Burris, "The Human Effects of Underemployment," *Social Problems* 31 (Oct. 1983): 100.
50. Gavriel Salvendy, "Human-computer Communications with Special Reference to Technological Developments, Occupational Stress and Educational Needs," *Ergonomics* 25 (June 1982): 439.
51. Richard Matteis, "The New Back Office Focuses on Customer Service," *Harvard Business Review* 57 (March/April 1979): 158.
52. Baran, "Technological Innovation and Deregulation," 136–37.

53. 9to5, *Hidden Victims*, 43.
54. Fusselman, "Computer Skills, Higher Pay, Better Jobs?" 14.
55. Zuboff, "New Worlds of Computer-Mediated Work," 458.
56. OTA, *Electronic Supervisor*, 54.
57. Kenneth M. Drange, "Office Productivity Factors," *Journal of Systems Management* 36 (Nov. 1985), 8.
58. 9to5, *Hidden Victims*, 36.
59. Shoshanah Zuboff, "Why Do Employees Misuse, Even Sabotage, Computer Systems?" *Facilities Design and Management* (May 1982): 61.
60. Ibid.
61. Roslyn L. Feldberg and Evelyn Nanako Glenn, "Incipient Workplace Democracy among United States Clerical Workers," *Economic and Industrial Democracy* 4 (Feb. 1983): 64.
62. Cynthia Costello, "The Office Homework Program at the Wisconsin Physicians Service Insurance Company" (Typescript).
63. Barbara Garson, *All the Livelong Day: The Meaning and Demeaning of Routine Work* (New York: Penguin Books, 1975), 152.

Chapter Three

1. Karen Nussbaum, "Office Automation: Jekyll or Hyde?" in *Office Automation: Jekyll or Hyde?*, ed. Daniel Marschall and Judith Gregory (Cleveland: Working Women Education Fund, 1983), 17.
2. "Restructuring Work for Health," *WOHRC News* [Women's Occupational Health Resource Center, School of Public Health, Columbia University] 7 (April/July 1986): 3.
3. National Research Council of the National Academy of Sciences, *Video Displays, Work and Vision* (Washington National Academy Press, 1983), 174.
4. Alan Westin, *Changing Workplace*, 7–7. Emphasis in original.
5. Edward Wakin, "The Jury's Still Out on Office Systems Safety," *Today's Office* (Sept. 1985): 39.
6. VDT Facts (White Plains, NY: March of Dimes Birth Defects Foundation [1275 Mamaroneck Ave., White Plains, NY 10605], n.d.).
7. These two types of non-ionizing radiation are different from the higher-frequency ionizing radiation that many people associate with the word *radiation*.
8. Marilyn Goldhaber, Michael Polen, and Robert Hiatt, "The Risk of Miscarriage and Birth Defects among Women Who Use Visual Display Terminals during Pregnancy," *American Journal of Industrial Medicine* 13 (1988): 704–705. Researchers also caution that their results may have been influenced by recall bias. In this case, women who suffer miscarriages may have been more likely to "recall" and report heavy use of VDTs during their troubled pregnancies.
9. Peter Lewis, "Questions on Health and PCs," *New York Times*, 5 July 1988, C6.

10. 9to5, National Association of Working Women, *9to5 Campaign on VDT Risks, Analysis of VDT Operator Questionnaires of VDT Hotline Callers* (Cleveland: National Association of Working Women, 1984), 2.

11. Susan Klitzman and Jeanne Stellman, "FactPack: Information on Stress" (Brooklyn, NY: Women's Occupational Health Resource Center, 1985), 1.

12. M. J. Smith et al., "A Review of NIOSH Psychological Stress Research—1977," in National Institute for Occupational Safety and Health, *Proceedings of the Conference on Occupational Stress* (Washington: Government Printing Office, 1978), 26–36.

13. Suzanne G. Haynes and Manning Feinleib, "Women, Work and Coronary Heart Disease: Prospective Findings from the Framingham Heart Study," *American Journal of Public Health* 70 (Feb. 1980): 136.

14. Teresa Schnorr et al., "Chest Pain in Users of Video Display Terminals," *Journal of the American Medical Association* 257 (6 Feb. 1987): 627.

15. Michael J. Smith et al., "An Investigation of Health Complaints and Job Stress in Video Display Operations," *Human Factors* 23 (1981): 387–400.

16. 9to5, National Association of Working Women, *National Survey on Women and Stress, Office Automation: Addendum,* 6.

17. Ibid., 9.

18. G. Johansson et al., "Social Psychological, and Neuroendocrine Stress Reactions to Highly Mechanised Work," *Ergonomics* 21 (Aug. 1978): 594.

19. Ibid., 595. The subjects in this study were not female clerical workers; they were male workers in an automated sawmill.

20. 9to5, *Stress Survey, Addendum,* 5.

21. R. Chris Knight, "Can Stress Make You Sick?" *Working Woman* (April 1984): 144.

22. R. A. Karasek, "Job Decision Latitude, Job Design, and Coronary Heart Disease," in *Machine Pacing and Occupational Stress,* ed. Gavriel Salvendy and M. J. Smith (London: Taylor and Francis, Ltd., 1981), 48.

23. Barbara G. F. Cohen, "Organizational Factors Affecting Stress in the Clerical Worker," in *Human Aspects in Office Automation* (Amsterdam: Elsevier, 1984), 36.

24. Robert A. Karasek, Jr., "Job Demands, Job Design Latitude and Mental Strain: Implications for Job Redesign," *Administrative Science Quarterly* 24 (June 1979): 292.

25. Robert Karasek et al., "Job Decision Latitude, Job Demands, and Cardiovascular Disease: A Prospective Study of Swedish Men," *American Journal of Public Health* 71 (July 1981): 694–705.

26. Knight, "Can Stress Make You Sick?" 148.

27. Cary L. Cooper and Judi Marshall, "Occupational Sources of Stress: A Review of the Literature Relating to Coronary Heart Disease and Mental Ill Health," *Journal of Occupational Psychology* 49 (1976): 15–16.

28. Cohen, "Organizational Factors Affecting Stress in the Clerical Worker," 37–38.

29. Judith Gregory, "Results from *Working Women's* Office Worker Health and Safety Survey," in *Human Aspects in Office Automation,* ed. Cohen, 198.

30. Michael J. Smith et al., "An Investigation of Health Complaints and Job Stress in Video Display Operations," in National Institute for Occupational Safety and Health, *Select Research Reports on Health Issues in Video Display Terminal Operations* (Washington: Government Printing Office, 1981), 8.

31. S. L. Sauter et al., "VDT-Computer Automation of Work Practices as a Stressor in Information-Processing Jobs: Some Methodological Considerations," in *Machine Pacing and Occupational Stress*, ed. Salvendy and Smith, 357.

32. Marianne Frankenhaeuser, "Coping with Stress at Work," *International Journal of Health Services* 11 (1981): 491–510.

33. Chaya S. Piotrkowski, "Impact of Women's Work on Family Health," in *Human Aspects in Office Automation*, ed. Cohen, 189.

34. Ibid., 191.

35. Haynes and Feinleib, "Women, Work and Coronary Heart Disease," 137.

36. Gregory, "Results from *Working Women's* Survey," 198, 200-1.

37. Lois M. Verbrugge, "Physical Health of Clerical Workers," in *Human Aspects in Office Automation*, ed. Cohen, 226.

38. "Stress on Your Job—A Major National Survey," *Ms.*, April 1984, 84.

39. Suzanne G. Haynes and Manning Feinleib, "Clerical Work and Coronary Heart Disease in Women: Prospective Findings from the Framingham Study," in *Human Aspects in Office Automation*, ed. Cohen, 243–46. There were no direct questions about income included in the survey.

40. Linda Williams, "Stress of Adapting to White Society Cited as Major Cause of Hypertension in Blacks," *Wall Street Journal*, 28 May 1986, 37.

41. Leith Mullings, "Minority Women, Work, and Health," in *Double Exposure: Women's Health Hazards on the Job and at Home*, ed. Wendy Chavkin, (New York: Monthly Review Press, 1984), 121.

42. Julianne Malveaux, "Black Women and Stress," *Essence*, April 1984, 152.

43. Mullings, "Minority Women, Work and Health," in Chavkin, *Double Exposure*, 122.

44. Ibid., 128.

45. Malveaux, "Black Women and Stress," 75.

46. 9to5, *Survey on Stress, Addendum*, 2.

47. Ibid. 7.

48. "Stress on Your Job," *Ms.*, 84.

49. Malveaux, "Black Women and Stress," 152.

50. Lynn O'Conner Gardner, "Strategic View of the Labor Force," quoted in Catharine A. MacKinnon, *Sexual Harassment of Working Women* (New Haven: Yale Univ. Press, 1979), 19.

51. MacKinnon, *Sexual Harassment of Working Women*, 18.

52. Peggy Crull, "The Stress Effects of Sexual Harassment in the Office," in *Human Aspects in Office Automation*, ed. Cohen, 181.

53. Ibid.

54. Malveaux, "Black Women and Stress," 76.

55. Crull, "The Stress Effects of Sexual Harassment," 181.

56. C. W. Fontaine, "The Relationship between Catecholamine Excretion as a Measure of Psychological Stress and the Variables of Job Performance and Gender," in *Machine Pacing and Occupational Stress*, ed. Salvendy and Smith, 117–23.

57. B. Beith, "Work Repetition and Pacing as a Source of Occupational Stress," in *Machine Pacing and Occupational Stress*, ed. Salvendy and Smith, 199.

58. Gavriel Salvendy, "Classification and Characteristics of Paced Work," in *Machine Pacing and Occupational Stress*, ed. Salvendy and Smith, 11.

59. M. J. Smith et al., "Stress and Health Effects in Paced and Unpaced Work," in *Machine Pacing and Occupational Stress*, ed. Salvendy and Smith, 266.

60. Salvendy, "Classification and Characteristics of Paced Work," 8.

61. "Stress on Your Job," 86.

62. Women's Occupational Health Resource Center, "The Stress of 'Women's Work,' " WOHRC Fact Sheet, 1983.

63. B. G. F. Cohen et al., "Psychosocial Factors Contributing to Job Stress of Clerical VDT Operators," in *Machine Pacing and Occupational Stress*, ed. Salvendy and Smith, 337–45.

64. Michael J. Smith et al., "An Investigation of Health Complaints and Job Stress in Video Display Operations," 397.

65. Gregory, "Results of *Working Women's* Survey," 197.

66. Haynes and Feinleib, "Women, Work and Coronary Heart Disease," 138.

67. Malveaux, "Black Women and Stress," 75–76.

68. James S. House and James A. Wells, "Occupational Stress, Social Support and Health," in National Institute for Occupational Safety and Health, *Proceedings: Reducing Occupational Stress* (Washington: Government Printing Office, 1978), 24.

69. Ibid., 26–27.

70. Ibid., 24.

Chapter Four

1. John C. Bennett, *The Radical Imperative* (Philadelphia: Westminster Press, 1975), 151.

2. Beverly Wildung Harrison, *Making the Connections: Essays in Feminist Social Ethics* (Boston: Beacon Press, 1985), 68.

3. J. Philip Wogaman reviews some of these factors in "Emerging Issues in Economic Ethics," in *The Annual of the Society of Christian Ethics, 1984*, ed. Larry L. Rasmussen, 94–97. Wogaman is more confident than I that the "return to economic ethics is on in earnest."

4. Michael Harrington, *The Other America: Poverty in the United States* (New York: Macmillan, 1962).

5. Henry Clark, *The Christian Case against Poverty* (New York: Association Press, 1965); Lyle E. Schaller, *The Churches' War on Poverty* (Nashville: Abingdon Press,

1967), and J. Philip Wogaman, *Guaranteed Annual Income: The Moral Issues* (Nashville: Abingdon Press, 1968).

6. Bruce C. Birch and Larry Rasmussen, *The Predicament of the Prosperous* (Philadelphia: Westminster Press, 1978), Ronald J. Sider, *Rich Christians in an Age of Hunger: A Biblical Study* (New York: Paulist Press, 1977), Robert L. McCann, *World Economy and World Hunger: The Response of the Churches* (Washington: University Press of America, 1982), John V. Taylor, *Enough Is Enough* (Minneapolis: Augsburg Press, 1977), Monica Hellwig, *The Eucharist and the Hunger of the World* (New York: Paulist Press, 1976).

7. Thomas C. Oden, *Conscience and Dividends: Churches and the Multinationals* (Washington: Ethics and Public Policy Center, 1985); Charles W. Powers, ed. *Social Responsibility and Investments* (Nashville: Abingdon Press, 1971); Oliver F. Williams and John W. Houck, eds. *The Judaeo-Christian Vision and the Modern Corporation* (Notre Dame, IN: Univ. of Notre Dame Press, 1982).

8. Feldberg and Glenn, "Incipient Workplace Democracy among the United States Clerical Workers," *Economic and Industrial Democracy* 4 (Feb. 1983): 60.

9. Jacob Viner., *Religious Thought and Economic Society* (Durham, NC: Duke Univ. Press, 1978), 50.

10. Ibid., 107.

11. Peter James Klassen, *The Economics of Anabaptism: 1525–1560*, (The Hague: Mouton, 1964), 64.

12. John Calvin, *Institutes of the Christian Religion*, trans. Ford Lewis Battles (Philadelphia: Westminster Press, 1960), 1: 725.

13. Ernst Troeltsch, *Social Teaching of the Christian Churches* (New York: Harper and Row, 1931), 2: 605.

14. Winthrop S. Hudson, "The Weber Thesis Reexamined," *Church History* 30 (1961): 93.

15. Troeltsch, *Social Teaching*, 2: 611.

16. See R. H. Tawney, *Religion and the Rise of Capitalism* (New York: Harcourt, Brace, 1926), 113–32; 211–27.

17. Walter Rauschenbusch, *Christianity and the Social Crisis* (New York: Macmillan, 1919), 233.

18. Elisabeth Schüssler Fiorenza, *In Memory of Her* (New York: Crossroad, 1983).

19. Elizabeth A. Clark, *Women in the Early Church* (Wilmington, DE: Michael Glazier, 1983), 16.

20. George H. Tavard, *Woman in Christian Tradition* (Notre Dame, IN: Univ. of Notre Dame Press, 1973), 87. For a similar divisions of public and domestic duties affirmed by a Latin Father, see Ambrose, *On Paradise*.

21. Rosemary Ruether, *New Woman/New Earth: Sexist Ideologies and Human Liberation* (New York: Seabury Press, 1975), 18.

22. Martin Luther, *Enarrationes in I Mose*, quoted in Jane Dempsey Douglass, "Women and the Continental Reformation," in *Religion and Sexism*, ed. Rosemary Ruether (New York: Simon and Shuster, 1974), 295.

23. Martin Luther, "Lectures on Genesis," *Luther's Works*, ed. Jaroslav Pelikan (St. Louis: Concordia Publishing House, 1958) 1: 203.

24. Practice in Luther's household departed from theory, particularly for money management. Luther, who was given to heedless generosity, found his magnanimous impulses restrained by his more provident wife. Luther reported: "In domestic affairs, I defer to Katie. Otherwise I am led by the Holy Ghost." Roland Bainton, *Women of the Reformation in Germany and Italy* (Boston: Beacon Press, 1971), 27.

25. Jane Dempsey Douglass, *Women, Freedom and Calvin* (Philadelphia: Westminster Press, 1985), 55.

26. Washington Gladden, *Working People and Their Employers*, 112.

27. Ibid., 114. Emphasis added.

28. Rauschenbusch, *Christianizing the Social Order* (New York: Macmillan, 1915), 136.

29. Ibid., 128.

30. Dorothy Bass Fraser, "The Feminine Mystique: 1890–1910," *Union Seminary Quarterly Review* 27 (Summer 1972): 232.

31. Rosemary Ruether and Eugene Bianchi, *From Machismo to Mutuality: Essays on Sexism and Woman-Man Liberation* (New York: Paulist Press, 1976) 49–50.

32. "Economic Justice for All: Catholic Social Teaching and the U.S. Economy," *Origins*, 5 June 1986, par. 90.

33. Michael Walzer, *Spheres of Justice: A Defense of Pluralism and Equality* (New York: Basic Books, 1983), 165–66.

34. "Economic Justice for All," par. 293.

35. *Laborem Exercens*, par. 19.

36. *Mater et Magistra*, par. 105. An important question would be: To what extent have unstable economic conditions in the 1970s and 1980s undermined programs to guarantee the financial security of workers? The social welfare programs in Western European nations have been attacked as too costly. Employers throughout the industrialized nations are under pressure to keep "fringe benefit" costs down. Both these trends imperil programs to guarantee the welfare of sick and disabled workers and retirees.

37. J. Philip Wogaman, *Economics and Ethics: A Christian Inquiry* (Philadelphia: Fortress Press, 1986), 60.

38. John C. Raines and Donna C. Day-Lower, *Modern Work and Human Meaning* (Philadelphia: Westminster Press, 1986), 93.

39. Dorothee Soelle with Shirley A. Cloyes, *To Work and to Love: a Theology of Creation* (Philadelphia: Fortress Press, 1984), 71.

40. Walter G. Muelder, *Religion and Economic Responsibility* (New York: Scribner's, 1953), 1.

41. *Quadragesimo Anno*, par. 71. Emphasis added.

42. "Closing homily," *Catholic Mind* 79 (1981): 62.

43. *Gaudium et Spes*, par. 52.

44. Muelder, *Religion and Economic Responsibility*, 47.

45. Raines and Day-Lower, *Modern Work and Human Meaning*, 85–93.

46. See, for example, Wogaman, *Economics and Ethics*, 40–44; 81–82, or "Economic Justice for All."
47. Robert Coles and Jane Hallowell Coles, *Women of Crisis: Lives of Work and Dreams* (New York: Delacorte Press, 1980), 2: 94.
48. A non-employed wife tends to have a greater say over day-to-day household decisions including immediate decisions about child rearing. If the husband of a working wife takes on more household chores, he may make more of certain kinds of decisions, such as what to purchase at the grocery store. Russell Middleton and Snell Putney, "Dominance in Decisions in the Family," in *American Journal of Sociology* 65 (1960): 605–9, and Lois Hoffman, "Parental Power Relations and the Division of Household Tasks, in *The Employed Mother in America*, ed. F. I. Nye and L. W. Hoffman (Chicago: Rand McNally, 1963).
49. Stephen J. Bahr, "Effects on Power and Division of Labor in the Family," in *Working Mothers: An Evaluative Review of the Consequences for Wife, Husband, and Child*, ed. Lois Wladis Hoffman and F. Ivan Nye (San Francisco: Jossey-Bass, 1974), 178.
50. Joan Aldous, "Wives' Employment Status and Lower-Class Men as Husband-Fathers: Support for the Moynihan Thesis," *Journal of Marriage and the Family* 31 (1969): 469–76.
51. Ronald J. Burke and Tamara Weir, "Relationship of Wives' Employment Status to Husband, Wife and Pair Satisfaction and Performance," *Journal of Marriage and the Family* 38 (May 1976): 279–86.
52. Lillian B. Rubin, *Worlds of Pain: Life in the Working-Class Family* (New York: Basic Books, 1976), 176.
53. Roberta Goldberg, *Organizing Women Office Workers: Dissatisfaction, Consciousness, and Action* (New York: Praeger, 1983), 103.
54. Ibid.
55. *Statistical Abstract of the United States: 1988* (Washington: Government Printing Office, 1988), Table 653.
56. Goldberg, *Organizing Women Office Workers*, 67–68.
57. U. S. Department of Labor, Women's Bureau, "Women Who Maintain Families," Facts on U.S. Working Women, Fact Sheet 86–2, 1986.
58. 9to5, National Association of Working Women, *Hidden Victims*, 5.
59. Ibid., 41.
60. New federal legislation concerning health insurance plans may prompt many employers to provide health insurance coverage for all employees who work 17.5 hours per week or more. See Milt Freudenheim, "Discrimination in Benefit Plans," *New York Times*, 11 Nov. 1986, D2.
61. John Paul frequently refers to this call to participate in God's creative activity as the command to "subdue the earth." He briefly acknowledges that such language can lead to an arrogant destruction of the natural world, and he repudiates all such ecologically irresponsible actions. However, I suggest that the concepts of subduing the earth and taking dominion over it are hopelessly compromised, in

light of our continuing ecological crises. Therefore, I have not used such concepts here.

62. John Raines and Donna Day-Lower offer some similar reflections about work as a uniquely human activity. See their discussion of the human capacity to create tools, *Modern Work and Human Meaning*, 14–17.

63. *Laborem Exercens*, par. 3.

64. Soelle, *To Work and to Love*, 85.

65. Ibid.

66. Michael Beer, "Needs and Need Satisfaction Among Clerical Workers in Complex and Routine Jobs," *Personnel Psychology* 21 (Summer 1968): 218–19.

67. Goldberg, *Organizing Women Office Workers*, 70.

68. Elinor Langer, "Inside the New York Telephone Company," in *Women at Work*, ed. William L. O'Neill (New York: New York Times Books, 1972), 358.

69. Louise Kapp Howe, *Pink Collar Workers* (New York: Avon Books, 1977), 143.

70. Karen Brodkin Sacks, "Computers, Ward Secretaries, and a Walkout in a Southern Hospital," in *My Troubles Are Going to Have Trouble with Me*, ed. Sacks and Remy, 173–90. These ward secretaries appreciated the computer system which they used, because it streamlined tedious routine paperwork and protected the ward secretary from being scapegoated for the errors of others, 177.

71. Ibid., 180.

72. Soelle, *To Work and to Love*, 56.

73. Ibid., 93.

74. Raines and Day-Lower, *Modern Work and Human Meaning*, 108.

75. Howe, *Pink Collar Workers*, 145.

76. Shoshanah Zuboff, "Why Do Employees Misuse, Even Sabotage, Computer Systems?" *Facilities Design and Management* (May 1982): 61.

77. Cathy Trost, "Three Labor Activists Lead a Growing Drive to Sign Up Women," *Wall Street Journal*, 29 Jan. 1985, 1.

78. Jean Tepperman, *Not Servants, Not Machines: Office Workers Speak Out* (Boston: Beacon Press, 1976), 2.

79. Sacks, "Computers, Ward Secretaries and a Walkout," 181.

80. Goldberg, *Organizing Women Office Workers*, 72.

81. *Laborem Exercens*, par. 12

82. Robert Nozick, *Anarchy, State, and Utopia* (New York: Basic Books, 1974). For comments on the rights of inventors, see especially p. 182.

83. Tracy Kidder, *The Soul of a New Machine* (Boston: Little, Brown, 1981), 106.

84. Bernard Murchland, "Sin: the Old and the New," in *Sin* (New York: Macmillan, 1962), viii.

85. Robert Benne, *The Ethic of Democratic Capitalism* (Philadelphia: Fortress Press, 1981), 29.

86. Kenneth Himes, "Social Sin and the Role of the Individual," in *The Annual of the Society of Christian Ethics, 1986*, ed. Alan Anderson, 208.

87. Langdon Gilkey, *Message and Existence; An Introduction to Christian Theology* (New York: Seabury Press, 1979), 128.

88. Gregory Baum, "Critical Theology," in *Religion and Alienation: A Theological Reading of Sociology* (New York: Paulist Press, 1975), 197–208.

89. Charles E. Curran, *Themes in Fundamental Moral Theology* (Notre Dame, IN: Univ. of Notre Dame Press, 1977), 151.

90. Feldberg and Glenn, "Incipient Workplace Democracy," 60.

91. Rauschenbusch, *Christianizing the Social Order*, 31.

92. Bruce C. Birch and Larry L. Rasmussen, *The Predicament of the Prosperous* (Philadelphia: Westminster Press, 1978), 172.

Chapter Five

1. Walzer, *Spheres of Justice*, 165–66.

2. For more suggestions about the sort of social science data which is needed, see Hartmann et al., eds., *Computer Chips and Paper Clips*, 1: 179–81.

3. The language "plant closing" used to describe this bill reflects the continuing power of the image of the assembly line worker as the archetypal American worker. This common terminology obscures the job loss experienced by clerical workers when *office* operations are relocated or closed.

4. Japan Information Processing Development Association, *Research Survey Concerning the Social Effects of Office Automation*, quoted in OTA, *Automation of America's Offices*, 135.

5. Terrence Deal and Allen Kennedy, *Corporate Cultures: The Rites and Rituals of Corporate Life* (Reading, MA: Addison-Wesley, 1982).

6. Shoshanah Zuboff, "Why Do Employees Misuse, Even Sabotage, Computer Systems?" 61.

7. Feldberg and Glenn, "Technology and Work Degradation," 73.

8. This category includes clerical workers.

9. United States Department of Labor, Bureau of Labor Statistics, *Employment and Earnings* 35 (Jan. 1988), Table 60, 223.

10. John C. Kilgour, "Union Organizing Activity among White-Collar Employees," *Personnel* 60 (March/April 1983): 19.

11. Cathy Trost, "More Family Issues Surface at Bargaining Tables as Women Show Increasing Interest in Unions," *Wall Street Journal*, 2 Dec. 1986, 70.

12. William, Serrin, "Union's Success at Yale: New Focus on White-Collar Women," *New York Times*, 10 April 1984, B24.

13. "Working at the Margins," *9to5 Newsletter*, Sept./Oct. 1986, 1.

14. "Why Clerical Workers Resist the Unions," *Business Week*, 2 May 1983, 126.

15. William Serrin, "Computers in the Office Change Labor Relations," *New York Times*, 22 May 1984, B2.

16. Marc Levinson, "On the White-collar Assembly Line," *Commonweal*, 1 June 1984, 335.

17. The English title for this organization—International Federation of Clerical, Professional and Technical Employees—makes clearer that it covers clerical workers.

18. "World Conference Set On Common Union Approach to Video Display Terminals," *White Collar Report* 56 (24 Oct. 1984): 501.

19. 9to5, National Association of Working Women, *Hidden Victims*, 23.

20. "Changing 45 Million Jobs," *Business Week*, 3 Aug. 1981, 67.

21. Heather Menzies, *Women and the Chip*, 65; Barbara Bergmann, *The Economic Emergence of Women* (New York: Basic Books, 1986), 75, 80, 113.

22. Judith Gregory, "New Technology in the American Workplace," in Jeanne Stellman and Mary Sue Henifin, *Office Work is Dangerous to Your Health* (New York: Pantheon Books, 1983), 209. Gregory cites *Vanished Dreams: Age Discrimination and the Older Woman Worker* (Working Women Education Fund, 1980).

23. United States Department of Labor, Women's Bureau, *Women and Office Automation*, 16.

24. Thierry J. Noyelle, "The New Technology and the New Economy," in *Computer Chips and Paper Clips*, ed. Hartmann, 2: 385.

25. United States Department of Labor, Women's Bureau, *United Nations Decade for Women, 1976–1985: Employment in the United States* (Washington: Government Printing Office, 1985), 11.

26. Bergmann, *The Economic Emergence of Women*, 172.

27. "Justice in the World: Synod of Bishops, 1971," par. 44.

28. *Statistical Abstract of the Unites States: 1988* (Washington: Government Printing Office, 1988), Table 653.

29. Westin, *Changing Workplace*, 13–14.

30. Henry J. Aaron and Cameran M. Lougy, *The Comparable Worth Controversy* (Washington: Brookings Institution, 1986), 28.

31. Bergmann, *Economic Emergence of Women*, 182

32. Frances C. Hutner, *Equal Pay for Comparable Worth: The Working Woman's Issue of the Eighties* (New York: Praeger, 1986), 97.

33. Jennifer Roback, *A Matter of Choice: A Critique of Comparable Worth by a Skeptical Feminist* (New York: Priority Press Publications, 1986), 35.

34. Stellman and Henifin, *Office Work Can Be Dangerous to Your Health*, 50.

35. Eric Schmitt, "Businesses Assess Impact of Law on Video Terminals," *New York Times*, Long Island edition, 19 June 1988, section 12, 1.

36. Lee Schore, "Occupational Stress: A Union-Based Approach," in *Human Aspects in Office Automation* ed. Cohen, 298.

37. For an extended discussion of this problem, see Barbara Andolsen, "A Woman's Work Is Never Done: Unpaid Household Labor as a Social Justice Issue," in *Women's Consciousness, Women's Conscience: A Reader in Feminist Ethics* (Minneapolis: Winston/Seabury, 1985), 3–18.

38. Barbara G. F. Cohen, "Organizational Factors Affecting Stress in the Clerical Worker," in *Human Aspects in Office Automation*, ed. Cohen, 34. Emphasis added.

39. E. Mumford and D. Henshall, *A Participative Approach to Computer Systems*

Design (London: Associated Business Press, 1979), K. D. Eason and R. G. Sell, "Case Studies in Job Design for Information Processing Tasks," in *Stress, Work Design and Productivity*, ed. E. N. Corlett and J. Richardsen (Chichester, Eng.: John Wiley, 1981); Joyce Ranney, "QWL in the Office," *Training and Development Journal* 36 (April 1982): 74–84.

40. 9to5, National Association of Working Women, *Hidden Victims*, 38.
41. OTA, *Electronic Supervisor*, 44.
42. Westin, *Changing Workplace*, 6/1–6/14; 15/4–15/5.
43. OTA, *Electronic Supervisor*, 38.
44. Ibid., 54.
45. 9to5, National Association of Working Women, *Dirty Tricks*, 9.
46. *Scientific Management, Job Redesign and Work Performance* (London: Academic Press, 1982), 211–12.
47. Paul Champagne and Curt Tausky, "When Job Enrichment Doesn't Pay," *Personnel* 55 (Jan./Feb. 1978): 33.
48. Ibid., 31.
49. J. Richard Hackman and Greg R. Oldham, *Work Redesign* (Reading, MA: Addison-Wesley, 1980), 152.
50. Feldberg and Glenn, "Incipient Workplace Democracy," 64.
51. E. A. Sturgis Hiller, Jr., "Stepping Up for Secretaries," *Management World* 12 (July 1983): 35.
52. Hackman and Oldham, *Work Redesign*, 233–34.
53. Robert Benne, *The Ethic of Democratic Capitalism* (Philadelphia: Fortress Press, 1981), 223.
54. Ibid.
55. Ibid.
56. 9to5, *Hidden Victims*, 39.
57. Beverly Harrison, *Making the Connections: Essays in Feminist Social Ethics*, ed. Carol S. Robb (Boston: Beacon Press, 1985), 241.

Bibliography

••••••••••••••••••

••••••••••••••••••

••••••••••••••••••

Aaron, Henry J., and Cameran M. Lougy. *The Comparable Worth Controversy*. Washington: Brookings Institution, 1986.

Acker, Joan, and Donald R. Van Houten. "Differential Recruitment and Control: the Sex Structuring of Organizations." *Administrative Science Quarterly* 19 (June 1974): 152–63.

Alderfer, Clayton P. "An Empirical Test of a New Theory of Human Needs." *Organizational Behavior and Human Performance* 4 (May 1969): 142–75.

Aldous, Joan. "Wives' Employment Status and Lower-Class Men as Husband-Fathers: Support for the Moynihan Thesis." *Journal of Marriage and the Family* 31 (1969): 469–76.

Alvarado, Anthony J. "Computer Education for all Students." *Computing Teacher* 11 (April 1984): 14–15.

Anderson, Ronald E., Wayne W. Welch, and Linda J. Harris. "Inequities in Opportunities for Computer Literacy." *Computing Teacher* 11 (April 1984): 10–12.

Andolsen, Barbara. "A Woman's Work Is Never Done: Unpaid Household Labor as a Social Justice Issue" In *Women's Consciousness, Women's Conscience: A Reader in Feminist Ethics*, ed. Barbara Andolsen, Christine Gudorf, and Mary Pellauer. Minneapolis: Winston/Seabury, 1985.

Andrisani Paul J., and Mitchell B. Shapiro. "Women's Attitudes Towards Their Jobs: Some Longitudinal Data on a National Sample." *Personnel Psychology* 31 (Spring 1978): 15–34.

Appelbaum, Eileen. "Technology and Work Organization in the Insurance Industry." *ILR Report* [Industrial and Labor Relations Report, Cornell University] (Fall 1985): 21–26.

Bainton, Roland H. *Women of the Reformation in Germany and Italy*. Boston: Beacon Press, 1971.

Baran, Barbara. "Office Automation and Women's Work: the Technological Transformation of the Insurance Industry." Typescript.

Baran, Barbara, et al. "Technological Innovation and Deregulation: the Transformation of the Labor in Process in the Insurance Industry." Working Paper, Berkeley Roundtable on International Economy, Jan. 1985.

Bibliography

Barnett, Rosalind, Lois Biener, and Grace Baruch. *Gender and Stress.* New York: The Free Press, 1987.

Baum, Gregory. *Religion and Alienation: A Theological Reading of Sociology.* New York: Paulist Press, 1975.

Beer, Michael. "Needs and Need Satisfaction Among Clerical Workers in Complex and Routine Jobs." *Personnel Psychology* 21 (Summer 1968): 209–22.

Bellah, Robert, et al. *Habits of the Heart: Individualism and Commitment in American Life.* New York: Harper and Row, 1985.

Benne, Robert. *The Ethic of Democratic Capitalism: A Moral Reassessment.* Philadelphia: Fortress Press, 1981.

Bennett, John C. "Christian Ethics in Economic Life." In *Christian Values and Economic Life,* ed. John C. Bennett et al. New York: Harper, 1954.

Bennett, John C. *The Radical Imperative.* Philadelphia: Westminster Press, 1976.0

Bensahel, Jane G. "How Much Longer Will Managers Have Secretaries?" *International Management* (Dec. 1978): 37–41.

Bergmann, Barbara R. *The Economic Emergence of Women.* New York: Basic Books, 1986.

Birch, Bruce C., and Larry Rasmussen. *The Predicament of the Prosperous.* Philadelphia: Westminster Press, 1978.

Blair, Jon. "Three Studies in Improving Clerical Work." *Personnel Management* 6 (Feb. 1974): 34–37.

Blum, Albert A. "Hard-Core Unemployment: A Long-Term Problem." *Business and Society* 22 (Spring 1983): 14–17.

Bradley, Gunilla. "Computerization and Some Psychosocial Factors in the Work Environment." In National Institute for Occupational Safety and Health, *Proceedings: Reducing Occupational Stress,* 30–40. Washington: Government Printing Office, 1978.

Braverman, Harry. *Labor and Monopoly Capital: the Degradation of Work in the Twentieth Century.* New York: Monthly Review Press, 1974.

Brief, Arthur P., et al. "Sex Differences in Preferences for Job Attributes Revisited." *Journal of Applied Psychology* 62 (Oct. 1977): 645–46.

Buchanan, David A., and David Boddy. "Advanced Technology and the Quality of Working Life: The Effects of Word Processing on Video Typists." *Journal of Occupational Psychology* 55 (1982): 1–11.

Burke, Ronald J., and Tamara Weir. "Relationship of Wives' Employment Status to Husband, Wife and Pair Satisfaction and Performance." *Journal of Marriage and the Family* 38 (May 1976): 279–86.

Burns, Alan. *The Microchip: Appropriate or Inappropriate Technology.* New York: John Wiley, 1981.

Burris, Beverly H. "The Human Effects of Underemployment." *Social Problems* 31 (Oct. 1983): 96–110.

Calvin, John. *Institutes of the Christian Religion,* trans. Ford Lewis Battles. Philadelphia: Westminster Press, 1960.

Cassidy, Edward W., Robert J. Edelman, and Robert P. Kelly, "Progress Report on Management Aides." *Personnel* 55 (Jan./Feb. 1978): 21–29.

Good Work at the Video Display Terminal

Champagne, Paul J. and Curt Tausky. "When Job Enrichment Doesn't Pay." *Personnel* 55 (Jan./Feb., 1978): 30–40.

"Changing 45 million Jobs." *Business Week*, 3 August 1981, 62–67.

Chavkin, Wendy, ed. *Double Exposure: Women's Health Hazards on the Job and at Home.* New York: Monthly Review Press, 1984.

Chenu, M. D., *The Theology of Work*, trans. Lilian Soiron (Dublin: Gill and Son, 1963).

Christensen, Kathleen E. "Impacts of Computer-mediated Home-based Work on Women and Their Families." *Office: Technology and People* 3 (1987): 211–30.

Clark, Elizabeth A. *Women in the Early Church.* Wilmington, DE: Michael Glazier, 1983.

Clark, Henry. *The Christian Case against Poverty.* New York: Association Press, 1965.

Coates, Joseph F. "Computers and Business—a Case of Ethical Overload." *Journal of Business Ethics* 1 (Aug. 1982): 239–48.

Cohen, Barbara G. F., ed. *Human Aspects in Office Automation.* Amsterdam: Elsevier, 1984.

Coleman, John A. *An American Strategic Theology.* New York: Paulist Press, 1982.

Coles, Robert, and Jane Hallowell Coles. *Women of Crisis: Lives of Work and Dreams.* Vol. 2. New York: Delacorte Press, 1980.

Connell John J. "The Future Office: New Technologies, New Career Paths," *Personnel* 60 (July/Aug. 1983): 23–32.

Cooper, Cary L., and Judi Marshall. "Occupational Sources of Stress: A Review of the Literature Relating to Coronary Heart Disease and Mental Ill Health," *Journal of Occupational Psychology* 49 (1976): 11–28.

Coronato, Richard J. "The Psychology of Office Mechanization." *Buildings* 77 (Aug. 1983): 60–62.

Costello, Cynthia. "The Office Homework Program at the Wisconsin Physicians Service Insurance Company." Typescript.

Curran, Charles E. *Themes in Fundamental Moral Theology.* Notre Dame, IN: Univ. of Notre Dame Press, 1977.

Davies, Margery W. *Woman's Place is at the Typewriter: Office Work and Office Workers 1870–1930.* Philadelphia: Temple Univ. Press, 1982.

Deal, Terrence, and Allen Kennedy. *Corporate Cultures: the Rites and Rituals of Corporate Life.* Reading, MA: Addison-Wesley, 1982.

Delgado, Alan. *The Enormous File: A Social History of the Office.* London: John Murray Ltd., 1979.

Dodd, John. "Secretaries Today: Expanding Roles, Higher Expectations." *Personnel Journal* 61 (Feb. 1982): 114–17.

Drange, Kenneth M. "Office Productivity Factors." *Journal of Systems Management* (Nov. 1985): 6–9.

Draper, Roger. "The Impact of Automation on Labor: An Interview with Faye Duchin." *Managing Automation* (May 1986): 69–71.

Douglass, Jane Dempsey. *Women, Freedom and Calvin.* Philadelphia: Westminster Press, 1985.

Eason, K. D., and R. B. Sell, "Case Studies in Job Design for Information Processing

Bibliography

Tasks." In *Stress, Work Design and Productivity*, ed. E. N. Corlett and J. Richardsen. Chichester, Eng.: John Wiley, 1981.

"Economic Justice for All: Catholic Social Teaching and the U.S. Economy." *Origins* 16 (5 June 1986).

Edwards, Carol. "Achieving Equity." *Computing Teacher* 11 (April 1984): 62–64.

Edwards, Richard. *Contested Terrain: The Transformation of the Workplace in the Twentieth Century*. New York: Basic Books, 1979.

English, Carey W. "Is Your Friendly Computer Rating You on the Job?" *U.S. News and World Report*, 18 February 1985, 66.

Feldberg, Roslyn L., and Evelyn Nanako Glenn. "Incipient Workplace Democracy Among United States Clerical Workers." *Economic and Industrial Democracy* 4 (Feb. 1983): 47–67.

Feldberg, Roslyn L., and Evelyn Nanako Glenn. "Technology and Work Degradation: Effects of Office Automation on Women Clerical Workers." In *Machina Ex Dea: Feminist Perspectives on Technology*, ed. Joan Rothschild, 59–78. New York: Pergamon Press, 1983.

Fiorenza, Elisabeth Schüssler. *Bread Not Stone: the Challenge of Feminist Biblical Interpretation*. Boston: Beacon Press, 1984.

———. *In Memory of Her: A Feminist Theological Reconstruction of Christian Origins*. New York: Crossroad, 1983.

Fiorenza, Francis Schüssler, "Work and Critical Theology." In *A Matter of Dignity: Inquiries into the Humanization of Work*, ed. W. J. Heisler and John Houck. Notre Dame, IN: Univ. of Notre Dame Press, 1977.

Ford, Robert N. "Job Enrichment Lessons from AT&T." *Harvard Business Review* 51 (Jan./Feb. 1973): 96–106.

Form, William, and David Byron McMillen. "Women, Men, and Machines," *Work and Occupations* 10 (May 1983): 147–178.

Frankenhaeuser, Marianne. "Coping with Stress at Work." *International Journal of Health Services* 11 (1981): 491–510.

Fraser, Dorothy Bass. "The Feminine Mystique: 1890–1910." *Union Seminary Quarterly Review* 27 (Summer 1972): 225–39.

Fusselman, Kay. "Do Computer Skills Mean Higher Wages?" *The Secretary* (June/July 1986): 14–23.

Garson, Barbara. *All the Livelong Day: The Meaning and Demeaning of Routine Work*. New York: Penguin Books, 1975.

Gilkey, Langdon. *Message and Existence: An Introduction to Christian Theology*. New York: Seabury Press, 1979.

Gillett, Richard W. *The Human Enterprise: A Christian Perspective on Work*. Kansas City: Leaven Press, 1985.

Gladden, Washington. *Working People and Their Employers*. Boston: Lockwood, Brooks, 1876.

Glenn, Evelyn Nakano, and Roslyn L. Feldberg. "Degraded and Deskilled: The Proletarianization of Clerical Work." *Social Problems* 25 (Oct. 1977): 52–64.

Goldberg, Roberta. *Organizing Women Office Workers: Dissatisfaction, Consciousness, and Action.* New York: Praeger, 1983.

Goldhaber, Marilyn, Michael Polen, and Robert Hiatt. "The Risk of Miscarriage and Birth Defects among Women Who Use Visual Display Terminals during Pregnancy." *American Journal of Industrial Medicine* 13 (1988): 695–706.

Grandjean, Burke D., and Patricia A. Taylor. "Job Satisfaction among Female Clerical Workers: 'Status Panic' or the Opportunity Structure of Office Work?" *Sociology of Work and Occupations* 7 (Feb. 1980): 33–53.

Greenawalt, Kent. *Religious Convictions and Political Choice.* New York: Oxford Univ. Press, 1988.

Greenbaum, Joan M. *In the Name of Efficiency: Management Theory and Shopfloor Practice in Data-Processing Work.* Philadelphia: Temple Univ. Press, 1979.

Gregory, Judith, and Karen Nussbaum. "Race Against Time: Automation of the Office." *Office, Technology and People* 1 (1982): 197–236.

Gurin, Gerald, et al. *Americans View Their Mental Health.* New York: Basic Books, 1960.

Hachey, Marilyn. "A Check List for In-House Secretarial Training." *Personnel Journal* 59 (Jan. 1980): 59–60.

Hackman, J. Richard, and Greg R. Oldham. "Motivation through the Design of Work: Test of a Theory." *Organizational Behavior and Human Performance* 16 (Aug. 1976): 250–79.

Hackman, J. Richard and Greg R. Oldham. *Work Redesign.* Reading, MA: Addison-Wesley, 1980.

Harrison, Beverly Wildung. *Making the Connections: Essays in Feminist Social Ethics,* ed. Carol S. Robb. Boston: Beacon Press, 1985.

Hartmann, Heidi, et al., eds. *Computer Chips and Paper Clips: Technology and Women's Employment.* 2 vols. Washington: National Academy Press, 1986.

Hauerwas, Stanley, with David Burrell. *Truthfulness and Tragedy: Further Investigations Into Christian Ethics.* Notre Dame, IN: Univ. of Notre Dame Press, 1977.

Haynes, Suzanne G., et al. "The Relationship of Psychosocial Factors to Coronary Heart Disease in the Framingham Study: I. Method and Risk Factors." *American Journal of Epidemiology* 107 (May 1978): 362–81.

Haynes, Suzanne G., and Manning Feinleib. "Women, Work and Coronary Heart Disease: Prospective Findings from the Framingham Heart Study." *American Journal of Public Health* 70 (Feb. 1980): 133–41.

Haynes, Suzanne G., Manning Feinleib, and William B. Kannel. "The Relationship of Psychosocial Factors to Coronary Heart Disease in the Framingham Study." *American Journal of Epidemiology* 111 (1980): 37–58.

Hellwig, Monica. *The Eucharist and the Hunger of the World.* New York: Paulist Press, 1976.

Hengel, Martin. *Property and Riches in the Early Church: Aspects of a Social History of Early Christianity.* Philadelphia: Fortress Press, 1974.

Herzberg, Frederick. *Work and the Nature of Man.* Cleveland: World Publishing Company, 1966.

Bibliography

Hill, A. B. "Work Variety and Individual Differences in Occupational Boredom."
Journal of Applied Psychology 60 (1975): 128–31.

Hiller, E. A. Sturgis, Jr. "Stepping Up for Secretaries." *Management World* 12 (July 1983): 35, 44.

Hilliard, Vera J. "What Your Secretary Wants to Tell You." *Supervisory Management* 23 (July 1978): 2–9.

Himes, Kenneth. "Social Sin and the Role of the Individual." In *The Annual of the Society of Christian Ethics, 1986,* ed. Alan Anderson, 183–218. Washington: Georgetown Univ. Press, 1987.

Hitt, Michael A., and Dennis R. Cash. "Task Technology, Individual Differences, and Job Satisfaction." *Review of Business and Economic Research* 17 (Winter 1981–82): 28–36.

Hoffman, Lois Wladis. "Parental Power Relations and the Division of Household Tasks." In *The Employed Mother in America,* ed. F. I. Nye and L. W. Hoffman. Chicago: Rand McNally, 1963.

Hoffman, Lois Wladis, and F. Ivan Nye. *Working Mothers: An Evaluative Review of the Consequences for Wife, Husband, and Child.* San Francisco: Jossey-Bass, 1974.

Hollenbach, David. *Claims in Conflict: Retrieving and Renewing the Catholic Human Rights Tradition.* New York: Paulist Press, 1979.

Hollenbach, David. "Unemployment and Jobs: A Theological and Ethical Perspective." In *Catholic Social Teaching and the United States Economy,* ed. John Houck and Oliver Williams. Washington: University Press of America, 1984: 110–38.

House, James S., and James A. Wells. "Occupational Stress, Social Support and Health." In National Institute for Occupational Safety and Health, *Proceedings: Reducing Occupational Stress,* 8–29. Washington: Government Printing Office, 1978.

Howe, Louise Kapp. *Pink Collar Workers: Inside the World of Women's Work.* New York: Avon Books, 1977.

Hudson, Winthrop S. "The Weber Thesis Reexamined." *Church History* 30 (1961): 88–99.

Hunt, H. Allan and Timothy L. Hunt. *Clerical Employment and Technological Change.* Kalamazoo, MI: W. E. Upjohn Institute for Employment Research, 1986.

Hunter, Carman St. John, and David Harman. *Adult Illiteracy in the United States: A Report to the Ford Foundation.* New York: McGraw Hill, 1979.

Hunting, W., Th. Laübli, and E. Grandjean. "Postural and Visual Loads at VDT Workplaces: I. Constrained Postures." *Ergonomics* 24 (Dec. 1981): 917–31.

Hutner, Frances C. *Equal Pay for Comparable Worth: The Working Woman's Issue of the Eighties.* New York: Praeger, 1986.

Jaschinski-Kruza, Wolfgang. "Transient Myopia after Visual Work." *Ergonomics* 27 (Nov. 1984): 1181–89.

Johansson G., G. Aronsson, and B. O. Lindstrom. "Social Psychological and Neuroendocrine Stress Reactions to Highly Mechanised Work." *Ergonomics* 21 (Aug. 1978): 583–99.

Kanter, Rosabeth Moss. *Men and Women of the Corporation.* New York: Basic Books, 1977.

Karasek, Robert, Jr. "Job demands, Job Design Latitude and Mental Strain: Implications for Job Redesign." *Administrative Science Quarterly* 24 (1979): 285–308.

Karasek, Robert, et al. "Job Decision Latitude, Job Demands, and Cardiovascular Disease: A Prospective Study of Swedish Men." *American Journal of Public Health* 71 (July 1981): 694–705

Kelly, John E. *Scientific Management, Job Redesign, and Work Performance.* London: Academic Press, 1982.

Kidder, Tracy. *The Soul of a New Machine.* Boston: Little, Brown, 1981.

Kilgour, John C. "Union Organizing Activity among White-Collar Employees." *Personnel* 60 (March/April 1983): 18–27.

Klassen, Peter James. *The Economics of Anabaptism: 1525–1560.* The Hague: Mouton and Company, 1964.

Knight, James L., and Gavriel Salvendy. "Effect of Task Feedback and Stringency of External Pacing, Environmental Load and Work Performance. *Ergonomics* 24 (Oct. 1981): 757–64.

Knight, R. Chris, "Can Stress Make You Sick?" *Working Woman* (April 1984): 142–49.

Kozol, Jonathan. *Illiterate America.* Garden City, NJ: Doubleday, 1985.

Krois, Paul A., and Phillip G. Benson. "Word Processing and Personnel." *Personnel Journal* 59 (Dec. 1980): 992–95, 1008.

Langer, Elinor. "Inside the New York Telephone Company." In *Women at Work*, ed. William L. O'Neill, 307–60. New York: Quadrangle Times Books, 1972.

Lazzaro, Joseph J. "Talking Instead of Typing," *High Technology* 6 (Jan. 1986): 58–59.

Lebacqz, Karen. *Six Theories of Justice: Perspectives from Philosophical and Theological Ethics.* Minneapolis: Augsburg Publishing House, 1986.

Leffingwell, William Henry. *Making the Office Pay.* Chicago: A. W. Shaw, 1918.

———. *Office Management: Principles and Practice.* Chicago: A. W. Shaw, 1925.

———. *Scientific Office Management.* Chicago: A. W. Shaw, 1917.

Leontief, Wassily, and Faye Duchin. *The Future Impact of Automation on Workers.* New York: Oxford Univ. Press, 1986.

Levin, Howard S. *Office Work and Automation.* New York: John Wiley, 1956.

Levinson, Marc. "On the White-collar Assembly Line." *Commonweal*, 1 June 1984, 334–35.

Lockheed, Marlaine E., and Steven Frakt. "Sex Equity: Increasing Girls' Use of Computers." *Computing Teacher* 11 (April 1984): 16–18.

Lockwood, David. *The Blackcoated Worker: A Study in Class Consciousness.* London: George Allen and Unwin Ltd., 1958.

Luther, Martin. *Luther's Works.* ed. Jaroslav Pelikan. St. Louis: Concordia, 1958.

MacIntyre, Alasdair. *After Virtue: A Study in Moral Theology.* Notre Dame, IN: Univ. of Notre Dame Press, 1981.

MacKinnon, Catharine A. *Sexual Harassment of Working Women.* New Haven: Yale Univ. Press, 1979.

MacNeil/Lehrer News Hour, 28 Dec. 1983, transcript no. 2153: 7–14.

Major, Michael. "Partners or Pawns?" *Modern Office Technology* (June 1984): 96–104.

Malveaux, Julianne. "Black Women and Stress." *Essence* (April 1984): 74–76, 151–53.

Bibliography

Malveaux, Julianne M. "Moving Forward, Standing Still: Women in White Collar Jobs." In *Women in the Workplace*, ed. Phyllis A. Wallace, 101–34. Boston: Auburn House, 1982.

Margolis, Bruce L., et al. "Job Stress: An Unlisted Occupational Hazard." *Journal of Occupational Medicine* 16 (Oct. 1974): 659–61.

Marschall, Daniel, and Judith Gregory, eds. *Office Automation: Jekyll or Hyde?* Cleveland: Working Women Education Fund, 1983.

Matteis, Richard J. "The New Back Office Focuses on Customer Service." *Harvard Business Review* 57 (March/April 1979): 146–59.

McCann, Dennis P. *Christian Realism and Liberation Theology*. Maryknoll, NY: Orbis Books, 1081.

McCann, Dennis P. *New Experiment in Democracy: the Challenge for American Catholicism*. Kansas City: Sheed and Ward, 1987.

McCann, Robert L. *World Economy and World Hunger: the Response of the Churches*. Washington: University Press of America, 1982.

McNally, Fiona. *Women for Hire: a Study of the Female Office Worker*. London: Macmillan Press, Ltd., 1979.

McPhail, Irving P. "Computer Inequities in School Uses of Microcomputers: Policy Implications," *Journal of Negro Education* 54 (Winter 1985): 3–13.

Menzies, Heather. *Women and the Chip: Case Studies of the Effects of Informatics on Employment in Canada*. Montreal: Institute for Research on Public Policy, 1981.

Mercer, D. E., and D. T. H. Weir. "Attitudes to Work and Trade Unionism among White-Collar Workers." *Industrial Relations* 3 (Summer 1972): 49–61.

Middleton, Russell, and Snell Putney. "Dominance in Decisions in the Family." *American Journal of Sociology* 65 (1960), 605–9.

Miller, Donald B. "How to Improve the Performance and Productivity of the Knowledge Worker." *Organizational Dynamics* 5 (Winter 1977): 62–80.

Mills, C. Wright. *White Collar: the American Middle Classes*. New York: Oxford Univ. Press, 1951.

Muelder, Walter G. *Religion and Economic Responsibility*. New York: Scribner's, 1953.

Mumford, E. and D. Henshall. *A Participative Approach to Computer Systems Design*. London: Associated Business Press, 1979.

Murchland, Bernard, ed. *Sin*. New York: MacMillan, 1962.

Murphree, Mary C. "Rationalization and Satisfaction in Clerical Work: A Case Study of Wall Street Legal Secretaries." Ph.D. diss., Columbia University, 1981.

Nash, June, and Maria Patricia Fernandez-Kelly. *Women, Men and the International Division of Labor*. Albany: State Univ. of New York Press, 1983.

National Institute for Occupational Safety and Health. *Potential Health Hazards of Video Display Terminals*. Washington: Government Printing Office, 1981.

————. *Proceedings of the Conference on Occupational Stress*. Washington: Government Printing Office, 1978.

————. *Select Research Reports on Health Issues in Video Display Terminal Operations*. Washington: Government Printing Office, 1981.

National Research Council. *Video Displays, Work and Vision*. Washington: National Academy Press, 1983.

Neuhaus, Richard John. *The Naked Public Square: Religion and Democracy in America*. Grand Rapids, MI: Eerdmans, 1984.

9to5, National Association of Working Women. *Computer Monitoring and Other Dirty Tricks*. Cleveland: National Association of Working Women, April, 1986.

———. *Hidden Victims: Clerical Workers, Automation, and the Changing Economy*. Cleveland: National Association of Working Women, Sept. 1985.

———.*9to5 Campaign on VDT Risks: Analysis of VDT Operator Questionnaires of VDT Hotline Callers*. Cleveland: National Association of Working Women, Feb. 1984.

———. *The 9to5 National Survey on Women and Stress, Office Automation: Addendum*. Cleveland: National Association of Working Women, 1984.

Nora, Simon, and Alain Minc. *The Computerization of Society: A Report to the President of France*. Cambridge: MIT Press, 1980.

Noyelle, Thierry J. "The New Technology and the New Economy: Some Implications for Equal Employment Opportunity." In *Computer Chips and Paper Clips*, ed. Heidi Hartmann et al., 2: 373–94.

Nozick, Robert. *Anarchy, State and Utopia*. New York: Basic Books, 1974.

Oden, Thomas C. *Conscience and Dividends: Churches and the Multinationals*. Washington: Ethics and Public Policy Center, 1985.

Osbaldeston, Michael D. "Skandia Insurance Group: Restructuring the Work and Enriching the Job." *Management International Review* 16 (Feb. 1976): 9–22.

Osterman, Paul. *Internal Labor Markets*. Cambridge: MIT Press, 1984.

Pierce, Jon L., and Randall Dunham. "Task Design: A Literature Review." *Academy of Management Review* 1 (Oct. 1976): 83–97.

Pollock, Michael, and Aaron Bernstein. "The Disposable Employee is Becoming a Fact of Corporate Life." *Business Week*, 15 December 1986, 52–53, 56.

Powers, Charles W., ed. *Social Responsibility and Investments*. Nashville: Abington, 1971.

Raines, John C., and Donna Day-Lower. *Modern Work and Human Meaning*. Philadelphia: Westminster Press, 1986.

Ranney, Joyce M. "QWL in the Office." *Training and Development Journal* 36 (April 1982): 74–84.

Rauschenbusch, Walter. *Christianity and the Social Crisis*. New York: Macmillan, 1919.

———. *Christianizing the Social Order*. New York: Macmillan, 1915.

Rawls, John. *A Theory of Justice*. Cambridge: Belknap Press, 1971.

Regan, Elizabeth. "Managing a New Generation of Office Jobs." *Words* (April/May 1983): 25–27.

Roback, Jennifer. *A Matter of Choice: A Critique of Comparable Worth by a Skeptical Feminist*. New York: Priority Press Publications, 1986.

Roessner, J. David. *The Impact of Office Automation on Clerical Employment, 1985–2000*. Westport, CT: Quorum Books, 1985.

Bibliography

Rubin, Lillian B. *Worlds of Pain: Life in the Working-Class Family.* New York: Basic Books, 1976.

Ruether, Rosemary. *New Woman/New Earth: Sexist Ideologies and Human Liberation.* New York: Seabury Press, 1975.

————. *Sexism and God-talk.* Boston: Beacon Press, 1983.

Ruether, Rosemary and Eugene Bianchi. *From Machismo to Mutuality: Essays on Sexism and Woman-Man Liberation.* New York: Paulist, 1976.

Sachs, Randi T. "Should You Send Your Input Overseas?" *Office Administration and Automation* 44 (March 1983): 70–74.

Sacks, Karen. "Work." In *The Women's Annual 1982–83,* ed. Barbara Haber. Boston: G. W. Hale, 1983.

Sacks, Karen Brodin, and Dorothy Remy. *My Troubles Are Going to Have Trouble with Me: Everyday Trials and Triumphs of Women Workers.* New Brunswick: Rutgers Univ. Press, 1984.

Salancik, Gerald R., and Jeffrey Pfeffer. "An Examination of Need-Satisfaction Models of Job Attitudes." *Administrative Science Quarterly* 22 (Sept. 1977): 427–56.

Sales, Stephen M. and James House. "Job Satisfaction as a Possible Risk Factor in Coronary Heart Disease." *Journal of Chronic Diseases* 23 (May 1971): 861–73.

Salvendy, Gavriel. "Human-computer Communications with Special Reference to Technological Developments, Occupational Stress and Educational Needs." *Ergonomics* 25 (June 1982): 435–57.

Salvendy, Gavriel, and M. J. Smith. *Machine Pacing and Occupational Stress.* London: Taylor and Francis, Ltd., 1981.

Sanders, Jo Shuchat. "The Computer: Male, Female or Androgynous?" *Computing Teacher* 11 (April 1984): 31–34.

Schaller, Lyle E. *The Churches' War on Poverty.* Nashville: Abington Press, 1967.

Schnorr, Teresa, et al. "Chest Pain in Users of Video Display Terminals." *Journal of the American Medical Association* 257 (6 Feb. 1987): 627–28.

Schoonenberg, Piet. *Man and Sin: A Theological View,* trans. Joseph Donceel. Notre Dame, IN: Univ. of Notre Dame Press, 1965.

Seeger, John A., et al. "First City Bank Operating Group (B)." Boston: Harvard Business School Case Services, 1975. Case number 474–166.

Shapiro, H. Jack, and Louis W. Stern. "Job Satisfaction: Male and Female, Professional and Non-Professional Workers." *Personnel Journal* 54 (July 1975): 388–89, 406–7.

Sider, Ronald J. *Rich Christians in an Age of Hunger.* New York: Paulist Press, 1977.

Silverstone, Rosalie, and Rosemary Towler. "Secretaries at Work." *Ergonomics* 27 (May 1984): 557–64.

Silvestri, George T., and John M. Lukasiewicz. "Occupational Employment Projections: the 1984–85 Outlook." *Monthly Labor Review* 108 (Nov. 1985): 42–59.

Smith, M. J., et al. "A Review of NIOSH Psychological Stress Research—1977" In National Institute for Occupational Safety and Health, *Proceedings of the Conference on Occupational Stress,* 26–35. Washington: Government Printing Office, 1978.

Good Work at the Video Display Terminal

Smith, Michael J., et al., "An Investigation of Health Complaints and Job Stress in Video Display Operations." *Human Factors* 23 (1981): 387–400.

Soelle, Dorothee, with Shirley A. Cloyes. *To Work and To Love: A Theology of Creation.* Philadelphia: Fortress Press, 1984.

Stead, Bette A. "The National Secretarial Shortage: A Management Concern." *MSU Business Topics* (Winter 1980): 43–47.

Stellman, Jeanne, and Mary Sue Henifin. *Office Work is Dangerous to Your Health.* New York: Pantheon Books, 1983.

"Stress On Your Job—A Major National Survey." *Ms.*, April 1984, 83–86.

Tavard, George H. *Woman in Christian Tradition.* Notre Dame, IN: Univ. of Notre Dame Press, 1973.

Tawney, R. H. *Religion and the Rise of Capitalism.* New York: Harcourt, Brace, 1926.

Taylor, John V. *Enough Is Enough.* Minneapolis: Augsburg, 1977.

Tepperman, Jean. *Not Servants, Not Machines: Office Workers Speak Out.* Boston: Beacon Press, 1976.

Tracy, David. *The Analogical Imagination: Christian Theology and the Culture of Pluralism.* New York: Crossroad, 1981.

Troeltsch, Ernst. *The Social Teaching of the Christian Churches.* 2 vols. New York: Harper and Row, 1931.

Trost, Cathy. "More Family Issues Surface at Bargaining Tables as Women Show Increasing Interest in Unions." *Wall Street Journal,* 2 Dec. 1986, 70.

U. S. Congress, Office of Technology Assessment. *Automation of America's Offices, 1985–2000.* Washington: Government Printing Office, 1985.

———. *The Electronic Supervisor: New Technology, New Tensions.* Washington: Government Printing Office, 1987.

U. S. Department of Labor, Women's Bureau. *Women and Office Automation: Issues for the Decade Ahead.* Washington: Government Printing Office, 1985.

Viner, Jacob. *Religious Thought and Economic Society,* ed. Jacques Melitz and Donald Winch. Durham, NC: Duke Univ. Press, 1978.

Wakin, Edward, "The Jury's Still Out on Office Systems Safety," *Today's Office* (Sept. 1985): 39–40.

Wallace, Phyllis A., ed. *Women in the Workplace.* Boston: Auburn House, 1982.

Walsh, Diane Chapman, and Richard H. Egdahl, eds. *Women, Work, and Health: Challenges to Corporate Policy.* New York: Springer-Verlag, 1980.

Walzer, Michael. *Spheres of Justice: A Defense of Pluralism and Equality.* New York: Basic Books, 1983.

Weaver Charles N. "Relationships among Pay, Race, Sex, Occupational Prestige, and Supervision, Work, Autonomy, and Job Satisfaction in a National Sample." *Personnel Psychology* 30 (Autumn 1977): 437–45.

Werneke, Diane. *Microelectronics and Office Jobs: The Impact of the Chip on Women's Employment.* Geneva: International Labour Office, 1983.

Wertheimer, Barbara Mayer. *We Were There: The Story of Working Women in America.* New York: Pantheon Books, 1977.

Bibliography

West, Jackie. "New Technology and Women's Office Work." In *Work, Women and the Labour Market*, ed. West. London: Routledge and Kegan Paul, 1982.

Westin, Alan, et al. *The Changing Workplace: A Guide to Managing the People, Organizational and Regulatory Aspects of Office Technology*. White Plains, NY: Knowledge Industry Publications, 1985.

"Why Clerical Workers Resist the Unions," *Business Week*, 2 May 1983, 126–28.

Williams, Fannie Barrier. "The Intellectual Progress of the Colored Women of the United States Since the Emancipation Proclamation." In *Black Women in Nineteenth-Century American Life*, ed. Bert James Loewenberg and Ruth Bogin. University Park: Pennsylvania State Univ. Press, 1976: 270–79.

Williams, Oliver F., and John W. Houck, eds. *The Judaeo-Christian Vision and the Modern Corporation*. Notre Dame, IN: Univ. of Notre Dame Press, 1982.

Wogaman, J. Philip. *Economics and Ethics: A Christian Inquiry*. Philadelphia: Fortress Press, 1986.

——. *Guaranteed Annual Income: The Moral Issues*. Nashville: Abington, 1968.

"World Conference Set on Common Union Approach to Video Display Terminals." *White Collar Report* 56 (24 Oct. 1984): 501–2.

Wright, Barbara Drygulski, et al., eds. *Women, Work and Technology: Transformations*. Ann Arbor: Univ. of Michigan Press, 1987.

Wright, Marc B. "Work Measurement System Monitors the Output of a Word Processing Operation." *Industrial Engineering* (July 1982): 70–72.

Zuboff, Shoshanah. "Why Do Employees Misuse, even Sabotage, Computer Systems?" *Facilities Design and Management* (May 1982): 60–61.

——. "New Worlds of Computer-Mediated Work." In *Catching up with the Computer Revolution*, ed. Lynn M. Salerno, 451–66. New York: John Wiley, 1983.

——. "Computer-mediated Work: The Emerging Managerial Challenge." *Office: Technology and People* 1 (Sept. 1982): 237–43.

Index

Index

Index

Index

Index

Index

Index

Index

Index

Index